1000
Ways to Amuse
Children

1000
Ways to Amuse
Children

Pam Harris
Toni Arthur

Contents

Part One Pam Harris
For children up to 7 years

Part Two Toni Arthur

For older children up to 11 years

Note

‼ This symbol appears throughout the book. It is used in three circumstances: beside a particular item in the lists of 'Useful things to have', at the start of a hint or at the beginning of a particular sentence in a hint. It means that the item or the activity could possibly be harmful if not handled carefully. It also means that it is best to supervise your child in these cases.

First published in Great Britain in 1984 by
Octopus Books Limited
59 Grosvenor Street
London W.1.

© 1984 Hennerwood Publications Limited

ISBN 0 86273 130 5

Printed and bound in Great Britain by
Collins, Glasgow

Illustrations by Mary Budd and Colin Mier

Part One

Safety Note

Young children and babies have no experience to tell them what is harmful or dangerous, so the responsibility for protecting them lies totally with you. Make sure that anything that a baby or young child can reach:

1. Has no easily detachable dangerous parts;
2. Is not small enough to be swallowed or cause choking;
3. Is not heavy enough to hurt little fingers and toes when dropped;
4. Has no sharp edges or pointed bits;
5. Is not dangerous if licked or chewed;
6. Cannot strangle or suffocate;
7. Is clean.

Always stay near babies when they are playing, and keep within earshot of older children. Never leave *any* child playing with water, even for a minute, since children can drown in just a few inches of water. If play is interrupted by the telephone or the door bell, take your child(ren) with you to answer it.

Only use P.V.A. adhesive or water-based glues.

Introduction

The activities in the first part of this book are intended for children from babyhood to seven years, but where ages are given they are simply for guidance. Children vary so much in their rate of development, it would be a shame not to try an activity simply because 'the book says' it is meant for children older than your own. For instance, a 2 year old will enjoy play-dough as much as a 4 year old or a 7 year old, it is just that older children will do different things with it. You will find the terms 'older' and 'younger' used throughout the book: in this part 'older children' refers to children aged about 4 to 7, and younger children refers to the under 3's.

The instructions in this part are directed at adults and suggestions are made as to what children can do for themselves, although in many cases you will be the best judge of how much or how little your child(ren) can manage. At all ages, it is important to take account of individual differences in interests and abilities. Activities that are easy for one child may be difficult for another of similar age; things that fascinate one child may be found boring by another. Don't be put off trying – you will find something enjoyable – and don't expect too much or too little: children will give up if the activity is too hard, and get bored if it is too easy.

While children are playing with whatever equipment you have provided, don't feel compelled to give them your unrivalled attention all the time. Children very often like to play, or experiment, and think without interruptions, and enjoy the freedom to do as they wish. Their enjoyment may be spoiled if they are badgered with questions such as 'How many cakes are there?', 'How many are needed?', 'How many are there each?', 'What colour is this icing?', 'What else can you see that is blue?'. We adults do not like being endlessly questioned as we are coming to terms with new experiences; in fact we often choose to try them out alone. Although you cannot leave young children physically alone, you can leave them verbally alone, sitting down nearby but out of their way somewhere and getting on with something else while they make their own little discoveries. One of the main aims of this book, after all, is to give *you* a little peace!

1.Babies

Useful things to have

Interesting pictures[1]
Pieces of fabric[2]
Small soft toys
‼ Milk bottle tops[3]
Brushes (small hairbrush, toothbrush, nailbrush, pastry brush)
‼ Different types of ball (ping-pong, large fluffy, tennis, rubber)
Aluminium foil dishes
Yogurt pots
Rubber glove
‼ Ribbon or braid

Bells (available in pet shops)
Balloons
‼ Bright paper shapes[4]
Cotton reels
‼ Buttons (strung together and securely tied)
‼ Shirring elastic
‼ Strong cotton
‼ String
Stand for mobiles (bought, or made from plastic hanger)
Christmas decorations
‼ Safe household objects[5]

Notes

1. Postcards are particularly good. If you use pictures cut from magazines they will need to be stuck on card: put one picture on each side. Use mainly brightly coloured ones but have a few paler, more subtly coloured pictures for contrast. Only use ideas involving magazine pictures with 18 month old children upwards, otherwise the printed paper might be chewed and swallowed.

2. Any dye-fast fabric will do, but try to provide different colours, plain and patterned, and different textures, for example, velvet, silk, wool, hessian, P.V.C., fur, 'bumpy' tweed material, thin nylon, fine lacy material, corduroy or lurex.

3. Use these only for two year olds upwards, under close supervision.

4. As the paper might be swallowed, use these shapes only with 18 month old children upwards and watch that they do not try to eat them.

5. All objects are new to babies, and to a baby it does not matter what an item is *supposed* to be used for. There are so many interesting things to find out about. What a baby cares about is how things look and feel and sound. You can use whatever you have as long as it does not have an easily detachable part, is not small enough to be swallowed or cause choking, nor heavy enough to hurt little fingers and toes when dropped. You will also have to ensure that there are no sharp edges or pointed bits, nothing that can strangle or suffocate and nothing on the object that could be dangerous if licked. Remember, some paint is toxic. Everything must be clean too. Here are some possibilities, all of which should only be used while you are supervising:

Containers Metal containers of different shapes and sizes: tin mug, saucepans with their lids, new wastepaper bin, biscuit tins, large coffee tins, teatrays, bun tins, egg-poaching pans (worth getting one just for play even if you don't use it for cooking – it will be far cheaper than many bought toys, and provides far more entertainment value), foil freezer containers (including those intended for whole meals, with 3 sections); plastic containers with and without lids, transparent bottles, mixing bowls, picnic cups, paper cups, egg cartons, yogurt pots (but throw them away as soon as they break, because the edges will be sharp).

Things to put in and out of containers Any type of smallish ball, keys, construction bricks, plastic cutlery, oranges, any small toys from toy cupboard.

Bangers Things to make a noise with, such as wooden spoons/spatulas, metal teaspoons and tablespoons, rolling pin, any small lengths of (well-sandpapered) wood, rulers (wood, metal or plastic).

Other interesting items Tea-towel, (new) dishcloth, sponge (wet or dry), picnic plates, clean comb, table mats, sieve, fish slice, ladle, objects with holes in to put hands through (plastic cake cutters, sticky tape rolls).

General hints

When do you start? It is possible that very young babies have enough entertainment getting accustomed to the world outside the womb and getting to know their parents. Certainly, faces and voices provide the greatest fascination for a baby under 3 months. The hints in this chapter are described with babies aged 3 to 18 months in mind.

In the mood: To those so young and inexperienced, most objects and events are entertaining **if babies are in a receptive frame of mind.** If they are hungry, thirsty, tired or miserable, they will not want to play at all; food, drink, bed or a nice cuddle will be needed first.

We all like different things: Right from the start babies are individuals with their own likes and dislikes. Things that cause some babies to chuckle with utter delight will bore or even frighten others. You will soon get to know what yours loves and hates – babies are generally extremely good at letting you know!

Make sure it can be seen: Brightly coloured objects with clear features rather than a blurred fluffy mass are easiest for a young baby to see. Hang them 20-30 cm (8-12 inches) from the baby's face. During the first few weeks the objects need to be at the **side** of the baby, since most very young babies lie with their heads turned to one side.

(A little) variety is the spice of a baby's life: From about 2 months of age, babies tend to be more excited by something familiar presented in a slightly different way than they are by something totally new. Just a small change on a hanging mobile, for example changing one of the objects from patterned to plain, provides a more interesting view than a completely new mobile (see 'ideas' page 16).

Touching is fun: Between around 3 and 6 months, the tactile qualities of objects become important – softness, hardness, smoothness or roughness. **!!** A baby will often explore this with the more sensitive mouth rather than the hands, so make sure everything is clean, nothing is small enough to be swallowed or dangerous to chew or lick.

One at a time: Before about 6 months, babies tend to concentrate on only one object at a time; more just confuses them. Therefore, you will have more success if you provide one or two interesting toys, which are replaced frequently, rather than putting a whole array in front of them. Otherwise they see just enough of the objects to get bored with them, without appreciating and enjoying the detail.

Patience, please: Babies often take a little while to respond to what you are saying, or doing, or offering. It is important to allow them **time** to show how they feel. Try not to get fed up and turn away; your baby might end up smiling expectantly at your back.

Somewhere to play: You are the most important part of your baby's surroundings, so there needs to be a safe place near you for activities other than those centred on a cot. This is much easier before crawling starts, so make the most of it! Once babies can reach cupboards, the easiest thing to do is to accept this and fill low cupboards with safe household objects (see page 13). Failing this, cupboards are better locked.

Letting go: It is fairly late in the first year that babies can first **deliberately** let go of objects in their hand. If you want your baby to play with something else, the easiest way of achieving this is to offer it: in taking the second object, the first object is usually dropped.

Old favourites: Don't forget all the traditional baby amusers such as 'this little piggy went to market'. Amusing babies is not just a matter of providing interesting objects and there will be times when all they want is a warm cuddle and a song or a rhyme with you. 'Knee rides' are a perennial favourite, too.

Ideas

MAKING MOBILES: A mobile is simply a hanging object or set of objects that will move slightly in surrounding air currents, although if the object is interesting enough, it does not have to have the additional quality of movement. For young babies who cannot yet stand up in their cots and therefore who cannot reach the objects, the choice is endless. Just tie a piece of string across the cot and hang objects from it. The items listed in the ingredients will give you some ideas. Some will just be nice to look at (because they are shiny, or have bright colours, or pretty patterns), others (for example a string of keys, cotton reels or bells) will make nice noises when the baby wriggles, or when you shake the cot gently. Generally, 4 or 5 objects will be enough, depending on size. The trick with mobiles is to keep changing them, and of course this is the great advantage of home constructed versions. Here are some suggestions:

▲ One day you could change one of the (firmly-fixed) flapping fabric pieces from soft fur to shiny P.V.C., the next day to sparkling lurex.

■ A piece of lace hanging down could have a bell put on the end.

● A bright rubber glove could suddenly appear right in the middle.

▲ You could add bought toys which may have been given as presents – a rattle, or one of those baby toys that bounces up and down at the end of a long spring.

■ ‼ Hang some Christmas decorations across the cot, even if it is not Christmas, but only if they are not fragile or sharp and if they are dye-safe.

● Emphasise the contrast – a soft blue fluffy rabbit, next to a hard shiny teaspoon for example, or a big bright plastic mug with a small foil dish on each side.

▲ If you do not have anything to hand one day, then just remove one of the objects to change the outline.

■ For older babies, who spend less time in a cot and who can in any case sit up, it is best to hang the mobiles from a ceiling hook.

PUNCHBALL: Hang a large soft ball from a ceiling hook at a height where it can be kicked or patted.

PRETTY POSTCARDS: Tuck any clear, bright postcard in the side of the cot or pram for the youngest babies to inspect. ‼ Only do this for babies who cannot yet grasp. It will need to be changed frequently and it is most interesting to watch the reaction to a new one, or the original one used again.

FUN TO FEEL: Collect squares of material of different colours and textures (see note 2 page 12) and sew them together. When you have done this, either put on a piece of backing fabric (any large piece of material will do) or, if you have enough material squares, you could make a double-sided one using another texture. The baby will enjoy just feeling the different textures.

A FEELY CUSHION: Using slightly larger pieces and backing fabric, sew the squares of material as above, but then stuff with old tights (which you have first boiled to remove the dye) or use a small ready-made cushion if you have one. This can then be tied to the cot bars, or just played with on the floor.

FINGER FOODS: For the 6-12 month old baby, picking tiny objects up can become an absorbing occupation and there are many safe foods that can be provided – breadcrumbs, grated cheese, cooked peas or other cooked diced vegetables, in fact any food that is enjoyed and that can be picked up between finger and thumb.

EXCITING BOX: Provide a box or basket containing a few interesting items from round the house. Let your baby explore as he pleases, changing discarded objects for something else from the list (see note 5 page 12) to postpone boredom.

WHAT A NOISE: Provide an empty biscuit tin (any shape) and a bunch of old keys on a ring, then substitute a wooden spoon, then a metal one. This is for days when you don't already have a headache.

SPLASH, SPLATTER: Water poured into the tin from a plastic bottle or a smallish plastic jug also makes a lovely noise. This is good fun at bathtime. You will need a towel or something similar on the floor.

NOW YOU SEE IT, NOW YOU DON'T: A selection of cardboard tubes of different lengths and widths and a ping-pong ball or smallish rubber one create interesting possibilities for disappearing acts to baffle a baby of 18 months old upwards.

RATTLES: Fill some small transparent plastic bottles with rice, pasta or lentils and secure the top with tape. Glue the tops before taping them too, if you have older children as well as a baby.

RATTLES WITH A DIFFERENCE: Fill a small transparent plastic bottle with water and add a tablespoon of cooking oil and seal well. The oil will do exciting things as the baby moves the bottle around.

RATTLES AND BUBBLES: Put some water and washing up liquid in a transparent plastic bottle and shake it up to get bubbles.

COLOURED RATTLES: After either of the above two rattles have been played with for a while, open the bottle and add some food colouring for variety. Make sure the tops are well secured.

I WANT TO DO IT TOO: Provided you don't mind a bit of a mess, here is a useful combination of objects to amuse older babies in their high chairs, while you are washing up or cooking. Provide a plastic mixing bowl, a bit of greaseproof paper, some brushes (pastry brush, toothbrush) and a small plastic jug of water, and let them explore the objects themselves, **‼** but watch that the paper is not eaten.

GIVING IN: When you tire of saying no, empty out one of your low level cupboards and fill it with harmless unbreakable objects (see note 3). Choose one that you don't have to keep walking past, unless you **want** to keep falling over!

PEEP-BO: **‼** Give your baby a clean teatowel to put over his head. You may need to demonstrate first and join in the game endlessly.

STOP THAT WRIGGLING: Older babies nearly always go through a stage when it is inordinately difficult to change their nappies. A selection of varying household items (again, harmless, unbreakable and clean) in a square ice cream box kept in the bedroom, or wherever you change nappies, helps tone down the wriggling (a bit). Keep your empty talc tins and cleaned cream jars for this – especially if the lid comes off.

BABIES AND BROTHERS AND SISTERS: Although this chapter is just for babies, many of the ideas in other chapters can be adapted for the very young, which is useful if you have older children at home to amuse at the same time. Having young children of different ages at home is normally the time when amusing them becomes particularly difficult, since the youngest tends to sabotage any sensible activity the older one(s) may become involved in. The same sorts of ingredients provided for the baby (selected, of course, with safety in mind) will often calm things down a bit. If you can get away with it, strap the youngest in a high chair. In particular, you will find ideas in the chapters on music, play-dough, dressing-up (shoes and hats are particularly popular) and water. The same materials are relevant, babies under 18 months or so will just do different (and more messy) things with them.

2. Painting And Drawing

Useful things to have

Paper approx. 50 cm × 45 cm (20 in × 18 in)[1]

Brushes 8, 10 or 12 size hoghair (one for each pot of paint)

Toothbrushes or old household paintbrushes or even paint rollers for variety

Containers[2]

Paint, ready-mixed or powder[3]

Emulsion paint for cardboard models[4]

Powder paints for finger paints[5]

Aprons[6]

Armcuffs worn with a pinafore type of apron are useful to protect sleeves

Optional extras

Straws

‼ Eye dropper

Graph paper

Printing materials

Piece of foam (cut to fit the lid of a jar or pot)

Cork

Comb

Cotton reel

Toothbrush

Wooden brick

Haircurlers (plastic, bristles or foam)

Piece of real sponge

Leaves, feathers

Pastry cutters

Potato masher

Cotton wool buds

Cut up fruit and vegetables (allow to dry out for a few minutes before use), e.g. halved potato, the end of a leek, chopped swede or parsnip, halved apple, orange or lemon.

Cut up polystyrene, cardboard tubes

A blown-up balloon (for printing 'clouds')

‼ Any other small household objects which seem suitable for interesting shapes e.g. odd jigsaw pieces glued on to a small block of wood for a handle

bits of old construction kit

tyres from a broken toy car

Stamp pad[7]

Drawing materials

Thick wax crayons[8]

Magic markers

Chalk

Pieces of charcoal

Coloured pencils

Thick black pencils

Optional extras

Piece of bark

Curtain rings

Old spice containers with perforated lids

Flour shaker

Milk bottle stand (2-4 size)

Workplace:
An easel of plasterboard fixed to a wall or cupboard at an angle.[9] Bulldog clips or drawing pins (for you to fix the paper and a damp cloth (to wipe off unintentional murals!).[10]

Notes

1. With young children, the rougher the paper, the better, e.g. old wallpaper, lining paper, sugar paper, computer paper, newspaper (several thicknesses and preferably with a few photos), blotting paper, embossed paper, coloured paper and brown wrapping paper. (Cut some pieces into triangles, strips, circles, or any shape for variety).

2. Use containers with lids, so paint can be kept for another session e.g. non-spill pots, margarine tubs; shallow plastic dishes, old saucers (for printing and for mixing colours). Pots can be carried safely in a milk bottle container if they will fit.

3. The paint needs to be thick enough not to run, for little ones, so it is worth buying by the pound, even for one child. Alternatively, runny powder paint can be thickened with cold-water paste, (non-fungicidal), good quality washing-up liquid or flour (this is the most economical). Make sure you have some white paint for mixing with other colours to make them paler. If you put a tablespoon of washing-up liquid in the paint, it will wash off more easily.

4. Mix emulsion paint with enough sand to give it a coarse texture for covering cardboard models.

5. Mix powder paints with either wallpaper glue or soapflakes and cold water starch or soapflakes and cornflour (see recipes page 26).

6. An old shirt worn back to front either with the sleeves cut out or with the sleeves cut down to fit or an old plastic mac cut down. You can buy P.V.C. aprons or overalls, but it may be better to spend the money on a cheap, thin plastic mac since this will give the best coverage.

7. Soak a sponge or piece of foam in paint and put in a shallow dish or saucer.

8. Large wax crayons are probably best to start with, although small children seem to be able to manage felt-tips very well and love using them (under supervision, if you want to avoid a thin line of ink everywhere your child has been in the last ten minutes).

9. An angled surface is best as with a flat surface, children tend to rest their tummies on the bottom half of the painting while they complete the top. A blackboard easel is a possibility.

10. A damp cloth is an absolutely essential ingredient since young children tend to paint very enthusiastically, leading to the 'flick-effect'. If you are being fairly vigilant you can wipe the flicked paint spots off immediately rather than finding them days later when they have become infuriatingly hard. For finger painting, have a bowl of water near by to avoid smears on the way to the sink.

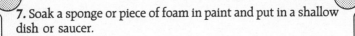

General hints

Impending boredom: The major factor which puts parents off painting activities with the under sevens is that it can take half an hour to get things ready, another half an hour to clear up afterwards and there is a strong possibility that your child will only paint for five minutes in between. To avoid this, let him or her help you get things ready, then watch for signs of impending boredom and introduce something new – a new piece of paper with a different shape or texture, a different object to splosh the paint on with – and you will sustain interest much longer.

In the beginning: Younger children tend to experiment with the paint by covering the whole paper with blobs of colour. This develops into more organized stripes as children gain more control over their movements. Eventually animals, people and houses start to take shape.

Painting for pleasure: Young children paint because they enjoy playing with the painting materials, rather than because they want to produce a picture, although they soon learn that they are supposed to call the finished product something, and often oblige your queries by inventing a name or agreeing to a suggested title.

The finished product: Some children screw up finished paintings and drawings in the same way that they might knock down a tower or break up a creation from construction bricks – once they have had the enjoyment of creating it, there is not much else to do with it. However, some children create carefully painted pictures which they obviously intend to be something and which they like you to recognise, perhaps by pinning them on the kitchen wall. You soon learn at what stage your own child is and the sort of responses he or she likes best.

Preparation hints

The painting box: If you keep all the necessary ingredients in a box, preparation is simply a matter of getting the box out and distributing a selection of its contents. With younger children particularly, just one implement or type of paint at a time works best, and not too many colours, then you can produce a new item as interest wanes (see 'Impending boredom' page 24).

Cover up: Protect the floor with old sheets, or newspapers, or a large polythene sheet covered with towels or old towels on their own and the child with an apron, old shirt, etc. Make sure sleeves are either rolled up or protected.

Setting up: Firstly, attach the chosen piece of paper to a board. Next, position this either on the floor, for finger painting or printing (you may get some unexpected knee prints though) or on a suitable table, or at an angle (see page 23).

Starting off: For straightforward painting you will need 3 or 4 pots of mixed paint, with a brush in each pot. The primary colours go down well at first.

Finger painting

FINGER PAINT RECIPES: Below are four recipes for making paint suitable for finger painting.

Recipe 1
Make up wallpaper glue according to instructions and put in old washing up liquid bottles. The children can then squeeze small amounts of it into a shallow dish or saucer, add dry powder paint to colour and stir it in.

Recipe 2
Mix equal quantities of flour and powder paint, then add water until the mixture is smooth and thick.

Recipe 3
Mix together ½ cup soapflakes, ½ cup cold water starch and ¾ cup cold water until the mixture has the consistency of mashed potatoes. Food colouring can then be used to make a range of colours.

Recipe 4
Dissolve 1 cup of cornflour in a little water as if making custard. Add 1 litre (2 pints) of boiling water and boil until thick. Away from the heat, beat in 1 cup of soapflakes. Cool (it will thicken as it cools) and colour as desired.

KEEP IT CONTAINED: Finger painting is best done on thick paper (such as wallpaper) in a large baking tray, or on an old piece of plastic laminated board, or the kitchen table. Put the paint in old margarine cartons or small bowls, then sit back and watch.

FIRST TIME NERVES: Some children are a bit nervous and gingerly put just a fingertip in the paint the first time, others dive in up to both elbows. If you think your child might be nervous, make up the paint in pastel colours – a soft blue or pink doesn't seem quite so off-putting to a child who is cautious about messy activities.

ORGANIZED FINGER-PAINTING: If you draw the outline of a dalmatian or a leopard, your child can make spots all over the inside with a finger dipped in paint. Alternatively, draw the outline of a flower and it can be filled in in the same way.

FILL ME IN: You could draw half a picture and your child could use finger-prints to fill in the missing bits, for example if you draw a man with his umbrella up and some clouds, then the rain and puddles can be added with a finger.

Printing

THICK OR THIN?: For printing make up a few colours of powder paint and either put a thicker mixture in bowls or margarine tubs or make it thinner and soak pieces of sponge or foam to act as pads.

TYPE OF PAPER: Don't use thin lining paper for vegetable prints: it will crinkle because of the water in the vegetable.

STARTING OFF: Try starting with blob prints. First fold over a piece of paper and crease the fold, then open it out and put a blob of paint to one side of the fold. Fold over the paper again. When the paper is opened out a second time, you will see that the blob has been reproduced on the other side of the paper making a weird shape, which you can then have fun in interpreting.

REPRODUCING: If the blob print is still very wet, you can take further prints from it by putting a clean piece of paper on top and running a rolling pin over the lot. If you cover the rolling pin in foil, it seems more like a 'printing machine', as well as ensuring you don't get paint in your next lot of apple pies.

OFF ON THEIR OWN: Once older children have become familiar with the basic idea, you can choose one of the printing materials listed in the ingredients and one of the following ideas and leave them to explore the possibilities themselves.

POTATO SHAPES: Find potatoes that are unusual in shape and cut across the unusual section. Curved potatoes can make moons, pear shapes can make men, circles make faces for people. Either cut holes for eyes, nose and mouth, or cut away the background, so that the eyes and mouth stand up in relief.

CROWD SCENE: Use potato print faces as described above (hollowed and in relief) to make a crowd picture – print the different faces on one large sheet of paper, in different colours if liked, with smaller 'faces' at the back.

STILL LIFE WITH FRUIT AND POTATO: Draw a fruit bowl on a piece of paper, then using green paint and half a round potato, or the cross section of a large carrot, let your child make a bowl of apples. Go round again afterwards with the printer dipped in red paint. Draw or paint on leaves, or stick on dried ones.

PRINTED PAPER: Cut some basic shapes in halved potatoes – square, circle, triangle – and print all over a large piece of paper. The finished print could be used to cover a box.

NATURE STUDY: Draw or paint a tree. Cut a simple bird out of the potato and print lots of birds of different colours perching on the tree. Leaves can be added (see leaf prints, page 31).

GIFTED WORK: Using any of the printers, make small gift tags, or Christmas/birthday cards by printing on to stiff paper or card. For the gift tags, all the printing could be done on one large piece of card, and later cut into small squares/rectangles/triangles.

BLACK BACKGROUNDS: Use black paper and print in white or other light colours.

CHRISTMAS DECORATIONS: Cut out bell, star or Christmas tree shapes from stiffish card and print over these for hanging up as decorations.

MOBILE ART: Print lots of brightly coloured shapes all over a large piece of paper, then cut round the individual shapes. Use these to make a mobile for the baby's room (see page 16).

SCENE PRINTING: Use a rectangular shape to make the body of a car/lorry, leek ends or cotton reels for wheels and steering wheel, vertically halved carrot for tree trunk, sponge for foliage, a balloon for clouds and a cut out potato for people. There are endless variations on this theme and if your imagination runs out, use a picture from a book or magazine for ideas. The end result of a print picture is unfailingly impressive.

HAND PRINTS: Make a hand print of all the people (and paw prints of animals if they are fairly docile and long-suffering) in the family. Try to get them all on one piece of paper/card, label and date them and put on the wall.

FOOT PRINTS: If you have a garden, or are extremely easy going, you could suggest hand or foot prints, although they may beat you to it.

A CIRCLE OF HANDS: If other members of the family are unavailable or unwilling, try printing one hand lots of times, so that all the handprints form a circle. Alternatively put them round the edge of a large piece of paper to make a frame for another print picture in the middle. The 'hard' printers (such as bricks) used in a repeated design make particularly effective frames too.

PAINTED LEAF PRINTS: Choose a leaf that has veins which stand out clearly and stick it upside down on a piece of card. Using a brush or sponge, cover with a thick layer of paint and use to print. Leaf prints make particularly pretty greetings cards or gift tags, especially if you add small pressed flowers (see collage chapter, page 40, for ways of pressing flowers).

STRING PRINTS: Dip a length of string in paint and drag it across the paper in swirls. This works best if it is lifted off vertically, but it does not really matter.

More ideas

PAINTING BY BLOWS: Using fairly runny paint, put a large blob on a clean sheet of paper, then give your child a straw and let him blow through it to change the shape of the paint blob into trickles, spiders, etc. He or she may get fed up and draw with the straw but it doesn't matter. !! Make sure that the paint isn't sucked up though.

EXPERIMENT WITH COLOURS OF PAINT: Mix some white into your paint colours to make them interestingly pale, or with black to darken them if you are brave enough to stock black paint. Let your child experiment with mixing colours too.

CONSTRUCTIVE IDEAS: Make a fort with corrugated card, then paint the outside with emulsion paint which you have mixed with a little sand. This creates a nice stone effect.

APPRENTICE DECORATOR: Children will feel very grown up if you allow them to 'paint' the outside of your house. Give them a proper paint brush and a paint tin filled with water.

PRETTY PRINTS: Pin a paper doily securely to a sheet of paper, then paint over the top of it to produce instant prints.

MAGIC PAINTING: Cut out a large picture from a glossy magazine. Tape it to the table and cover with tissue paper or absorbent kitchen paper towels. Let your child gradually apply water from a non-spill paint pot with a brush, thus revealing the picture as he paints.

WAXING MAGICAL: Another magic painting can be made by either you or your child drawing a picture on a piece of paper with white or light wax crayon, or a candle. The child can then paint over the whole surface of the paper with one colour of paint and the invisible picture will come to life.

A CHANGE OF SHAPE: If your child has run out of ideas for what to paint, cut some paper into the shape of a bird, flower, butterfly or fish. Your child can then decorate these shapes with exotic colours.

ABSTRACT PAINTING: Once your child has slightly more control over where the paint goes on the paper, draw an abstract pattern with lots of curvy lines, so that the pattern can be filled in using lots of different colours, with either paint or crayons.

PAINTING ON: There are many other activities involving painting in the chapter on making things, so it is worth looking at these before putting the paint away.

Drawing

HOW TO START: The same general comments hold for drawing as for painting (see page 24) but the advantage of drawing over painting is that it requires very little in the way of preparation. Once your child is three years old or so, you can give her paper and pencils and leave her to get on with it.

DEVELOPING IDEAS: For older pre-schoolers, you could try drawing an outline and letting the child make it into something. Next time your child can draw the outline and you can make it into an animal or object to be guessed.

PRESSED PATTERNS: Grate old wax crayon stubs on to a piece of paper, put another piece of paper over and press with a warm iron. !! Now let your child peel off the top sheet to reveal the picture under-

neath. If the crayons are fairly thin, you can use a pencil sharpener to obtain the shavings.

RUBBINGS: Rubbings can be made from any object which has a raised or indented surface, for example textured wallpaper, coins, textured floor or wall tiles, engraved names (as on cutlery or a dog's name tab), piece of bark. Just cover the object with a piece of thin plain paper (greaseproof paper is better for younger children, because it is stronger; older ones can use typing copy paper) and rub all over the surface with the side of a wax crayon, or the end of a stubby one, or older children could use a soft pencil.

COINING IT IN: Make rubbings from coins, cut out and stick on card, to make loose change for playing shops.

DESIGN REPEATS: Whatever object you use, try moving the paper along each time, so that you get a whole sheet of repeated rubbings. Either leave them as they are for an interesting picture, or cut them out for use as gift tags, or greetings cards. The advantage of cutting them out is that this gets rid of the crayon which overshot the object. Once the cut-outs are stuck on a piece of plain card, they make a most unusual impression.

OUTDOOR RUBBINGS: Try a trip out to find different objects to 'rub' – water hydrant lids, markings on lamp posts, sign posts, any name plates (with the permission of the owner!); walls and the bark of trees can make fascinating rubbings.

DESIGNS ON BARK: Bring a piece of bark home and use it to make rubbings all over large pieces of paper. These can then be used to decorate boxes or waste paper bins, or as wrapping paper.

LEAF MAGIC: Older children can try leaf prints using the rubbing technique. Collect a number of different leaves and from each type choose the best one. Lay each leaf, veins uppermost, on newspaper, cover with thin plain paper, and rub a soft pencil or crayon over the top. These actually work best if the rubbing is done all in the same direction, since this encourages children to be more gentle. Because leaves are fragile, if you do not have an over-five you could do the rubbing yourself, and the leaves can then be cut out. Very young ones can stick them on the drawing of a tree after the prints have been cut out.

COLLAGE DRAWINGS: There are ideas in the collage chapter (see page 36) for other activities involving drawing and painting. The general idea is to draw an outline picture then make grass, rooftiles, trees, etc., in the ways suggested, but younger children would enjoy just covering a sheet of paper with paste and sprinkling on any of the small collage ingredients listed in that chapter. It's a nice idea to use outlines, such as curtain rings, pastry cutters or other open shapes to create patterns of particular ingredients, but your child may just want to sprinkle it anywhere (on the paper!) with a teaspoon or an old spice container with holes in the top, or just chuck it all on.

KEEPSAKES: You may like to date a few drawings and keep them in a scrapbook.

A FREER APPROACH: Some children who don't take at first to 'free' drawing will spend a long time drawing round shapes or filling in colouring books and dot-to-dot pictures, so these can provide excellent entertainment value and do no harm as long as they have plenty of opportunity for drawing freely too.

SQUIGGLES: Draw swirly lines all over the paper. The 'holes' can then be coloured in using different colours to make a pattern.

COLOURING BOOKS AND STENCILS: Although some people criticise these because they do most of the work for the children and thus, perhaps, discourage their own creative instincts, there is no sound evidence for this view, and many children thoroughly enjoy the non-demanding nature of colouring books, particularly when recovering from an illness or generally feeling a bit under the weather.

A SAMPLER: Using graph paper with large squares, outline the letters of a name, or the shape of a house to be filled in. Different colours can be used in the squares around the edge to make a frame.

MORE HAND AND FOOT PRINTS: This time, instead of dipping the hand in paint, place a hand or a foot on paper and draw around it.

ME: You will need newspaper, lining or wallpaper for this, so that your child can lie full length on it. Draw around to make an outline, which can then be filled in with eyes, nose, mouth, clothes and so on.

3. Collage

Useful things to have

Large pieces of paper, the stiffer the better, in different colours
Corrugated card
Sheets of card
Fabric pieces[1]
Containers for all the bits and pieces[2]
‼ Glue[3]

‼ Brush or lolly stick to spread glue
‼ Small, round-ended scissors that will cut efficiently
Framing material[4]
A selection of items to make the pictures[5]
Preserved leaves and flowers[6]
Damp cloth

Notes

1. Any and every type of fabric will come in useful: velvet, fur, P.V.C., carpet samples or left-overs, corduroy, printed cottons, lurex fabric, smooth nylon, wool, tweed (particularly the highly textured type), hessian, lace, wadding (used for quilting, makes wonderful clouds and smoke).

2. Collect plenty of the following, with lids if possible. Margarine tubs, yogurt pots, small plastic containers with lids (freezer shops and catalogues usually have a good selection), foil freezer containers (intended for individual pies, or try the sectioned ones intended for whole meals), picnic trays, egg poachers, bun tins. Some of these, particularly those with lids, will be useful for storing items, others for putting items in while the collage picture is in progress. For instance, items like lentils and spices which will be available in the kitchen any-way do not need to be stored separately in a collage box; they can be distributed in bun tins or egg poachers at the beginning of the collage session.

3. Probably the best buy is a large pot of P.V.A. glue. It is milky when wet (so you can see where it is going), but dries clear, and it is washable. If it should get on jumpers, put them in the freezer for a couple of hours, after which the glue will become crisp enough to chip off. If you do not have a freezer, leave the jumper somewhere cold until it is completely dry before attempting to remove the glue. Wallpaper paste is adequate for many purposes and is cheaper. When using the glue, transfer some to a shallow dish – if you leave it in the large pot it could tip up, and anyway would end up with a selection of lentils, bits of twig and eggshell in it. Put it on with a glue spreader – it will ruin brushes. If glue is a new experience for your child, a demonstration session with a few rules laid down is called for.

4. If you would like to frame some of the finished products, you can do this with stiff card (from art shops), cutting out a suitable sized centre square or rectangle with a Stanley knife. This is fairly fiddly, so you may prefer to buy the frames ready cut – you can get thin cardboard frames in picture-framing shops fairly cheaply, including oval ones that are very difficult to cut yourself, although a cheese-portion box makes a good round one. Alternatively, you can use old picture frames, or simply trim the edges of the finished collage and lay on a larger piece of coloured paper. If you have some dress-maker's pinking shears, a trim round the edge of the finished collage with these will look most effective.

5. Choose from the following list of possibilities. Keep the items that are not already in the kitchen in separate containers in one large box ready for action. Particularly if you have young children, provide just a few at a time, otherwise the whole session may get out of hand.

Possibilities:

Fabric pieces (see note 1)
Bits of wool
Embroidery silks
Bits of string (of different thicknesses, e.g. include green garden twine)
Drinking straws
!! Woodshavings
!! Sawdust
!! Bits of wood
!! Used matchsticks
!! Bottle tops
!! Odd beads or buttons

!! Seeds (sunflower, melon, marrow, and seed heads)
Cones
Sand
Lentils, macaroni, rice, any shaped pasta
Salt, semolina, ground spices, herbs, cocoa, coffee, tea
Any breakfast cereal
!! Lollipop sticks
!! Twigs
Wadding
Shells

Feathers
Ribbon
Ric-rac braid, lace and other
    trimmings
Tape used instead of zip
    fastenings that pulls apart and
    reseals
Pictures cut from old card or
    magazines
Tissue paper
Glitter
Talcum powder
Powder paint
Kitchen foil and coloured foil
Paper doilys

Grated wax crayons (use a
    pencil sharpener if the
    crayons are small enough)
‼ Very small pieces of cling film
    or cellophane for windows
Sweet papers
Sequins
Small stones
‼ Brass split pins (e.g. for 'clock'
    hands)
Egg shells (washed and allowed
    to dry)
Gummed coloured paper (in
    sheets; the shapes are usually
    too fiddly for little fingers)

The possibilities are endless – but many of the items are interchangeable in terms of the purposes they can serve in a picture. As you progress with these beautiful collages together, you will develop an eye for bits and pieces that are just right for particular aspects of the picture. You will probably find that your children do the same, and nothing in the house will be safe again!

6. Preserving leaves and flowers:

i) Lay between sheets of blotting paper under a pile of books for a week or so.

ii) If you want to use natural looking leaves, use the glycerine method: collect the leaves late in the year, just before they begin to fall. Squash the ends of the twigs and stand in a mixture of 1 part glycerine, 2 parts water, about 10 cm (4 inches) deep, for 2 weeks. Old Man's Beard is particularly successful prepared like this, then sprayed with hair lacquer to protect it.

iii) Preserving good flowers by the borax method: flowers should be fully open, in perfect condition and absolutely dry, with all the leaves removed. Cover the bottom of a box with borax, place the flowers on it, heads facing downwards, then sprinkle more powder on until the flowers are covered. Leave the box in a warm dry place for a week or so after which the

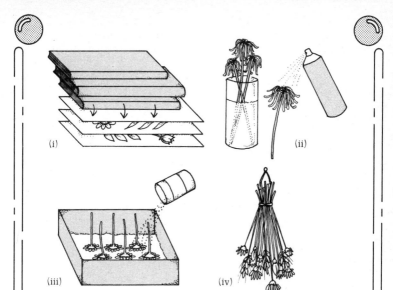

(i)　　(ii)

(iii)　　(iv)

flowers should be quite dry. You can use the same borax over and over again.

iv) Flowers, grasses and seed heads can be dried by hanging upside down in bunches in a dry, airy cupboard away from bright light.

v) To dye dried flowers, put in hot (not boiling) household dye, leave half an hour, then rinse and hang up to dry. Grasses can be dyed before drying by standing them in the dye until they have soaked it up to the tips.

General hints

Let them decide: Once you have provided all the ingredients, it is probably best to sit firmly on your own urge to create and leave your child to it, unless you have the sort of child who prefers lots of help and ideas – you can always have a go after bedtime!

Individual creations: Different children will want to manage their collage in different ways – some will just enjoy experimenting, others will like to fill in or copy a picture, older ones will be able to draw their own, and some younger children will just throw everything on the floor, in which case try again in a few months (or years).

Starting off: Try to keep the table (covered with newspaper) fairly organized with one place for the glue, another for the ingredients (on a tray, for example), another for the damp cloth. The child will need protection for clothes (see Chapter 2, note 6, page 23), and newspaper or an old curtain on the floor is fairly essential, unless you want to tread on escaped lentils for weeks to come. At first you may have to make a lot of suggestions; how many depends both on the age and the personality of your child, and on the idea you choose to start with. 'Decorating the box' and 'Making patterns' are good ones to begin with, since children can become familiar with the possibilities of collages, without the constraints of 'making a picture'. Using the glue rather than where to put the objects is the main attraction at first.

Coming back to it: Older children particularly may want to have a rest and come back to their picture at another time. Leaving the materials out can cause problems, particularly if you are short of working surfaces or have even younger children around. Keeping things organized should make it easier to collect up the bits and pieces quickly. The picture can be put on the wall while it is waiting to be finished, although keep it flat until the glue has dried, or everything will fall off.

Framing it: However non-creative you may feel you or your child is, collage will always produce something special which will last a surprisingly long time. See note 4, page 39, for framing suggestions.

Ideas

DECORATING THE BOX: You could begin by helping to decorate a large box to keep all the bits in. Cover three sides with pretty paper, old paintings, prints or drawings (see chapter 2, Painting and Drawing). Cover the 4th side with plain paper, which can then be decorated with a selection of the collage ingredients. Use as many as possible, then this side can serve as a reminder of what is in the box, and what it looks like when glued as part of a picture. If collage ingredients are used to cover more than one side, the other sides will need to be done at different times, because of the need to dry flat, and they may be vulnerable in storage. One decorated side, kept at the front, will stay fairly intact for as long as required.

MAKING PATTERNS: Some children, particularly younger ones and those who have never tried collage before, may just like to make patterns with the smaller items, such as semolina and cocoa, perhaps using outlines such as pastry cutters to control the spread. Put blobs of glue on the paper, spread it thinly, and lay the cutter over before sprinkling with whatever is fancied inside.

FILLING IN: If you draw a simple outline (cat, house, tree, path, dog, flowers), your child can paint it with glue and fill it in with suitable ingredients. Below are some suggestions for individual outlines.

MY TEDDY: Draw an outline of teddy; he can be filled in with fur fabric, and given bead or button eyes and black fabric paws. You will get ideas on what to use from the 'real' teddy – he may have a tartan 'hat', or a check tie, or 'he' may be a 'she' with a skirt or pinafore. Just cut out the shape to be stuck over the fur, or if you are short of fur fabric, you can use other fabrics to dress the teddy picture.

MY TOYS: Ask your child to choose some favourite toys and make a picture of them. You can use catalogue pictures of the actual toy, where available, otherwise draw or trace the outlines and choose some suitable ingredients to represent them.

FLOWERS: Collage pictures of flowers always look beautiful. The centres can be filled in with lentils, small dried beans, peas or barley, sequins or beads. The petals can be larger beans, such as coffee beans or haricot beans !! (do not use red beans, they are poisonous when not thoroughly cooked), pieces of macaroni, pasta shells, or even dried flower petals, although younger children will find these too fragile; leaves can be felt, green fabric, or dried leaves. Try a collage of some snowdrops made with pieces of white lace, or a bunch of pasta flowers tied with real ribbon at the bottom. Alternatively, use a cheese-portion box, which has been painted and which has a paper doily flower in the middle.

DRIED LEAF/FLOWER PICTURE: Arrange leaf sprays (oak, ferns) or flower sprays of different colours, shapes and sizes in an attractive pattern and stick them in place with small blobs of glue. You can then fit this into an old picture frame.

A BIG FAT CAT: Draw the outline of a large cat. Glue over it, then use some crushed brown or white eggshells to fill it in. Whiskers can be lengths of wool, eyes can be black felt ovals and/or shiny beads or sequins, the nose can be black P.V.C. and more wool can be used to shape the mouth. String can be glued around the outline for an even more special effect.

A VERY PRETTY DRESS: Draw the basic outline of a dress, then fill in using beads or buttons, various fabrics and trimmings, and perhaps a P.V.C. belt. If you sew, you could use fabrics left over from your own or your child's clothes.

OTHER POSSIBLE OUTLINES: You could draw any person your child knows well, including himself; any food which is particularly enjoyed, either an individual item (such as an iced cake), or a whole dinner; any favourite animal, or a character from a favourite television programme, comic or book.

A COMPLETE PICTURE: Instead of just drawing one item, try a combination of elements to create a complete picture or scene. For younger children you will need to draw or trace an outline of all the components in the picture. If like me you are not particularly artistic, start off by copying or tracing a picture from a holiday brochure, magazine, or your child's favourite nursery-rhyme or story book. If you copy a magazine picture, bits of the actual picture can then be cut out and used to fill in part of the collage, choosing other ingredients for the remaining parts. You should ask your child to choose a favourite picture, and see if you can find together the best collage materials to represent each individual part. The following are some other ideas for creating whole pictures.

INDOOR TREE: Draw a large outline of a tree with bare branches and stick it on to a door, wall or cupboard. Paint the trunk, or stick on fabric, then every time you go out bring back some leaves to stick on the branches. (Paint them with P.V.A. glue if you want them to last.) If you are feeling particularly adventurous, this could be extended to create a complete country scene, with hedges, ponds, fences and walls, cattle and sheep.

MAKING GRASS: Spread glue over the required area, sprinkle with sawdust, and when it is dry shake the surplus back into the container. Paint the 'lawn' green. Another idea is to use old felt carpet underlay painted green, or cotton towelling in an appropriate shade.

PLOUGHED FIELDS: For country scenes, corrugated cardboard painted brown makes very acceptable, realistic, ploughed fields.

A PATTERN PICTURE: Draw stripes, swirls or geometric shapes on a piece of strong paper and fill each space with a different ingredient. You can either use one colour overall, or make it as bright and colourful as possible, with different textures in each space.

NIGHT SCENE: Use black or dark blue paper, silver foil or bought stars to create a night-time collage.

MY HOUSE: Draw an outline which approximates to the shape of your own house. The roof can be filled in with 'slates' of black paper rectangles (or grey or rust, depending on your own roof). It can have foil or cellophane windows, fabric or lace curtains, sand or tweed fabric walls and a bead handle on the door; a path can be 'cobbled' with lentils; a dog can be fur fabric or velvet with matchstick legs and a wool tail, bead eyes and a shiny black P.V.C. nose; flowers can be filled in with lace or other pretty trimmings; a tree could have thick brown fabric or coloured sawdust trunk and screwed-up bits of green tissue or crêpe paper leaves, or use dried leaves. You could add an outline of a postman's van to be filled in with shiny red foil, with milk-bottle top wheels. Finish off with wadding clouds and smoke.

GRANDMA'S HOUSE: As a special present, make a collage of Grandma's house in a similar way to 'My House' above, to frame for her. Instead of a frame, you could cut a piece of chipboard the correct size, paint the sides and back, and stick the finished collage on the front.

OTHER SCENES: Any building can be used as a model – playgroup, school, shops or Mum or Dad's workplace. A seaside scene provides lots of possibilities, or a camp site, anywhere your child has been recently. How about the park, hospital or doctor's surgery, a country garden or a farm, or even a scene from a television programme, in which case there may be a picture in the television press you could use as a guide?

STAINED GLASS WINDOW: Cut out a church window shape from black paper (see illustration), then use cellophane or colourful sweet papers for the window. Cut these into interesting shapes by folding them in half first; this will give a properly symmetrical shape. Glue the windows on to the black paper.

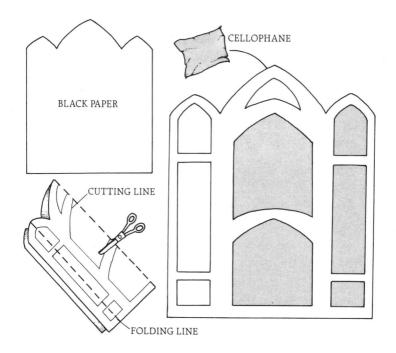

SCENTED PICTURES: Draw concentric circles on a sheet of paper. Each part can be filled in with a different, strong-smelling powdery item – cocoa in the middle, surrounded by a dried herb, then cinnamon or curry powder and lastly a strong smelling talcum powder. For this to be really successful, each circle needs to be painted with glue, sprinkled with the desired ingredient, then allowed to dry before shaking off the surplus (back into the container, ready for the next picture session) and doing the next one. It is therefore a convenient activity for a child who does not like doing any particular thing for very long.

A SPECIAL SELECTION: Choose just one or two things from the list on pages 39 and 40 and use as imaginatively as possible. For example, just use sand or sawdust, coloured all different colours (either mix colouring with water and add to sand/sawdust or mix dry powder paint with sand/sawdust, then add water – spread on a tray to dry in the oven). Or screw small pieces of different coloured tissue paper into tiny balls and use these to fill in a simple outline. Or dip eggshell bits in different coloured paints during a painting session and leave to dry; then use to fill in an outline, perhaps of geometric shapes. Or make a garden picture just using dried grasses, flowers, leaves and real bark (you will have to break the bark into small pieces, or it will not stick). Or use just magazine pictures; cut out pictures of heads, arms, legs, bodies, hats, shoes, handbags and clothes: older children will be able to stick them together to make a 'street picture' of silly people, younger ones can simply stick them all over the paper.

A NUMBER POSTER: If you are feeling particularly educational one day, make a number poster. Pencil 11 rows across a large piece of paper, and write '(Child's name)'s Number Poster' across the first. Number the others down the left hand side from 1 to 10, and glue the appropriate number of objects in a line beside each number, with equal space in between, so that it is easy to see, for example, that 6 is one more than 5. (See chapter 11 on Sorting and Threading, page 130, for ideas on small objects to use.)

CHRISTMAS AND BIRTHDAY CARDS: These are little complete pictures and any of the ideas in this chapter can be used. Glitter tends to be the main ingredient of Christmas cards, but make sure you give the finished card a good shake (over the container – it can be expensive when used enthusiastically) or the receiver will get an envelope full of glitter over her toast and marmalade when she opens it! Cotton-wool snowmen, and red foil breasted robins are nice and Christmassy – you can get ideas from purchased cards. For birthday cards you could do an outline of the receiver's name or age to be filled in with any of the ingredients, or even a picture of their house. **Any** collage card will be special for the receiver.

MY OWN IDEA: The nicest aspect of this particular activity is that once familiar with the concept of collage, children come up with some wonderful ideas themselves. Your only task will be to provide the necessary bits and pieces and offer a few suggestions now and again. The result will always be unusual and very pleasing to look at. For posterity, name and date the finished product; older children can sign their name on the picture and younger ones could put a special mark as their 'signature'.

4.Play-Dough

Useful things to have

To make the play-dough[1]
Self-raising flour
Plain flour
Salt
Cream of tartar
Oil (the cheapest cooking oil)
Food colourings
Powder paint
Cocoa

Equipment
Ice cream containers or similar for storage
!! Bluntish knives or plastic ones

!! Fork for making edges and patterns
Rolling pin[2]
Cutters of various shapes and sizes[3]
Cake trays and tins for 'biscuits'
Fish slice or spatula
Paper cake cases[4]
Flour sifter[5]
Things to stick in the dough[6]
Things to scent the dough[7]
Weighing scales for older children, if available
Apron or old shirt (flour spreads surprisingly!)

Workplace:
Table, or a large piece of lino-type floor covering, or a tray, with something to protect the floor if it is carpeted.

Notes

1. You will not need all these ingredients, just choose a recipe from the list on page 54 according to the type of play-dough you require. Although the dough looks appetizing, do not let children eat it.

2. If you have more than one child using the play-dough at one time, you will definitely need one rolling pin for each child. They will (probably) share cutters but will fight over the rolling pin. A cut up broom handle would do, although you can buy smallish rolling pins quite cheaply. Try to get ones without ridges at the ends, since in inexperienced hands these mark the dough, making a line right through the middle of a carefully cut out rabbit or whatever.

3. You can buy special small ones for children, shaped as animals, stars, hearts, but they are too fiddly for the very young. Use cheap plastic cake and biscuit cutters instead and keep them all together in one container.

4. Providing paper cake cases seems rather extravagant and of course they are not essential. However, children do seem to get a lot of pleasure out of them, and this is another example (like the egg poacher) of your money being better spent than it would be on an expensive commercial toy that may not be played with more than a couple of times.

5. Again, a flour sifter is not essential, but it is fun, and actually makes less mess than handfuls of flour taken from the bag; it also involves less of your time – if you are 'minding' the flour bag, you will be continually on call for more flour, usually when you have wet hands. You can buy cheap plastic sifters, or holes punched in the lid of a plastic tub (with a warmed knitting needle) would do the trick (*tape* the lid on!).

6. The sort of things you need include currants for eyes, buttons, bottle caps, wheels from broken toys, lolly sticks and used matchsticks for legs, black wool for spider legs, whiskers, cut-up drinking straws, pipe-cleaners or feathers.

7. To scent the dough (just for a bit of variety) you can use peppermint essence, rosewater (available from chemists – take your own bottle), orange flower water (also from chemists), almond flavouring, ground ginger, cinnamon powder, curry powder, in fact any food flavouring.

(Recipes)

Colouring suggestions: These apply to all the dough recipes:
  i) Add food colouring to the water before mixing – this makes a smooth overall colour.
  ii) Add food colouring or powder paint after mixing – this makes a streaky marbled interesting dough that gradually becomes one colour after a few sessions.
  iii) Use cocoa or brown powder paint.
  iv) Leave some a natural colour to remind the child of pastry.

Stretchy dough: This is the right consistency for exploring, rather than rolling and cutting. It does not keep more than a few days because there is no salt, but provides much entertainment value while it lasts. Simply mix 750 g (1½ lb) self-raising flour with 300-450 ml (½-¾ pint) water (you can of course halve the quantities, but a big stretchy mess is part of the fun of this one). Colour as desired. When this dough is held up, a large dollop hangs enticingly from it and can be pulled and stretched before finally breaking. If a finger is poked in, the holes gradually fill up again all by themselves. It is wonderfully squashy when squeezed in the hands, and oozes up between the fingers in a rather sensual way; it also makes a satisfyingly splatty noise when slapped on the table. As a change, you could use bread flour (strong flour) which makes an even more stretchy dough, from which long ropes can be made.

Rolling and cutting dough: If you make a dough with plain flour and salt, you end up with a quite different mixture which does not stretch or fill up holes by itself, and is meant for rolling, cutting and stamping imprints in. The salt preserves it, but makes it more brittle, so you need a little cooking oil to counteract this. Use 450 g (1 lb) plain flour, 150-300 ml (¼-½ pint) water, 2 tablespoons cooking salt and 2 tablespoons cooking oil to make it shiny and pliable. Mix all the ingredients together well. Colour as desired. This keeps well for several months in a lidded container, but keep a watch on it for signs of deterioration.

Smooth and wonderful dough: The smoothest play-dough of all is one made with cream of tartar, which rolls and cuts beautifully. It takes nearly a whole pot of cream of tartar, so you may like to try your child out on the above first. It is still a great deal cheaper than the commercial dough however and can provide enough peace and quiet to make it infinitely worthwhile. Stir 2 cups of plain flour, 1 cup of salt and 4 tablespoons of cream of tartar in a saucepan, then add 2 cups of water, colouring and 2 tablespoons of oil. Cook over a low heat for 3-5 minutes, stirring well. Any lumps will come out as it is kneaded and it feels wonderful in your hands when it is still warm – we have to take it in turns in our house to feel the play-dough just after it is cooked! If this play-dough is kept in a lidded plastic container, it will last for ages – we have some that is going strong after over a year and still shows no apparent signs of deterioration.

General hints

Enjoying the feel: Nearly all children enjoy play-dough from an early age. Much of the enjoyment comes from simply handling the dough, often children will not 'make' anything for ages. Leave them to it – they will start rolling/cutting/modelling when they are ready, according to either their age or their temperament.

Avoiding arguments: If you have more than one child, you will need to divide the dough up and give them each a container of dough. Put their names on 'their' containers, since younger children tend to mix up the colours and upset the older one. This is particularly applicable in the case of the last recipe ('smooth and wonderful'), because it keeps so long, and older children who are at school may only play with theirs once a month or so; they will be most upset if they come home to find the little one has mixed all their colours together to make a box of dirty brown mush.

The bought sort: Home-made play-dough is cheap and easy to make in large quantities, meaning your child can have more of it and a greater choice of colours. If you do buy play-dough, make sure you do not accidentally buy Plasticine instead – it is much too stiff for little fingers. Plasticine will come into its own once they are older.

Go on, make it!: It really is worthwhile making the small amount of effort required to produce play-dough. In terms of entertainment value, it is unbeatable, and if you introduce a new colour to revive flagging interest every so often, it becomes even better value, since the first colours are then played with again, with a renewed interest. Try it and see – it is a marvellous invention for busy parents.

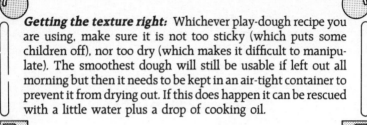

Getting the texture right: Whichever play-dough recipe you are using, make sure it is not too sticky (which puts some children off), nor too dry (which makes it difficult to manipulate). The smoothest dough will still be usable if left out all morning but then it needs to be kept in an air-tight container to prevent it from drying out. If this does happen it can be rescued with a little water plus a drop of cooking oil.

Ideas

STARTING OFF: Very young children who are unable to manipulate the 'rolling and cutting' dough will enjoy the 'stretchy dough'. Just let them play with it, although you may need to show them what it can do, if they are a little nervous at first.

NEXT TIME: Make a fresh batch using the smooth dough. Your child can watch or help (according to age) and as soon as it is cool enough to handle (but still warm) give him some to feel (you can keep a bit for yourself!). Once it has cooled down you can provide the other ingredients and perhaps demonstrate rolling and cutting if necessary. Your child might like to press objects into it to make patterns.

MAKING MONSTERS: Although younger children will not make models, they can use the dough to make snakes, gingerbread men, or anything else they fancy. The smoothest play-dough is best, although the 'rolling and cutting' recipe works too. Begin with simple ideas, such as a hedgehog made with a ball of play-dough stuck with spent matches and currant eyes, or a spider can be created from another ball, flattened and given 8 pipecleaner legs. A bird can be made with real feather wings. Older children can make little men, or monsters from outer space, perhaps copying a picture for ideas.

REALLY REVOLTING: A horrible colour change often incites children to greater action. Try black or brown colouring: the black makes super tarmac, and I leave you to discover for yourselves what they make with the brown! One of the less revolting creations is a very realistic bar of chocolate with which they can trick someone.

LUMPY DOUGH: Try changing the texture by adding 2 tablespoons of jumbo or rolled oats to the flour before mixing, or use the 'granary' type flour sold for bread-making. The new texture is most interesting.

WEIGHING IT OUT: If you have a set of kitchen scales with weights, or if you can find some old scales in a jumble sale, older children may enjoy weighing out their lumps of dough, or making pounds (kilos?) of apples, sprouts, carrots, pears, bananas, etc. These can also be used for playing shops (see chapter 7 'Dressing up and Fantasy play').

MAKING CAKES: For cakes and biscuits you need to provide cutters, cake or bun tins, paper cases and bits and pieces to decorate them. If you keep one batch of play-dough white or pink, it can be used for icing 'chocolate' cakes, although it is difficult to separate the different colours afterwards, so you may prefer to use the second, cheaper recipe for this. Flour is essential if biscuits are being cut and you will need to provide a spatula or similar to prise them off the table in one piece.

KEEPSAKES: Here is a dough which dries hard on exposure to air, so may be enjoyed greatly by those children (probably the older ones) who make models. It takes a lot of baking soda, but since it makes permanent objects, it does not seem so extravagant. Mix 1 cup of cornflour, 2 cups of baking soda and 1¼ cups of water. Cook over a medium heat until thickened. Knead well. This dough can be used to make food for doll's tea parties, or supplies for military men dolls, brooches, pendants, counters for games, dishes and so on. When the models are hard, they can be painted and/or varnished. Enamel paints do not need varnishing, but take a while to dry, and are not washable. Acrylic paints dry very quickly, are washable (fairly), but need varnishing.

PAINTING: If you are having a painting session, try winding a strip of play-dough round a cotton reel; stick a pencil through the centre of the cotton reel, engrave a pattern round the play-dough with a matchstick or another pencil, then dip in paint and use as a 'printing wheel'.

CLEAN UP: If you have still got a large portion of a rainy day to fill after a play-dough session, cleaning up the mess could lead to a bit of water play, washing up the equipment in bubbly water at the sink.

MAKING THINGS: Play-dough is also very useful for using as a base for sticking other types of models on to – see chapter 8 'Making things'.

5. Water Play

Useful things to have

Bowl[1]
Protection for the floor, if
  inside[2]
Container for equipment[3]
Equipment for pouring[4]

‖ A variety of objects for
  floating, sinking and
  absorbing[5]
Other items for added
  interest[6]

Notes

1. You can use a bowl, a baby bath, or a sink half full of water (at least 25 cm, 10 inches depth for pouring). ‖ **NEVER** leave young children alone with water, however shallow, even for a minute. If the telephone rings, or there is someone at the door, **take your child with you** to answer it, every time.

2. To protect your floor if inside, use old towels, newspaper, a small groundsheet or heavy duty polythene plus newspaper to prevent slipping. Towels are best, because they absorb the puddles and do not create a particularly slippery surface.

3. To keep the water play equipment together, use a bucket, laundry basket (plastic), or a plastic vegetable rack, in the bathrom if you have a bit of space there.

4. Containers for pouring **from** include: metal teapot, old whistling type kettle, small plant-watering can with a long spout, child's watering can (you can get these with different types of spouts), plastic squash bottle, jug, water container with a tap (available from camping shops or shops which sell home wine-making equipment); in fact any plastic container with a smallish pouring hole or lip. Equipment for pouring **through** can be a funnel (one which fits plastic tubing if possible), plastic tubing (from D.I.Y. or shops which sell home wine-making equipment), piece of hose, teastrainer, sieve, colander, coffee strainer, flower pots (plastic), toy water wheel, toy pump. Other containers which can be used include beakers, buckets, plastic egg cups, cream or yogurt cartons, washing up liquid container (which can be used as a squirter, a pourer, or a submarine in the bath, or you can cut across it and use it as a beaker and funnel); small or large tins make a nice noise, although they will need to be dried very thoroughly after use to prevent rusting. They could also be smeared with a little petroleum jelly if they are to be stored.

5. For floating and sinking, try corks, bottle tops, aerosol caps, ping-pong and other small balls, nailbrush, pieces of (sanded) wood, nutshells (for example, walnut shells for boats), fir cones, paper, pieces of polystyrene as used for packaging, open or closed plastic containers, stones, shells, toy boats, conkers, paper cake cases, pennies, a piece of paper; for soaking up water provide felt, natural sponges (available from the cosmetic section in the chemists), foam sponges or pieces of foam, or any scraps of fabrics.

6. For added interest, depending on your facilities, try a plant sprayer or small cosmetic spray bottle (if you are brave, or outside), straws (rigid looped ones are fun), medicine dropper, spoons and ladles, empty squeezy 'lemons', thin wire twisted into a loop for bubbles, cotton reels, washing up liquid, glycerine, wire egg beater, food colouring.

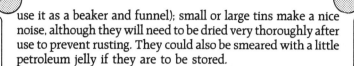

General hints

It's wonderful: Playing with water is lovely – relaxing and soothing and hypnotic. It also gives many opportunities for little scientific discoveries about the properties of water and of objects, but these are just additional advantages, secondary to the sheer enjoyment of pouring, squirting and splashing.

Preparation time: Like painting, there seems to be a lot of preparation and cleaning up, but the time is usually well rewarded in terms of the time children will play with water, and of course preparation time is much reduced if you can keep all the equipment somewhere together.

Extra materials: As you can see, looking through the list of equipment in notes 4, 5 and 6, all you are really doing is providing materials which do different things in the water –

they float or sink, absorb water in different ways and to various extents, they move the water around in different ways, so you may well have other objects around the house which could be enjoyed when children are exploring the possibilities of water. Have a look, too, in home wine-making, gardening and camping shops if you have the opportunity – yet again, your money may be better spent on an item not intended as a toy rather than on a less versatile 'proper' toy.

Chatting as you play: If you feel like watching your child playing, it can be very interesting to see their discoveries, and if your child is the kind who enjoys questions, there are many opportunities for 'prompting'. For example, the conversation might go: 'I wonder why the ping-pong ball floats?' ''Cos it's white' 'Let's try the white stone then'. **However,** partly because of the hypnotic nature of water play, there are many children who like to be quiet, to play to their heart's content. They will still make the discoveries, only in their own time. Of course prompts do not have to be questions requiring answers, often just a comment as you pass will set the child on a new course of thought.

Inside or outside?: If the weather is warm and you have some outside space, then naturally outside is the best place to be; you will feel more relaxed about the activity (**!! although again, do not leave your child alone outside playing with water**) and your child can be more enthusiastic in sploshing and splashing. However, water play works well inside, with very young children on the floor, and older ones standing on a chair at the sink with towels laid across the floor in front. You will have to rely on explanations and threats to protect the walls! There is no reason why you should not move up to the bathroom and use the bath although this may not be so convenient as regards your getting on with something else at the same time. As long as you are present (even if you are sewing, or reading a book, or cleaning the sink or decorating the bathroom) it does not matter where the water play goes on and the bath may suit your nerves better. A mid-day bath as a complete change of routine is most intriguing to a lot of young children.

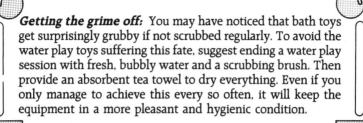

Getting the grime off: You may have noticed that bath toys get surprisingly grubby if not scrubbed regularly. To avoid the water play toys suffering this fate, suggest ending a water play session with fresh, bubbly water and a scrubbing brush. Then provide an absorbent tea towel to dry everything. Even if you only manage to achieve this every so often, it will keep the equipment in a more pleasant and hygienic condition.

Ideas

STARTING OFF: Just provide water, a few containers from the list, some items for pouring, floating and sinking. Older children can be encouraged to wipe up spills indoors with a handy towel as they go along. 'Tidy up' the water every so often if it gets too full of equipment – there needs to be some water available for pouring and filling, and if the bowl/sink/bath is chock-ablock with objects, this won't be possible.

BLOWING BUBBLES: Have a bubble session. Either use bubble bath mixture or good quality washing-up liquid (this will work better if you mix ½ cup with ⅓ cup of hot water and leave to stand overnight, when it will become a syrup). If you add a few drops of glycerine to the water, the bubbles come out better. !! Since some water is likely to end up in mouths, you could add some baby-bottle steriliser, to keep it hygienic. You can use any of the suggested equipment, although only provide straws if you child can be relied upon to **blow** not suck. Twisted wire loops or squares or triangles make interesting bubbles, and bubbles can also be blown through the ends of cotton reels. An egg beater for whisking bubbles into a froth is usually very popular – you can pick up the wire balloon-shaped hand whisks very cheaply nowadays.

COLOUR IT: Whether using bubbles or not, the addition of food colouring makes a fascinating variation. You could provide a number of transparent plastic bottles (with caps), with a different food colouring solution in each.

EXPERIMENTS: Make holes in plastic containers (with a warmed metal knitting needle to help prevent splitting) so your child can experiment with the effects of pressure on jets of water. Choose three or four similar containers and arrange the holes differently in each. For example, make one with a hole in the bottom, one with a line of holes from top to bottom, another with a ring of holes around the container, another with just a single hole, on the side, fairly near the base. You need to choose a fairly soft plastic if you are doing a number of holes close together – it is difficult to prevent yogurt-type pots from splitting between the holes.

WATER MUSIC: Fill some plastic cups or bottles with different levels of water and tap the rims with a spoon to make different sounds.

WASHDAY: Have a washing session for dolls or military men and their clothes, or for doll's house dishes, or toys, or anything else in the house that could do with a good clean and that could survive not-so-gentle treatment. If you have any space outside, garden toys (bike, car, tractor) could be washed, or spare flower pots may need a good clean, or the steps might benefit from a good scrub. Just have a look round to see what there is in the house or garden.

ON A SUNNY DAY: Again, if you have space outside, and you have a fridge or freezer that needs defrosting, put the ice that you clear out in a bucket and it can provide much entertainment outside.

GOING FOR A SAIL: Make boats with bits of wood, walnut shells, corks or the skin from halved or quartered oranges or grapefruits. Use a cocktail stick as a mast, stuck on with a tiny piece of play-dough, and make a paper sail. Alternatively, use paper cake cases and see what has to be put in them to make them sink; or float a piece of paper on the water and put things on it to see what happens.

PADDLING AMONG THE TOYS: A paddling pool with the water play equipment nearby (it will all end up in the pool) would happily fill a hot afternoon – you may even be able to get on with something in a chair nearby, or perhaps some gardening or D.I.Y. !! The latter may not be so successful though, since the D.I.Y. will probably appeal to the child more than the water and tools need very careful supervision.

6. Sand Play

Useful things to have

Dry sand[1]
Wet sand
Sand tray[2]
Dustpan (with straight edge) and brush

Large bucket to keep equipment in (with lid, if outside)
Equipment for play[3]

Notes

1. Fine silver sand can be bought from garden centres, or you can use washed builder's sand, but do not get the red type, since it tends to stain.

2. Some purchased sand pits have seats at the corners and can be used for water play too, so may be a worthwhile investment. However, an old baby bath (even a new one is cheaper than a commercial sand pit) will do just as well. Whatever you use, it is essential to have a cover that cannot be knocked off, to keep cats out. Even when the sand pit/bath is left for a short time, for example over lunchtime, it needs to be covered. Some people make their own sandpits, so this may be an idea if you have some space, but again remember to make a cover too. A small drain in the corner helps to keep the sand from becoming waterlogged.

3. Equipment includes small rubber or plastic spades, small rake or large comb, scoop, spoons, various large and small containers (small boxes, coffee tin, flower pot, foil dishes, mixing bowl, cartons from shopping (e.g. tea boxes), plastic jelly moulds, buckets sold for seaside play which often have interesting shapes at the bottom, sink tidy, bun tin, items to build with or just to add interest, any caps (toothpaste, aerosol, bottle), ruler or pieces of flat wood (sanded), lolly sticks, shells, stones, fork, wooden spoon, magnifying glass, cardboard and paper, toy cars, trucks, tractors, road signs, petrol pumps, toy animals, plastic flowers, twigs, fircones, flags, leaves, foil for rivers and foil dishes for ponds, feathers; for dry sand, many of the water play ingredients are suitable, for example a funnel, colander, water-wheel, pourers, transparent bottles (plastic).

For either wet or dry sand an old pair of weighing scales will add to the fun for older children.

General hints

Wet or dry?: Wet and dry sand provide two different kinds of play. Wet sand can be used for moulding, building and land-scaping and needs a large fairly shallow container: the bigger, the better. Dry sand provides a relaxing activity more akin to water play and can be kept in a smaller container, such as a biscuit tin.

Rules of the game: !! Whichever sand you use, it is a good idea to try to persuade children to keep to a few basic rules:

i) No throwing – if sand does get in the eyes, wash with plenty of cold water, or instil two drops of castor oil in the corner of the eye and the sand will float out.

ii) No eating of sand cakes, etc. – it will not actually hurt them if they eat it, but too much can cause diarrhoea.

iii) Have a cleaning up time at the end of each day (or play). This may sound ambitious, but children can easily shake sand off toys and put them into the container, or wash and dry those that have been in wet sand. Small metal toy vehicles will soon get rusty if left around in wet sand. Although spilling is inevitable, and a part of the fun, you can teach older children to sweep up with a dustpan and brush (see 'Ideas', page 73).

iv) Sand needs to be washed occasionally to keep it sparkling and free of smells. Use a solution of sterilizing liquid (intended for babies' bottles or wine-making equipment) and rinse the sand thoroughly. It also helps to sprinkle some of the solution on to the sand every so often.

v) Children should not play in a sandpit if suffering from a tummy bug – accidents can occur and the infection spread.

Ideas

EXPLORE AND DISCOVER: Just discovering the sand and its properties is usually the first much enjoyed activity. With a selection of the pieces of equipment from the list on page 68 this will keep younger children happy for some while. Slightly older ones may like to examine the sand more closely through a magnifying glass, which is an absorbing occupation.

BUCKETS AND SPADES: For children who only see the sea once a year, if at all, playing in sand with just a bucket and spade will be particularly pleasurable. Younger ones will probably just fill and empty the buckets; older ones can be shown how to make sandcastles and then they can start building.

POURING AND FILLING AND EMPTYING: Provide fine dry sand, a scoop, trowel or large spoon, some transparent plastic containers, a toy water wheel, a funnel and a sieve or colander. Children tend to find it very satisfying filling containers with dry sand by means of a scoop, and pouring the sand through the funnel, or sieve, or water wheel. Paper bags are also surprisingly satisfying to fill, although the younger ones will find this difficult to manage on their own. Older ones will enjoy 'weighing' their filled bags if you have some old scales with weights.

PLAYING SHOPS: Sand play can be combined with a dressing-up game to play shopkeepers. For this you need to provide empty quarter pound tea boxes or any other packaging from the shopping that can be filled with dry sand. Again, older children will be more sophisticated, demanding a counter, scales and perhaps a toy till and toy money (see chapter 7 'Dressing Up and Fantasy Play').

PLAYING COOKING: Dry sand plus water in a plastic jug are needed for this. You will also need to provide a mixing bowl, wooden spoon, fork, sieve, and perhaps a wire balloon hand whisk if you have an old one, or have bought one for water play. All sorts of cakes can be made, decorated with various twigs, small pretty stones, petals from flowers which have **dropped off** (emphasise this!) plants, and unusual small shells. Pies can be made in foil dishes. To make it really exciting you could provide coloured water, for example dark brown for chocolate cakes, bright pink for strawberry tarts, although unless you have the very silvery sand, they will not actually turn out amazingly pink.

COLOUR IT: Silver sand can be coloured, however, with a solution of food colouring and water. If you then want to use it dry, it can be spread on baking trays in a low oven (while you are cooking something else) for a while. Just do small quantities of two or three different colours and keep them in separate jars for a special treat. Alternatively, you can mix the dry sand with powder paint.

JELLIES: Provide different jelly moulds in different shapes and sizes, together with some coloured wet sand. Pressing sand into the moulds will make jellies which can then be used for a toys' tea party. The sand should be quite wet and pushed well down in the mould. Wash the moulds well before putting them to their normal use.

A MINIATURE TOWN: The whole sand pit or bath can be hollowed and shaped to make a miniature town or landscape. Rivers of foil can run down hills into a foil pond (you need to provide water to make this realistic), bridges can be made from toy bricks and a ruler or piece of flat wood or a strip of card; these can also be used for motorways and flyovers, using wider strips. Traffic lights can be made from a lolly stick with 3 circles of colour, stuck to the 'road' with a piece of play-dough. The roads themselves can be made from strips of cardboard, flat stones, black paper, haricot beans (for a village, cobbled effect) or just flattened strips of sand. The surface of sand roads could be sprinkled with black

powder paint or sand coloured black, for a special effect, or strips of cardboard could be painted with a mixture of sawdust and black paint during a painting session. Boxes for houses and garages could also be painted first, or use tins, bits of wood or toy bricks; shoeboxes and cereal boxes are useful here. Trees can be made from a cotton reel with pipe-cleaners, feathers or twigs stuck in the top, or just use twigs stuck in the sand; a windmill could be made from a small empty plastic bottle with 2 lolly sticks taped across; plastic flowers add an attractive touch. Apart from the pleasure in constructing their own village, this will provide endless new possibilities for playing in the sand pit.

WHERE ARE THE CARS?: The town needs to be busy, so toy cars, tractors, lorries, buses, petrol pumps and road signs can be added by older children who tend to expect more realism.

WHERE ARE THE PEOPLE?: As a final touch, bought toys such as construction kit accessories, small plastic people and animals could be used in the town, if you make it clear that they will need to be brought in and washed at the end of play.

FURTHER FURNISHING FOR THE TOWN: See chapter on 'Making Things' for more ideas on things you can create for your sand town, for example see: boats, trains, cowboy wagon, towns and land-scapes, defending the town.

A MINIATURE GARDEN: Five to seven year olds are often keen on miniature gardens. For these you need wet sand and a plate or tray into which go twig trees, foil-dish ponds, shell or stone rockeries, and plastic flowers or real ones if you have a source.

A COMPLETE CHANGE: Use sawdust instead of sand, if you can get hold of it, for older children who can be fairly relied upon not to make a meal of it. It behaves similarly to sand, and can be moulded when wet. It also has a supremely wonderful smell! If you only have a little, provide it in a bowl for using in a sand landscape – perhaps as a farmyard surface. Other possibilities are lentils and other dried pulses for building sites and gravelly surfaces, or for scooping, weighing, filling and emptying in exactly the same way as dry sand.

CLEAN-UP: Using a brush and dustpan requires more skill than you might imagine. It has to be taught in stages, first how to hold the pan steady, moving it back a little each time you sweep. You will probably have to hold the pan at first, so your child can use two hands for the brush, then swap over while the other end of the operation is mastered. On the other hand, it would be much quicker to do it yourself. . . .

7. Dressing Up And Other Fantasy Play

Useful things to have

Old clothes and accessories[1]
Items to make your own
props[2]

Notes

1. In fact, it is accessories which are important to collect, rather than clothes, since children of this age would just be swamped by a complete item of adult clothing. Here are some suggestions for items to obtain from jumble sales, grandparents, or from your own supplies: handbags and shopping bags, hats (old ladies' hats, felt hats, straw hats, caps, berets, policeman's/fireman's hats, workman's hats – probably bought from a toy shop), cloaks (made from curtains or the skirts of old dresses), wedding veil and princess's skirt (from old net curtains and elastic), frilly dresses and skirts (from old petticoats, dresses or nighties), shawls, chiffon scarves, belts, gloves, old bag for workman's tools, hairnet, slides, various materials with an interesting texture (velvet, fur, lace, chiffon, satiny material, sparkly material), tablecloths or old curtains (for brides' trains, cloaks, saris, ghosts, etc.).

Other props, which could be obtained by looking around a jumble sale together after the first rush is over, include: jewellery, saucepans, baking tins, plates, metal kettle and teapot, tray, pudding basins, plastic cutlery, cushions (to furnish a den), fish slice, colander, flour sifter, plates, wooden spoons, whisk, old scales, an old door knocker, an old pillow case (for a nurse's uniform, with a red cross on the front), blankets and sheets, breadboard (a round one makes a good steering wheel for a cardboard box car), spectacles without lenses, old shoes or wellies that are too big. Give any fabrics a wash before use.

2. To make your own props, you may need: cardboard boxes of all sizes, milk bottle tops (to make necklaces, brooches, badges or to decorate crowns), round cheese boxes or paper plates (to make clocks, masks or wheels on a cardboard box train), cardboard inners from toilet rolls (2 make good binoculars, or 1 for a telescope), macaroni (for making jewellery), feathers (for a

Red Indian Head-dress), corks or bottle caps (for knobs), empty food and other household goods packets for playing shops – biscuit, tea, cocoa, margarine tubs, cheese boxes, etc. Start a collection before you think you will need it so that you have time to build up a good choice of items. If you fill the boxes with scrunched up newspaper and tape or glue the ends down they will look more realistic and also will be more durable.

General hints

Where to keep it: The ingredients sound like a long list of other people's rubbish, and you probably will not have the space to store much in the way of dressing-up clothes and props, particularly the larger items like kettles and saucepans. Just get a few things to start with – you may have all you require in cupboards somewhere, or older relatives may have some hats and suchlike lurking in an attic. If at all possible, try to arrange materials so that they are accessible and look appealing, rather than in a crumpled heap at the bottom of a wardrobe somewhere. Cardboard boxes on their sides make functional, accessible, 'open-plan' storage or a plastic clothes airer is good for larger items.

The basics: Cloaks (or the material to make them – see below), and hats form the basis for most younger children's dressing up play (and the very young seem particularly fond of shoes), plus cardboard boxes for dens, trains, swords and shields, and also a few extras such as jewellery and scarves. These should provide plenty of scope for little ones. (**!!** Do not let under-fives have high-heeled shoes.)

Necklaces: Thread beads on shirring elastic, which when pulled does not snap.

Using the furniture: Bunk beds make a wonderful prop if you happen to have them and are reasonably easy going. They can be made into a den by hanging a blanket down from the top bunk, but even without this they can still be used as vehicles, such as a double-decker bus, a submarine or a boat.

Under threes: Since the imagination requires quite a lot of experience to fuel it, the under threes are unlikely to do an awful lot in the way of dressing up. They will naturally tend to copy the situations they **have** seen, such as household and D.I.Y. tasks, and perhaps shopping. They may also enjoy a 'den' in the corner of the room where you are.

In control: Much has been written about the way children 'play out' feared situations in fantasy play, but most children just enjoy it for its own sake. They are at the same time trying out what it feels like to be a doctor, dentist, patient, mother, father, shopkeeper or baby. Because it is a game, they have the added advantage of being in control of what happens in the particular situation they are imagining. They can say whatever they want, and the other 'participants' do what they want them to do – the baby doll, for instance, instantly stops crying when thrown headlong into a cot, ailing toy teddies always get better when they have seen the doctor, superman always wins his fights.

Preparation before an event: If there is a possibly worrying situation coming up, and your child is one who enjoys make-believe play, you could act out the event beforehand. You could join in a play hospital session, for example, or a teddy could have an interesting visit to the dentist, or the toys could start playgroup or school.

Coming to terms with an event: Some children play at hospitals a great deal after a stay in hospital themselves, partly because they now have lots of relevant new experiences to draw on and partly perhaps to sort out any confusion they may have felt, under conditions where they can decide what occurs and when.

Enjoying themselves: Whatever they may gain from dressing up, the main advantage, as with all these activities, comes if they are thoroughly enjoying themselves, and perhaps also leaving you to get on with something you would like to do, although you may have to do a bit of 'shopping' or take teddy's temperature now and again.

Children are different: Some children do not seem to enjoy imaginative play. They will look in amazement at other children (or parents) playing imaginative games and seem just not to see the point at all. Others will have complicated adventurous pretend fights or rush around shooting everyone with a few construction bricks stuck together as a gun, but 'playing shops' leaves them cold. Others love putting toys to bed or looking after them tenderly when they are crying or ill, but would never dream of using an imaginary gun.

Choice of props: It is worth providing a choice of props in order to find out what your particular child enjoys at the moment. Also, if you do not, you will probably find your four year old careering around the house with coat kept on by the hood, arms waving and shouting 'Batman' or similar. Not that there is anything wrong with that, it's just that once they have the idea of wearing a coat that way, you will have a job getting it on properly when it is pouring with rain or freezing cold outside. On the other hand they are just as likely to insist on wearing their cloaks outside instead of their coats. . . .

Ideas

A PRIVATE DEN: The easiest den is a blanket or old bedspread over a table, or you can fence off a corner of the room with chairs and put a blanket over the top (sheets usually let too much light in to make a 'private' hidey-hole). You could use a clothes horse, although unless yours happens to be very strong, boisterous children will collapse it every time they dash in or out. You could hang an old curtain on string or net curtain wire, or if you are outside, hang a bedspread or blanket over a washing line (if yours goes low enough) with stones to secure the edges. Often children will just take something in their den to play with but it could be furnished as a mini-house. A television can be made from a box with the front cut out and corks or caps for knobs, or leave it intact and stick on a picture cut in a television screen shape with rounded corners. Alternatively, cut slits in the sides of the box, cut away the front and draw some 'screens' on a strip of grey card. These can then be pushed through the slits. A picture, or a clock made out of a paper plate with hands kept on with a split pin can be put on a 'wall', and with a toy telephone, a few plastic cups and saucers, some books and a cushion, it will be just like home.

TRAINS AND BOATS AND PLANES: A row of cardboard boxes (painted if liked) can form a train with paper plate wheels and a bread board (or other round object – another paper plate would do) as a steering wheel. One on its own can be a car, with a drumstick stuck down with a piece of play-dough for a gearstick, some foil circles stuck on the front for lights and a radiator grill drawn on the front. A boat can be made from a box, with a broomstick mast; a blue-ish curtain can be the sea. For an aeroplane two extra pieces of cardboard will be needed for wings and the control panel can be made with bottle caps or corks on a drawn-on background panel.

LET'S PLAY COOKING: Real (old) sets of baking tins, bowls, plastic cups and saucers are more satisfactory for young children than miniature sets: the enjoyment of the specially designed miniature equipment tends to come later, as doll's houses begin to be appreciated. Have an old teapot and/or kettle, provide some water (coloured if desired), put everything on a tray to catch the drips and provide a dishcloth to mop up spills. Wooden spoons, balloon egg whisks, plastic cutlery, a spatula, colander and flour sifter are possible extras. If you are in the kitchen, you could provide a bit of flour or play-dough (see chapter 4, page 54) or a mixture of cornflour and water to stir around. Other kitchen things will probably be requested as needed.

PLAYING AT SHOPS: A counter will be required – two boxes with a tray or a piece of wood across, or you may have a suitable low table. If you do not have a toy till, a bun tin is a useful alternative (it makes a satisfying noise as the money drops in too) and buttons could replace toy money (although toy money is quite cheap to buy and provides useful experience for older children). The goods for sale can be used packets stuffed with newspaper and taped to seal, or you could use unopened tins and packets from your own cupboards, if you have not had time to build up a selection of old packets. (You will need to keep a closer watch if new packets are used.) Some loose 'goods' (from chapter 11 'Sorting and Threading'), a plastic scoop, some bags of various sizes and perhaps scales as well, are all much enjoyed and can be all sorts of different items for a pretend shopkeeper. Baskets or paper carriers are also much appreciated. If you only shop in supermarkets, your children will be used to self-service and so will probably only be prepared to serve out cheese and vegetables in 'their' shop unless you show them otherwise – they may not have had enough experience of traditional shops to use them in their imaginative play.

TURNING INTO SOMEONE ELSE: Here are a few ideas for changing identities:

▲ Doctors and nurses require (short) bandages (from old sheets), cotton wool for swabs and a white coat or apron.
  You can buy a plastic 5cc syringe (without a needle!) cheaply from a chemist – these are more durable than the type you get in toy doctor's kits, although a stethoscope from one of these would be useful.

■ Wellies can be temporarily disguised with coloured sticky tape to fit a superman – the tape will wash off in warm water. If you have some glitter, you could sprinkle a bit around the glued tops, too. (This will also wash off afterwards.)

● Princes can have woollen tights (pinched from sisters or cousins if necessary), Wellies with the tops turned over or a bit of fur or bright material stuck around the top, a fancy jumble sale blouse, a wide belt, cardboard sword and a hat with a feather.

▲ Fairies can be created by attaching a net curtain to the wrists (for wings) and closing at the front with self-fastening tape, or with a pretty brooch (with safety clip). A wand can be made from a piece of dowelling painted white, covered with glue and sprinkled with glitter. (See also, 'Making Things', page 90 for another wand.)

● ‼ Robots can appear by placing a large box over your child, with a square cut for the face and pieces of egg box, bottle caps or corks for knobs. Alternatively, put the box on the shoulders with a hole for the head. A cereal box can be made into a mask for the head, or use a number of 'heads' to create lots of different robots. (See also chapter 8 'Making Things' for more ideas.)

■ Hats can have wool stuck around the inside of the brim to turn your child into anybody at all.

● If the new character requires a horse, a broomstick with a sock or a Wellington boot pulled over the end makes a good one – tie a ribbon round the 'neck' and stick on a woollen mane.

▲ Abracadabra – a magician needs a capacious cloak or a large overcoat with stars and moons glued around the hem and a hat from a cone of stiff paper (see chapter 8, 'Making Things', page 89), decorated with more stars. Things can be hidden under the cloak to pull out with an abracadabra and a magical flourish.

▲ A colander stuck with greenery makes a good camouflage helmet for a foot soldier.

■ Kings and Queens must have a robe (old curtains), a crown (see chapter 8 'Making Things') and some sparkling extravagant-looking jewellery.

BE PREPARED: Once your child gets the dressing-up 'bug' you may be asked to provide all sorts of odd props to look just like a favourite television character or a particular animal. There are more ideas for making things to dress up in in chapter 8 'Making Things', including a selection of hats, which for young children is often the most effective way of changing identity.

CLEAN UP: Finally, you could occasionally wash, iron and mend the dressing up clothes together – they will be played with more often if they are kept reasonably respectable.

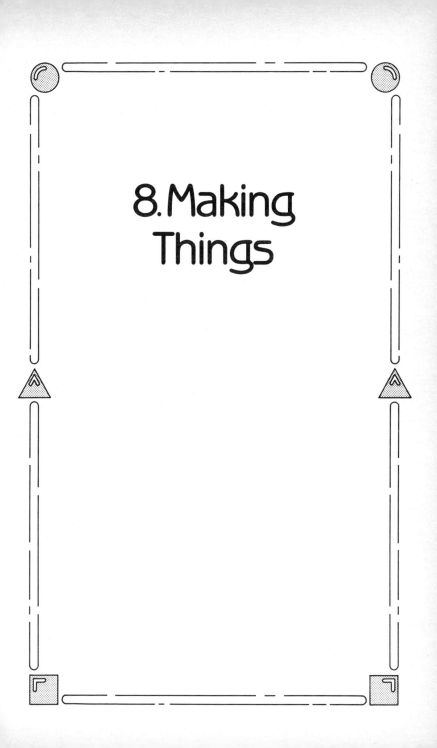

8. Making Things

Useful things to have

!! Glue (P.V.A.)
!! Sticky tape in different
   widths and colours
!! Scissors (round-ended)
Paperclips
!! Split pin paper fasteners
Cotton reels
Matchboxes
Cardboard boxes, food cartons,
   tins, cereal boxes, cheese-
   portion boxes
Paper, coloured card, graph
   paper
!! Lollipop sticks, spent
   matches
!! Milk bottle tops
Macaroni
Corrugated card
!! Buttons, beads, sequins
!! Ribbons, string, wool,
   covered pipe cleaners
Pieces of fabric and felt
   (fluorescent material makes
   good eyes)
Straws

Insides of toilet rolls, foil or
   kitchen rolls
Feathers
Egg boxes
Shells
Cotton wool
Modelling clay, play-dough
   (see page 54)
Large paper bags
Paper plates
Kitchen foil and coloured foil
Foil dishes
Odd gloves, odd socks
!! Ping-pong ball or plastic ball
   with holes in
Old wooden spoons
!! Bottle tops, well-washed
   aerosol lids and corks
!! Pipe cleaners
!! Elastic, elastic bands
Old magazines and
   newspapers, envelopes
Sponge
Paint and brushes for decorating
   models (see page 22)

General hints

How much guidance?: Try just providing a selection of cartons and other things from the list and let children do what they like with them. However, they may only start using the materials on their own after you have made a few things together. A number of ideas in this chapter would be too hard for little ones to make themselves, but they will enjoy helping you, making suggestions and playing with the finished product. If older children are making things, younger ones will usually amuse themselves with a selection of the ingredients.

Dramatic play: Puppets are often useful in mini-dramas to allay fears of hospital, dentists, going to school and to teach road safety or something similar. Again you will need to be fairly involved in both the making and in the play with them afterwards.

Television models: Get the ingredients box ready when you are watching model-making on a children's television programme which your child would like to copy. Having once made the start in this way, the ingredients will be more familiar, so that more things will be stuck together, boxes decorated, or hats and masks made.

Where to put them: Some of the items made can be rather on the bulky side, so you need to have somewhere to put them, at least for a short time. However, like many other activities with young children, the enjoyment is in the making, and children often lose interest in a model, once it has been created and admired, readily agreeing to (or not noticing) its dismantling fairly soon after creation. So, do not be put off by the thought of strange junk objects gradually taking over the house.

Ideas: Things to wear

ROBOT/SPACE SUIT: Find a large cardboard box and cut holes in it for the head and arms. Decorate with shiny bits and pieces, knobs (caps from bottles, tubes etc.), then be prepared to spend the rest of the day listening to a squeaky voice saying 'I am a robot. I will 'sterminate you'. A good game with robots can begin when you point out that robots do what you command, although even robots can get tired and grumpy after a while.

CHEAP AND CHEERFUL JEWELLERY: Thread pieces of macaroni on to wool or shirring elastic to make bracelets, necklaces, headbands or rings. If you like, the macaroni can be dyed first. Dip it in water coloured with food colouring, then allow it to dry out before use. For more instant effect, find some envelopes and paint them, or use patterned ones; stick down the flap, draw lines across, and cut into bracelets. For heavier, statelier accessories, thread some cotton reels (decorated if liked) on wool or elastic for bracelets, necklaces or mayoral chains.

HORRIBLE MASKS: Some children find masks frightening at first, so you may need to begin with a simple eye mask cut from coloured or foil covered card. An effective mask can be made from a large **paper** bag, big enough to fit right over the child's head. Cut eye holes in it, then decorate it as horribly as desired; a mouth hole can also be cut and the corners twisted to make ears. An interesting mask can be made by sticking some hand-drawn eyes on the bottom of a sieve and threading wool through the two holes opposite the handle. It can then be held in front of the face. For a simpler version, you can use paper plates, with eye and mouth holes cut and a length of elastic attached, which will fit round the head.

HEADGEAR: The simplest base for decorating is just a strip of card cut to fit round the head and fastened with sticky tape. This can be decorated with beads, milk bottle tops, shiny paper shapes, or further pieces of card (for example a superman 'flash' or a cut out feather) can be attached with more tape.

▲ A Red Indian hat can be made from feathers stuck in painted corrugated cardboard (left over from the ploughed fields in the collage chapter, page 46).

■ A crown can be made from cardboard and foil, with paper shapes, bits of glittery Christmas cards, coloured foil, bright buttons or beads, or milk bottle tops stuck on as jewels. Older children can cut V shapes around the top edge to make an even more realistic crown.

● A veil can be made from an old net curtain with elastic threaded through, or the bride could wear a headband of wide elastic with plastic or paper flowers attached.

▲ A witch's hat can be made from a sheet of black paper about 45 cm (18 inches) square. To make the conical shape, lay the tape measure along one side, hold it firmly in one corner and move it in an arc across the paper, marking the 45 cm (18 inch) length as you go, in a dotted line. Join up the dots and cut round this line – depending on age and abilities, children can do some or all of these things. When it is cut out the children can stick on star and moon shapes. Finally glue together and strengthen the inside seam with sticky tape – !! if you have a large stapler you could put staples in, **under** the sticky tape, so they do not scratch the head. To make the hat even more witch-like, stick strands of black or brown wool, or black material around the back inside edge for straggly hair.

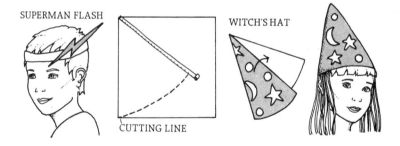

SUPERMAN FLASH

WITCH'S HAT

CUTTING LINE

SWIRLY CLOAKS: Often a curtain on its own will be just the job but you can make a cloak from fabric (black for a witch or magician). You need a large square folded in half, with a semi-circle cut out from the middle for the head. Depending on which character the cloak is for, various decorations can be stuck on the cloak.

BLUEBEARD: Beards can be made by cutting a beard shape from cardboard and sticking on woodshavings, cotton wool or knitting wool or string for a long straggly one. Make holes in the top corners and attach shirring elastic to go over the ears.

FINISHING TOUCHES: False teeth can be cut in the middle of a segment of orange peel. Ears can be created by making a basic headband of wide elastic, to which you can then attach old socks stuffed with paper or old tights, large paper shapes, or cut some odd-shaped ones from card. A nose can be made from a section of egg box with elastic to keep it on. Add some spectacles without lenses. Swords and shields can be cut from cardboard boxes and a wand can be a length of dowelling painted black with white ends for a magician. For a fairy's wand, cut two triangles of card, cover with foil and stick together to make a star, then paint with glue and sprinkle on some glitter. Attach this to the end of the dowelling.

Things to play with

BOATS: Take a small piece of wood or a walnut shell and stick on a matchstick mast with a tiny bit of play-dough plus a paper sail. This (or just a big leaf) can float in a water-filled tray with some islands made from more lumps of play-dough. The islands can be tropical, with pipecleaner palm trees, or hostile enemy islands surrounded by a circle of lolly sticks and toy soldiers fiercely guarding their territory. Tie some wool round a little plastic toy person who can be 'rescued' from behind enemy lines. Make some rivers using kitchen foil and then fill them with water so that it runs down to the 'sea'. Alternatively the scene could be constructed in sand (see chapter 6). If there is enough water, there can be a submarine made from an empty washing-up liquid bottle with a piece of play-dough as a conning tower. Fill it with water and replace the cap, then to make it surface, simply release the cap.

TRAINS: Cotton reels strung together make a good train, with a toothpaste tube cap as a funnel, or use matchboxes strung together, with another matchbox jammed into the first one to make the engine. For trains big enough to ride in, see chapter 7, page 80.

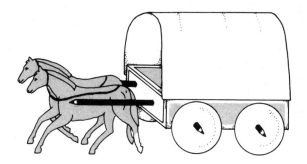

COWBOY WAGON: Use a large matchbox (from cook's matches) and bend a piece of paper over the top in the shape of a covered wagon. Push pencils or something similar through the sides to make the axles, fix card circle wheels on the pencils, then find two more pencils for shafts and add a toy plastic horse with wool reins. This is quite fiddly, so you may need to give a lot of help.

TRUCKS: Depending on the size required, you could either use a matchbox with card wheels stuck on the sides, or make a bigger truck by using a small cardboard box and fixing cheese portion boxes to the sides with split pins; knot some string through one end and the truck can be loaded up and pulled along.

TOWNS AND LANDSCAPES: Paint cereal or other largish boxes, cut out squares and rectangles for windows and doors, or stick bits of card on. Cotton reels are good as chimneys, with cotton wool smoke. A roof can be made by bending a square of cardboard in two. Cereal boxes make good flats, two or more large shoe boxes on their sides on top of each other make a doll's house in which can be put fabric carpets and some furniture (see page 94). A garage can be a shoebox, with petrol pumps made of matchbox covers stuck on their ends in a play-dough base, with a pipecleaner pushed in one side for a hose. Very realistic trees and hedges can be made from sponges: tear up a large sponge into small pieces, put green paint in one saucer and yellow paint in another, then dab the sponge pieces into both saucers, turn the sponges over and leave to dry. Twist six pipecleaners together, leaving the ends of each bundle free for branches and roots – these can be painted brown, and

when dry will stand up by flattening out the roots, then the sponges can be pushed on the 'branches' for leaves. For hedges, simply glue the sponges to pieces of card in strips. For fields and grass, see chapter 10, page 123.

DEFENDING THE TOWN: Make a fort quickly by fastening clothes pegs around the top of a box or tin; lolly sticks would do the trick, too. For a castle, take an ordinary square box and cut turrets around the top, then cut round three sides of a large 'drawbridge' but leave the bottom attached, so that it can be pulled up with string knotted through a hole in the middle. If the castle is put in the sandpit you could build a moat, lined with foil, around the bottom.

Making people and animals

LITTLE PEOPLE: Pipecleaners make the most versatile people (see below) or clothes' pegs make a simple version (see opposite). Alternatively, puppets can be used instead (see page 95), or the plastic people that come in commercial sets of toys. Younger children will usually find that making their own little people will be too fiddly and take too long.

PIPECLEANER PEOPLE: Take one pipe cleaner and bend it in half around your finger to make a loop for head and neck. Take two more pipecleaners and turn over 2 cm (1 inch) at one end of each. Hook these over the 'shoulders', then twist hooks and shoulders to make the arms. Twist the rest of these two pipecleaners together down to 2 cm (1 inch) from the end to make the body and leave the ends free for the legs. Stuff

the head loop with a ball of cotton wool, cover with a circle of thin pink material and tie tightly around the neck. Add facial features with a felt-tipped pen and make hair from wool, either stuck or sewn on. Fabric can be stuck on for clothes, for example, trousers can be made by laying the pipecleaner person on a square of adhesive covered fabric reaching to the 'waist'. Cover with another square and stick down. When dry cut around the 'trousers'.

CLOTHES' PEG PEOPLE: The old fashioned type of unsprung clothes' pegs make quite realistic people. You will need to drill a hole through just beneath the narrow 'neck'. The children can then thread a pipecleaner through for the arms, stick on wool for the hair and make clothes out of paper or material. Younger children will accept 'armless' peg people quite happily.

LARGER PEOPLE: Potato men can be made with matchstick arms and legs, or use a toilet roll inner, with a ball of newspaper covered in fabric and pushed in the top for a head, then all that is needed is a cloak, a paper crown (decorated) and some button eyes and a nose.

A WOOLLY LAMB: Use a stone or a cotton reel on its side and stick cotton wool all over. Two pieces of felt glued on will make the eyes.

A BIG SNAKE: Use one leg from a pair of tights and stuff it with newspaper or other cut up tights, then sew up. Glue a red paper tongue on the head end. A smaller snake can be made by threading cotton reels together. (See also page 95 for puppets.)

Making furniture
(best for 5+ but the small ones can help you)

A COMFY CHAIR: Cut down two corners of a ¼lb tea box and bend inwards at seat height, stuffing the base with crumpled newspaper. Cut the sides down to make arms about 2 cm (1 inch) higher than the seat and round off the top of the back. It can then be painted, or covered with stuck-on material or wallpaper.

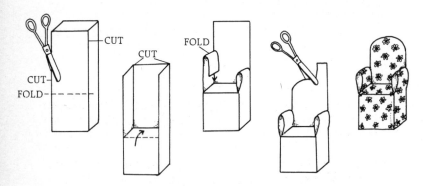

A POSH TABLE: Use a cheese-portion box stuck on two cotton reels glued one on top of the other, then the tablecloth can be a piece of lace, or other fine fabric. A 'glass' topped coffee table can be made from the plastic lid of a ground coffee tin stuck on one cotton reel.

MORE FURNITURE: The following are some ideas for other items of furniture. All the furniture can be placed in two or four stacked cardboard boxes painted or papered, as a doll's house, or if you give it a much sparser decor it can become a soldier's barracks/base.

▲ Chests of drawers can be made from matchboxes with split pins for knobs.

■ Foil-covered card makes mirrors.

● Tea cartons make wardrobes.

▲ A stool can be a painted cotton reel topped with fur fabric.

■ A standard lamp can be a cotton reel, pencil and a cut down paper cup or paper cake case.

● Beds can be made from small cartons or matchboxes, covered with fabric and with rectangles of fabric-covered wadding stuck on as pillows.

ON THE FLOOR: The floor of a doll's house can be covered in any of the following ways.

▲ A tiled floor can be made from graph paper, with the squares coloured in different shades.

■ Use left over bits of cushioned vinyl flooring.

● Carpets can be bits you have left over, or samples, or use material backed with iron-on stiffener, and velvet makes a particularly luxurious bedroom carpet.

▲ Rugs can be made from bits of material frayed at the edges, or with small pieces of wool or fringing stuck on the edges.

Puppets

A GLOVE PUPPET: An odd glove can make a spider or octopus puppet. Cut three triangles of material and glue or sew a face on one piece; sew three sides together (felt can be glued), stuff, then sew on the back of the glove. If you have two old gloves, put them on the hands and join the thumbs together with an elastic band (or you could sew them together for a more permanent puppet), then put an eye on each thumb and there's a spider.

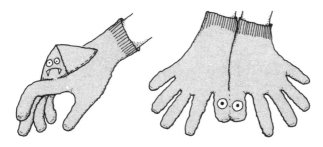

WOODEN SPOON PUPPETS: Draw a face on a wooden spoon and glue strands of wool hair around it. If you would like to 'dress' this puppet, push the handle through an upside down yogurt pot and paint it, or put a circle of fabric around the neck, neatening the edges with lace if liked. Arms can be made from pipe cleaners (see also page 92).

FINGER PUPPETS: These are particularly easy for younger ones to manage. They can be made from felt or card stuck on the fingers of an odd glove, or cut all the fingers off the glove and add eyes, nose, mouth and hair to make a finger family. Alternatively, just cut a hole in the middle and on each side of a paper bag. Draw a face on one side and one finger can be a nose (or a trunk, for an elephant) with the middle finger and thumb becoming arms, legs or ears. (See also page 236 for other finger puppet ideas.)

A PAPER BAG PUPPET: A bigger puppet can be made by stuffing a paper bag with some crumpled up newspaper. This, too, is good for younger children. Slip in a cardboard roll at the bottom and tie at the neck with string. Draw a face on a separate piece of paper, cut it out and glue on to the bag (it may be easier to do this before stuffing). Glue on wool or paper curls for hair, and add a fabric cloak to hide the cardboard roll. You can make animals this way by twisting the corners of the paper bag to make ears. (See also page 238 for a quick version.)

A MOP PUPPET: If you can pick up a cheap washing-up mop, it makes a ready-haired puppet. Push the handle through a perforated ball to make a head (these balls can be bought from golf, pet or toy shops), then stick or draw on a face and wrap some material round for a dress/cloak and to cover up the hand.

A POP-UP PUPPET: Cut a face from a magazine and stick it on a piece of cardboard; trim the edges, then stick on the end of a lolly stick. The face should not be wider than the diameter of a yogurt pot. Make a slit in the bottom of the yogurt pot and push the stick through it. Push up the stick and the face appears, push down – where has it gone?

Making things to do

A WALKIE TALKIE: Pierce a small hole in the bottom of each of two plastic tubs. Join the tubs together with about 10 metres of strong thin string, tying big knots on the ends. Stretch the string tight, making sure it does not touch anything, then take it in turns to talk and listen. One child speaks into one pot, while the other holds the pot on the opposite end of the string over his ear.

A WHIZZER: Thread a large button on a circle of string and make it whiz. Thread the string through one hole and back through another. Join the string and hold the circle with two hands, so that the button is in the middle. Twist the string by moving both hands in a skipping rope motion, then allow to slacken by moving the hands closer together. Now pull the hands back sharply and the button will whiz.

FEED THE MONSTER: Draw a horrible monster face on the front of a large paper carrier bag (if there is print on the bag, then draw the face on a separate piece of paper and stick it on the bag). Attach the bag to the back of a chair by one handle and cut off the other, so that the bag hangs open. Screw up small balls of newspaper for monster food. Stand back and throw the food to the monster. Instead of a bag, you could use an upturned box with a hole cut in for a mouth and lots of sharp monster teeth drawn around the hole.

EGG-BOX GAME: Stand a little way back from an egg box placed on the floor and try to throw buttons into it. Younger children will find it easier if they use an egg cup or empty yogurt carton to throw the buttons with. Older children might enjoy keeping a score, you could number the holes one to six and award that number of points for a successful throw.

SKITTLES: Make some balls from rolled-up newspaper and line up some small plastic people some distance away, then get your child to try to knock them over. Alternatively, use a real ball and some empty plastic washing-up liquid bottles.

Making presents

A PRETTY BOX: Paint an empty box or stick fabric on. Glue on shells, sequins or beads.

A STRING TIN: Use a syrup or custard powder tin or similar. Decorate with paper, put a ball of string inside and make a hole in the lid for the string to come out of. Alternatively, use a small decorated box in the same way.

A POMANDER: Give your child a whole orange and let him stud its skin with cloves. Leave this to dry in an airing cupboard for 3-4 weeks. It can then be used to make rooms and drawers smell sweet for months. At Christmas you could both make small tangerine ones to hang from the tree.

A TWISTER FOR THE BABY: Cut a circle of thin card about 30 cm (12 inches) in diameter. Draw concentric circles but cut along the lines in a continuous spiral. Pierce a hole in the centre. Decorate both sides with sequins or glitter, tie a knot in the end of a piece of string, thread through the hole and hang up over the baby's cot.

A COUNTING FRAME FOR A YOUNGER BROTHER OR SISTER: Paint a shoe box or cover with pretty paper and stand it on its end. Make ten holes down each long side. Thread a needle with strong thread, knotted at the end, and push through the top left-hand hole. Thread on one button, push the needle out of the opposite hole, in through the next one down and thread two buttons on before pushing out of the opposite hole. Continue with three on the next row, four on the next, until you get to the bottom, which will have ten.

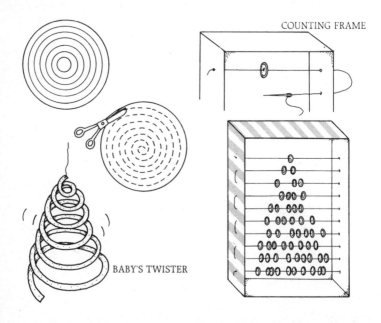

COUNTING FRAME

BABY'S TWISTER

YOGURT POT BELLS: Pierce the bases of several plastic tubs of different shapes and paint them white – they will probably need two coats. Pour some glue into one saucer and some glitter into another. Dip the open end of each pot into the glue, then into the glitter. The outside of the pot can be decorated with glued on sequins. Hang a small bell on the inside from a piece of wool, string or pretty Christmas thread if you have some.

SNOWMAN: Unroll a length of cotton wool and wind round a cardboard tube. Tie with ribbon to make a head and body, then add felt for eyes and nose and stick buttons down the front. A hat can be made from half a toilet roll inner painted black, with a ring of black paper stuck on the bottom.

MAKING LITTLE CLOTHES: If you like sewing, you and your child could choose some material together from your oddments to make some clothes or bedclothes for dolls or military men dolls. You can also get knitting patterns specifically for these. They do not need to be complicated – the major requirement for younger children is that they should be big enough to put on easily and have simple fastenings, such as self-fastening tape or large buttons and buttonholes. The tight-fitting clothes sold for military and teenage dolls are often too fiddly for little fingers, so it is worth making some bigger ones. If you are knitting, just add a few stitches on the width if your child is under 5-ish and make the button holes a bit bigger. Press studs almost always get pulled off. You will need to do the knitting or sewing, your child will enjoy choosing the materials and patterns and, of course, playing afterwards.

9. Sounds and Music

Useful things to have

Material for making
  instruments[1]
Containers for making rattles
  and drums[2]
Items for filling shakers and
  rattles[3]

Bought instruments[4]
Ready-made music (see IDEAS)
Clothes – a few swirly skirts
  and chiffon scarves for
  dancing
Books of songs[5]

Notes

1. For making the instruments in this chapter you will need: broom handle and lengths of dowelling, small bells (from pet or craft shops), other bells (such as bicycle bells, bell-rattles, door bells), flat pieces of wood for clappers (approximately 3 × 1 × ½ cm, 6 × 3 × 1 inches sanded smooth), cotton reels (for handles), ribbons, elastic, string, metal and wooden spoons for beaters, coconut shells, saucepan lids (for cymbals, if you can bear it!)

2. The sorts of containers required include yogurt pots or similar (the lidded sort in which salads and cream cheeses are sold are best), small tins (such as yeast or cough tablet tins), plastic lemons, margarine tubs, paint tins, large ice cream or ground coffee tins (for drums), bottles (plastic, if possible with a moulded handgrip as sold with some shampoos or fabric softeners) and cheap plastic salt and pepper containers.

3. For filling rattles and shakers you will need things like rice, split peas, sand, dried peas, lentils, pearl barley, small stones, milk bottle tops, marbles, paper clips and flowerseeds. Even water makes a good 'rattle' noise.

4. Bought instruments are completely optional according to your own resources – perhaps they would be good suggestions for presents (not the piano, unless you have very rich friends!). Possibilities include: tambourine, glockenspiel, triangle, tone block, chime bars (start with E and G, add A and finally C and D – you can accompany most nursery rhymes with the first three), guitar, piano. Have a look in toy catalogues, since new instruments are always appearing, often at a reasonable price. Beware, though, of cheap toy instruments, go to a reputable supplier for the best sounds and finishes.

5. Which books you buy will depend on the interests of your children. Try to find some time to look at the available books of nursery rhymes, action rhymes and music for children. There are a few rhymes at the end of the 'Ideas' section, if your memory is a bit rusty.

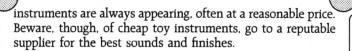

General hints

Raising the spirits: It is surprising what an uplifting effect a 'musical' session can have on jaded moods (yours and theirs). Most people sing nursery rhymes to their children and most children thoroughly enjoy them. The purpose of this chapter is to suggest additional ways in which to exploit the 'therapeutic' value of sounds and music, as well as to suggest ways of encouraging listening.

The ability to listen: In our normal day with young children we (parents and children) do a great deal of hearing but typically not a great deal of listening. Yet the ability to listen is an important skill, not only for learning, but also for the kind of enjoyment and escape which comes from involving yourself totally in a piece of music, or a particular rhythmic melody.

Rhythm to get rid of the blues: Young children generally respond to rhythm in a totally natural way that is enchanting to watch. It usually involves moving some part of their body – swaying or dancing. They usually like recurring melodies and rich, full-bodied sounds in the music they listen to. They may not want to 'make' rhythmic music in the traditional way at this age and may find it constricting to have to bang something at, and only at, a particular point in a tune.

Pre-music: In the same way that there are pre-reading activities (discriminating detail in different shapes, learning sequences that go from top to bottom, left to right), so there are pre-music activities – discriminating different sounds, making rhythms on their own, moving to music. At this age, most children simply appreciate the experience of various kinds of sound making from the voice and from instruments (although many can and do start to learn playing an instrument in a more formal way).

Your influence: The way you 'use' music with your children will vary a great deal according to your own experiences and expertise and perhaps also with the sorts of hopes and expectations you cherish regarding their future interest in music. However, even if you do not particularly enjoy music, or perhaps you did once but now rarely find a quiet moment to listen, it is worth trying some of the ideas on your children.

On a bad day ...: If the children have been especially horrible, or you have been especially snappy, try turning some music on (loudly, if this is possible where you live!) and dancing, clapping or singing, or turn something soft on and have a quiet few minutes (the first is more likely to work than the second, I'm afraid). Alternatively, try some of the other ideas in this chapter – one is almost sure to do the trick.

Making instruments: You can, of course, go to town making drums with tins and laced inner tubes, or dulcimers from bits of hardwood, guitar strings and glue, but here instrument making is limited to simple shakers, scrapers and beaters, which are very satisfying for younger children and also take very little money, time and effort to make.

Ideas

RATTLES AND SHAKERS: Just half-fill any of the suggested containers with any of the various ingredients from the list on page 102, glue or tape the top on, let the child paint the outside, and there you are. If using yogurt pots, use two for one shaker, filling and sticking together with glue and tape and decorating as wished.

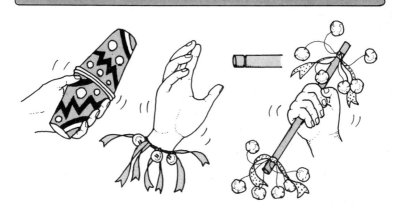

PERFECT PAIRS: To encourage listening and provide interesting opportunities for games, fill containers in pairs; you need to do this fairly accurately, weighing the lentils or whatever, so that each sounds the same as its twin. You can then ask the child to 'pick out the one that sounds the same as this', or variations on this theme.

MORE SHAKERS: Put a groove in each end of a 10 cm (4 inch) piece of dowelling, fasten bells on to the end with string and decorate with ribbons. Alternatively, put light objects (such as milk bottle tops) in small lidded cardboard boxes, to make a different sound.

WRIST SHAKERS: Stitch bells on to wristbands of elastic or elasticated ribbon and have a few extra lengths of ribbon hanging loose.

SCRAPERS: Cut notches on a 30 cm (12 inch) length of broom handle or thinner dowelling and run a teaspoon, 15 cm (6 inch) ruler or another piece of dowelling up and down the notches. Another version is to make 2 pieces of dowelling and rub them together, or cover two pieces of wood with sandpaper to make a very interesting noise when scraped together. You could also try rubbing two large, empty matchboxes together or corrugated card. As the noises made by these scrapers may not amuse the neighbours as much as it does your children, it is probably best not to do this outdoors!

GALLOPING HORSES: Small coconut shells with cotton reels tied on as handles (have a knot inside the shell) make a good clip-clop noise. Two plastic cups could be used instead but the sound is not quite so realistic. All these instruments can be decorated as desired.

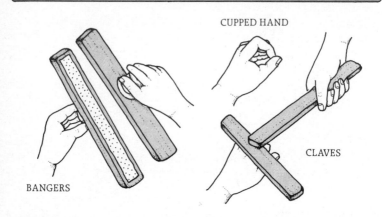

CUPPED HAND

CLAVES

BANGERS

BANGERS: Bits of wood (see the ingredients on page 102) banged together make a satisfying sound – !! stick or screw cotton reel handles on to the ends to prevent squashed fingers, and you could glue sandpaper on the banging surface for variation, or perhaps felt for a softer noise.

RESONANT BANGERS: Claves come into the banging category. To make a clave (a South American instrument for beating out dance rhythms) balance a piece of wood across thumb and forefinger, with the cupped hand forming a resonance chamber, and tap the wood with another piece.

DRUMS (GOOD FOR MARCHING SONGS): Simply use a beater (see below), an old ground coffee tin, ice cream container, empty saucepan, round cake tin, upturned plastic bowl or bucket, or food tin. If you have a left over cork tile, try cutting it to shape and glueing it to the top of the tin or container to vary (and subdue!) the noise.

BEATERS: You can use 15 cm (6 inch) lengths of dowelling, a small hammer with felt glued to the head, metal or wooden spoons or (even!) drumsticks. The dowelling ones can be varied by sticking the end on, or into, a small wooden ball, or tying and glueing a piece of cotton wool stuffed fabric around the end, or sticking the end into a cork. These beaters are easier for little hands to hold if you wrap the handles in insulating wire or glued felt. !! If using wire this can be fixed down at the ends with insulating tape.

SWISHERS: !! As an alternative to beaters, use a 15 cm (6 inch) piece of cable with 7 cm (3 inches) frayed out as a wire brush and the other half used as a handle, **although you may feel that children should not be encouraged to play with anything that looks electric** – you are obviously the best judge of this, it depends on the age and temperament of your child, and whether it is possible to explain the difference between his or her beater and the real thing.

BLOWERS: You can actually buy good whistles cheaply but these are not suitable for very young children. A horn can be made with a funnel and a length of tubing borrowed from the water play equipment and the cardboard insides from kitchen foil make good (if soggy) trumpets.

A MUSIC SESSION: Whatever instruments you use, it is probably best to provide just one or two at a time, either while listening to a record or tape of children's songs, or singing and dancing, with swirly clothes and scarves if available, to your own music.

Listening games

WHAT CAN YOU HEAR: Just try sitting still and asking your child what he or she can hear – clock ticking? car going past? fridge humming? washing machine churning?

WHAT MAKES THIS NOISE?: If you have a cassette recorder, record some interesting sounds for your child so that he or she can have fun trying to identify them later. You can either go round the house with your child, recording things you hear in each room (in which case you will get his/her voice too, which will probably be much enjoyed when played back later), or make the tape on your own, over a period of time. Possible noises include: clocks ticking, familiar voice (for example, Grandma's), water running or dripping, a door being shut, a window being opened, a squeaky floorboard, footsteps, an electric or hand mixer, an alarm clock ringing, telephone ringing, someone singing, a car, ambulance or lorry, the toilet flushing, someone cleaning their teeth, the doorbell or knocker, letters falling through the letterbox, someone sniffing, the baby chuckling or crying, anything at all that you know your child has heard before. Then all that has to be done is for the child to guess where the sounds come from. If you included a few that reflect his/her current passions (such as a snatch of music from a favourite television programme or the conversation of one of the characters, or one of his/her best friends' voices), it will be even more fun and you may find the tape is played just for enjoyment, long after all the sounds have been identified.

HOME PLAYGROUP: You could have a 'sound table' laid out one morning, with various home-made instruments, a musical box, a few baby's rattles and some unexpected noise-makers like a squeaky horn (from a cycle shop) or some noisy bits and pieces from a joke shop like the cushion that makes a rude noise when you sit on it. You only need a few extras, just to attract interest. It may be nice to do this on a day when a little friend is coming round, since sounds are often more fun with two or more children involved.

GUESS WHAT I'VE GOT: Remove one of the instruments from the 'sound table' without the child(ren) seeing what it is, so that they can try to guess what is missing. Make it sound, still without showing it. This requires a combination of observation (what was on the table before?) and listening (what noise does the mystery object make?). Once they have the hang of it two children can play this on their own, with one child covering his eyes while another takes a noise object to hide behind the back.

READY MADE MUSIC: Cassettes and records according to your children's taste can be bought cheaper than many toys; in fact a small cassette recorder compares favourably in price with commercial toys and can be extremely good value in terms of the time spent playing with it. A blank tape is also a good investment. For supervised sessions, you may have some suitable records – 3 and 4 year olds are often aware of the latest pop 'hits' and children of all ages often enjoy classical music, according to their mood. They may enjoy slow music (for example, 'Saturn', from the 'Planets' Suite), fast music ('Russian Dance' from Tchaikovsky's 'Nutcracker Suite') or be in the mood for something very loud, neighbours permitting ('Mars' from the 'Planets', or 'The Trumpet Voluntary') or soft ('Autumn' from Vivaldi's 'Four Seasons'.) They may enjoy a high-pitched tune ('Bird Theme' from Prokofiev's 'Peter and the Wolf') or a low pitch ('Wolf Theme' from 'Peter and the Wolf'). If you enjoy classical music, you may be able to point out various features in the records you have that will attract their interest, although don't expect wonders from the younger ones. Incidentally, my children are very keen on my keep-fit tape, so if you have one, try it!

A SINGING/ACTION RHYME SESSION: If you are singing, and do sing as often as you can, remember to pitch your voice fairly low, since children find it difficult to sing high. Vary the tempo – a marching song followed by a lullaby to cradle and sway dolly to sleep (or themselves, if you're lucky!). Here are a few action rhymes for starters:

THE GRAND OLD DUKE OF YORK

ACTIONS

Oh the grand old duke of York
He had ten thousand men

Marching on the spot

He marched them up to the top of
    the hill
And he marched them down again

Forward marching
Backward marching

And when they were up they were up

Forward marching

And when they were down they were
    down

Backward marching

And when they were only half way
    up

One step forward, one back

They were neither up nor down

HERE WE GO ROUND THE MULBERRY BUSH

ACTIONS

Here we go round the mulberry bush
The mulberry bush, the mulberry bush
Here we go round the mulberry bush
On a cold and frosty morning

Skipping round in a circle

This is the way we wash our hands
Wash our hands, wash our hands
This is the way we wash our hands
On a cold and frosty morning

Stand still and perform the
    action

VARIATIONS ON THE MULBERRY BUSH SECOND VERSE:
Endless! The traditional ones are wash our face, comb our hair, tie our shoes, and go to school. Others you may have heard are clean our teeth, wash the clothes, wave goodbye, clean our shoes, but you can ask for ideas from the children. In this case you may get ones like eat our toast, drink our drink or go to sleep. You could use the instruments instead – this is the way we bang the drum, etc.

PETER HAMMERS WITH ONE HAMMER	**ACTIONS**
Peter hammers with one hammer, one hammer, one hammer	Bang with 1 fist
Peter hammers with one hammer this fine day	
Peter hammers with two hammers ...	2 fists
Peter hammers with three hammers ...	2 fists, 1 foot
Peter hammers with four hammers ...	2 fists, 2 feet
Peter hammers with five hammers ...	2 fists, 2 feet, head nodding
Peter's getting tired now ...	Yawns, stretches
Peter's going to sleep now ...	(you could stop at this point) Curling up, close eyes
Peter's waking up now	Open eyes wide, starts frantic hammering again

INCY WINCY SPIDER	**ACTIONS**
Incy Wincy Spider climbed up the water spout	Fingers like spider creeping up
Down came the raindrops and washed poor Incy out	Fingers come down like rain
Out came the sunshine and dried up all the rain	Spread arms out wide in a circle
Incy Wincy Spider climbed up the spout again	As first time

CAN YOU WALK ON TIPTOE?

Can you walk on tiptoe, softly as a cat?	As described
Can you stamp along the road? Stamp! Stamp! Just like that	
Can you take some great big strides just like a giant can?	
Or walk along so slowly like a poor old bent old man – Can you?	

I CAN HEAR

I can hear my hands go (clap clap clap)
I can hear my feet go (tap tap tap)
I can hear my mouth go (click click click)
But I can't hear my head go (nod nod nod)

TEDDY BEAR TEDDY BEAR

Teddy bear, teddy bear dance on your   As described
  toes
Teddy bear, teddy bear touch your nose
Teddy bear, teddy bear stand on your
  head (more or less)
Teddy bear, teddy bear go to bed
Teddy bear, teddy bear wake up now
Teddy bear, teddy bear make your bow

JACK IN THE BOX   ACTIONS

Jack in the box is a funny wee man   Crouch and then jump up
Sits in his box as still as he can (wait)
Then UP he pops!

ME   ACTIONS

Eight big fingers standing up tall   Point to, clap or
Two big ears to hear Mummy call   wriggle the various
One little nose to blow and blow   parts of the body
Ten little toes in a wiggly row
Two fat thumbs that wriggle up and
  down
Two little feet to stand upon the
  ground
Hands to clap and eyes to see
Oh, what fun to be just me!

LIVING IN HARMONY: This chapter contains some starting ideas,
but with these ingredients and your mutual increasing familiarity with
them, you and your child should fill many a happy hour in relative (if
noisy) harmony together for years to come.

10. Growing Things

Useful things to have

Good soil, or (to be on the safe side for the plants), potting compost
Containers[1]

Muslin or fine perforated dishcloth
Selection of items to plant/sprout/colour[2]

Notes

1. You will need containers for many of the ideas: shallow dishes, saucers, plates, bowls, baking tins, trays, jam jars, seedtrays and flowerpots (plastic).

2. A selection of the following: pips from oranges, lemons, grapefruits, tangerines, mandarin oranges; fresh leafy top from a pineapple; tops from root vegetables like carrot, beetroot, parsnip, turnip or swede; bulbs – daffodil, tulip, hyacinth or grape hyacinth; plant cuttings from spider plant, African violet, mother-in-law's tongue, herb plants, cacti plants; any seeds which give reliable results – nasturtium, beans, peas, lettuce, marigold, parsley, sunflower, radish, forget-me-not, mustard seeds, cress seeds, or a packet of 'children's seeds'; seeds for drying your own flowers – honesty, straw daisy, Chinese lanterns; beans for sprouting – mung, aduki, fenugreek, alfalfa, unroasted coffee beans or peanuts; fresh sweet potato; underwater plants – bog arum, fairy moss, horn-wort, water fringe, pondweed; items to 'colour' – carrot, white flower, celery stalk; fruit stones – date, avocado, peach or plum.

General hints

How much do you know?: If you are a keen gardener with enough experience to know what will reliably grow in spite of children, you will have lots of ideas of your own to work from. If you do not know a great deal about how to grow things, all the suggestions in the ideas here are fairly reliable. ❙❙ To be on the safe side, it is worth pointing out the difference to children between things being grown just to look at (e.g. flowers) and things being grown to be eaten (e.g. vegetables).

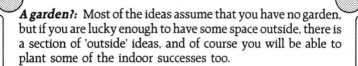

A garden?: Most of the ideas assume that you have no garden, but if you are lucky enough to have some space outside, there is a section of 'outside' ideas, and of course you will be able to plant some of the indoor successes too.

An added bonus: One of the greatest advantages of growing things at home is that it shows children where, for example, beans come from, or at least opens up discussion about it. Unless you do have growing space in a garden or an allotment, your children could quite reasonably assume that beans come from tins, packets or the greengrocer, without beginning to wonder how they got there.

Extra research: If you can find some books in your local library relating to how things are made/grown/shipped, these will be a useful addition to your own home growing experiments.

What about other foods?: All you are doing when growing things with children is introducing the **idea** of the origins of various produce. Obviously you will not be able to cover everything, like for example, where milk comes from (unless you happen to have a cow or a goat), but if resources run to it, there are various outings (to farms, for example) that could be arranged for a treat.

Just for fun: The main reason for growing things with young children, of course, is simply for their pleasure; as always, they will pick up a lot of information as if by accident, if they are enjoying the activity, and many older ones will ask lots of pertinent questions next time you are in a hurry at the green-grocer's with a long queue behind you.

Preventing tears: Once you have planted something, or started off a root garden together, remember that young children cannot be relied upon to remind you about the plant or whatever, yet they will still be reproving and disappointed if faced with a dried-up stick or shrivelled carrot top two weeks after planting. Children also need to be warned that things take time to grow.

Ideas: Pips

TROPICAL TREES: Choose a few pips from a citrus fruit with plenty of them (see note 2) and soak overnight in water. Poke some holes in the bottom of a margarine tub and fill with potting compost. Push several pips gently into the compost – you can reasonably expect a success rate of about 30% – then cover with another ½ cm (¼ inch) of soil or compost. Moisten with tepid water, label (with a piece of paper on a lolly or cocktail stick), and to be absolutely sure put the pots into a plastic bag loosely tied at the top. Put somewhere warm and dark and keep the soil moist by watering every one to two days. When the pips have germinated and little shoots are showing, transfer to a warm window sill. When the plants have grown two pairs of leaves, transplant them into their own little pots. In four to six weeks you should have lovely mini-plants, which if treated with some respect will, in a few months, have shiny dark green leaves. If well cared for, you will have an impressive bush after a few years, by which time the children will have forgotten all about it . . .

A QUICKER TROPICAL TREE: Choose a pineapple with fresh-looking green (not yellowing) leaves and cut about 5 cm (2 inches) off the top (eat the rest!). Scoop out the flesh, leaving the central core untouched, and leave a couple of days to dry out a bit. If you happen to have any hormone rooting powder, you could dip the central core in this, tapping off any excess, but it does not matter if you don't have any. Pot the pineapple top in potting compost or a mixture of potting compost and sand. Put the whole pot in a bag, tie the top, and put in a very warm place, keeping the soil moist. Eventually you should see new green shoots appearing in the middle of the cluster of old leaves. (It is obvious if it hasn't taken as it wrinkles up sadly.) An alternative method, and visually more interesting, is to place the pineapple top, prepared as above, in a jam jar, with the rim of the jar supporting the leaves and the core hanging in the water. Roots and new leaves will appear. You can plant it in a pot of compost at this stage if you like, or else just observe, through the glass jar, how the roots grow.

ROOT TOP GARDENS: Slice 1 cm (½ inch) off the top of a carrot, parsnip, beetroot, swede or turnip. If the root vegetables have leaves, trim to within ½ cm (¼ inch) of the top of the vegetable. Put the tops on a large plate or flattish cereal bowl, with just enough water to cover the bottoms. To make them look particularly garden-like, sprinkle some small stones or pebbles between them, then leave on a window sill. Water frequently, and in a few weeks you will have a leafy little garden. It is more interesting if you have a mixture of tops in your garden; for instance, the fine feathery tops of carrots contrast beautifully with richly coloured beetroot crowns.

Seeds and sprouts

MUSTARD AND CRESS: Put three or four squares of kitchen paper towelling on a large plate and wet it well, pouring off the excess water. Sprinkle some **cress** seeds thinly on one half of the paper, in a single layer. Cover with another square of paper and leave for 3 days with another plate over the top, keeping the paper moist (with a spray, if you have one). Then sow the **mustard** seeds on the other half of the paper and cover again. Keep the paper moistened, and when the cress is about 1 cm (½ inch) high, remove the cover and put on a window sill. When the shoots are about 7 cm (3 inches) high the mustard and cress can be cut with scissors and used for salad or sandwiches.

CRESS MAN: Put some cotton wool in egg shells with faces painted on and grow mustard and cress as above, in the moistened cotton wool. When it has grown, the person's 'hair' can be cut.

CRESS ANIMAL: Join two potatoes together with cocktail sticks to make the body, then add another round potato for the head. Use matchsticks for legs (it will need more than four!). Make shallow holes all over the back and head with a cocktail or matchstick. Then your child can push mustard seeds and cress seeds into the holes. You will

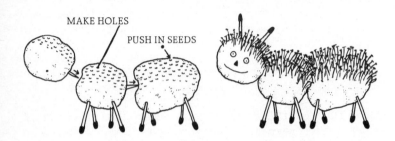

MAKE HOLES

PUSH IN SEEDS

not need to water your animal, there is enough water in the potato to sprout the mustard and cress. Draw a face on the head with felt-tip pen and wait for the 'hairs' to grow!

MORE SPROUTS: You can also sprout sunflowers, nasturtiums, beans or wheat on a bed of damp cotton wool in a saucer to watch, or . . .

SPROUTS TO EAT: For bean sprouts use mung beans (tiny green ones) or aduki beans (slightly bigger brown ones) to begin with. Put two tablespoons of the beans in a jar (larger than a standard jam jar and with a wide mouth if possible). Cover the jar with a circle of absorbent kitchen cloth or muslin kept on with an elastic band. Pour water through the cloth to cover the beans and leave overnight to soak. The next day, empty out the water (without removing the cover) and put the jar in a cupboard. Each day pour in some warm water and drain it off through the cover, twice if the weather is warm – if you keep the jar near your tea or coffee supply you will be reminded to water it. You will have a good jarful of crunchy beansprouts in a week, or less in warm weather, which can be used in salads, Chinese dishes or whatever you fancy. If you start when your children are young, they will just accept bean-sprouts as an everyday food, and will have the added pleasure of having grown them themselves. They make a delicious no-calorie alternative to rice as a 'bed' for numerous dishes, and are interesting in soups.

BIGGER BEANS TO SPROUT: Runner beans, broad beans or peas can be grown in a jar with a lining of moistened blotting paper, so that you can see the roots. Soak the beans or peas in water for 24 hours. Put the beans or peas between the blotting paper and the jar and fill the jar with water. Once it's soaked through, empty out the water, leaving just

BLOTTING
PAPER

WATER

a little in the bottom. Keep the blotting paper moist and keep the jar in the light, and you will be able to see the roots and shoots forming. The roots will grow in a fishbone shape because they are flattened against the jar by the blotting paper. You could start the bean off in a pot of damp potting compost, then remove it and the seedling and place in the top of a bottle filled with water, supporting the seedling with matchsticks; more roots will develop, the proper shape this time.

EXTENDING THE RANGE: Sweet potatoes, unroasted coffee beans or unroasted peanuts, started off in a pot inside a bag somewhere warm, will produce very interesting leaves. Peanuts produce a curious vine-like plant and sweet potato will produce scented flowers which make a pleasant indoor plant.

More seeds

GROWING FLOWERS FOR DRYING: Suitable flowers you can grow from packet seeds and which dry beautifully are listed below. They all make wonderful collage ingredients too (see chapter 3).

▲ Honesty – this has unique silver coloured seed pods. Take off the leaves and hang up to dry.

■ Straw daisy – bright yellow, orange, white, pink and red heads. Pick them when they are not quite fully open and hang in bunches to dry, somewhere without much light.

● Chinese lanterns – pick these colourful orange lanterns, take off the leaves and hang in bunches upside down.

▲ Poppies, love-in-a-mist – these have beautiful detailed seed heads that you can use without drying, sprayed with silver or gold paint for Christmas, or just left attractively natural.

Stones

DATE PALMS: Date stones can be planted straight into a pot of damp potting compost, but plant three or four to be on the safe side. Put the pot in a clear plastic bag, tie the top tightly and leave in a warm dark place, keeping the compost moist. Check it about once a week to see if it needs water. When the shoots begin to sprout (one to three weeks), bring the pot out, but keep the bag on until there are three leaves on each shoot. Each surviving plant can then be transferred to its own pot and each should produce leafy palms.

AVOCADO DELIGHT: Soak an avocado stone in water for two days, to encourage it to germinate more quickly. Then put the stone in the neck of a glass jar almost full of water – the size of the jar depends on the stone – the large end of the stone should just touch the water, and you may need to use matchsticks to wedge the stone in your particular jar. All being well, the stone will begin to split after about a fortnight, and a shoot and a root should appear. Wait until there are plenty of roots, then transfer to a pot of potting compost, so that the compost comes half way up the stone. As it grows, support the stem with a stick and repot the plant when necessary.

PEACHES AND PLUMS: For these hard stones, you will need to squeeze them gently in a nut-cracker until they just crack, before planting. This replaces the natural 'weathering' they would undergo in the 'wild' before germinating. Put them in a pot of potting compost, water and enclose in a plastic bag. Leave in a warm, dark place, watering as necessary. Shoots should appear in one to three weeks.

Bulbs

BALANCING ACT: Try balancing a bulb from a daffodil or a hyacinth on top of a wine carafe full of water, or use a pretty glass jar if you have one. Keep in the light, topped up with water. You can also use this method to grow a shoot from an acorn, or a conker, but soak them for 24 hours first; when they are developing strongly, transfer the little 'trees' to a pot of potting compost or good soil.

BABY BULBS: Bulbs like daffodils and tulips have small 'baby' bulbs which can be broken away to start a new one.

CUTTINGS: If you or any of your friends grow indoor plants, take a cutting. Spider plants usually appeal to children since they can easily cut off and plant one of the baby offshoots of the main plant. They can also plant a few leaves cut from an African Violet; put them round the edge of a pot of potting compost, and those that 'take' can be given their own pot later. You can grow a new mother-in-law's tongue (there's an exciting prospect!) from a single leaf to produce a very striking plant. Put the bottom of a healthy whole leaf in the compost. Ask any gardening friends if you can have some cuttings from whatever suitable plants they may have indoors, and perhaps they may be kind enough to pass on a few simple instructions too. Alternatively, they may have some little plants, for you to begin a herb garden (see below).

HERB GARDEN: You can begin from seeds and it will give you all a great sense of achievement. Plant the seeds in potting compost in a punctured margarine tub on a tin tray. Moisten with tepid water and start them off in a warm place, such as an airing cupboard. Keep them moist. If you have a garden or a window box, you can tip the pot upside down when the seedlings look strong enough, and plant the whole lot. Below are some suggestions. You can buy packs of children's herbs fairly cheaply to see which ones work best.

▲ Parsley – sow seeds in the spring, soaking them first in warm water for a day.

■ Rosemary – difficult from seed; try to get a cutting taken around September time. Not only delicious with lamb, but also a very pretty shrub especially when in flower.

● Chives – again, chives are much easier if you can beg a clump from someone else's plant, and this can be grown in a pot or in the garden if you have one. Chives are 'cut and come again' – they will actually grow **better** if your child gives them a snip with the scissors every so often. Lovely in salads.

▲ Mint – this tends to go a bit mad, so you should not find it difficult to find someone who will be only too glad to get rid of a clump. Start it off in the spring.

■ Thyme – try to obtain a cutting with some root and plant it in the spring for some scrumptious winter stews.

● Sage – also needs to be planted in spring. It is extremely pretty when growing and the plant will not miss the odd bit you pinch for the stuffing.

DRYING HERBS: Don't waste all the effort you have put into growing the herbs! Collect the herbs on a dry sunny day during the flowering period, tie in little bunches and simply hang up in a warm place to dry. Once dried, children can crumble the herbs up in their (clean) hands and pop them into little air-tight jars. They could perhaps help decorate some pretty labels too.

Cacti

FROM SEEDS: Although cacti take a long time to grow, they have very interesting shapes and prickles which appeal to children. (!! However, don't let children handle these.) Cacti grow best if you use a mixture of potting compost and coarse sand spread in a seed tray. Sprinkle the seeds in rows and cover with a very light layer of potting compost. Label each row, if they are different, with a lolly pop stick stuck through the seed packet, water well, cover, and keep in a warm place. They will need to be left in the tray for about a year (although you will see things happening before then!). You may prefer to begin instead with small ready grown plants, which you can buy in little pots or beg from someone else's mature plant. Either way, you can make a desert scene (see below) with the tiny cacti.

A DRY DESERT: Use a large shallow bowl and lay pebbles in the bottom, for drainage. Then cover these with a mixture of potting compost and sand, finishing with a layer of sand. Plant the cacti 8-10 cm (3-4 inches) apart. All you need now are a few plastic camels, a water-hole (a shallow plastic dish) surrounded by small stones and you have a real desert scene (do not let the water in the oasis get too near the cacti – they like a dry environment).

MINIATURE GARDENS: Spread a layer of pebbles in a dish/tray for drainage, then fill up with potting compost. Water thoroughly. Buy a packet of mixed flower seeds (sold for children), sprinkle on the soil and cover lightly with a sprinkling of potting compost. To increase the realism, you could sow good quality grass seed in the centre to make a lawn. Spray each day with water, and leave on the window sill, or at least in a very light place – outside in the summer, if possible. For variety, you could try scattering a few grains from a box of bird seeds on the soil and see what comes up! However, such experiments should be purely for show and not for consumption, as there is no knowing what may be contained in a packet of bird seed.

UNDERWATER GARDENS: For these you will need a fish tank or a large goldfish bowl. Cover the bottom with 2 cm (1 inch) of sand, then put a layer of compost, then finish with another layer (same depth) of sand. Fill with clean water and leave to settle. Underwater gardens are most successful if you buy the plants ready grown, from a pet shop or garden centre and include some floating plants too. There are some suggestions in note 2, but any water weeds will do. Put the plants in, pushing the roots into the potting compost under the first layer of sand, then push a few pretty pebbles or stones round the stems, otherwise they will float back up to the surface. If you keep the tank outside, or on a balcony, you could buy water lilies in pots, which you stand on the base of the tank. The lily will grow upwards to float its leaves and flowers on the surface. For finishing touches, decorate the sand with more pebbles and unusually shaped, clean shells; when the plants have definitely taken root, you can add a few water snails (from a pet shop) which do not require feeding and will keep the water clean. If you are

prepared to feed them, put a couple of goldfish in too. There is a complementary relationship between the plants and the other living things – the plants put oxygen in the water for the snails and fish, the snails and fish fertilize the soil and breathe out carbon dioxide for the plants to use.

If you have a garden

GET DIGGING: Clear a patch in the garden by removing weeds, digging the soil and taking out large stones (because the small roots cannot get round them to find soil). Rake well. Most seeds are planted in the spring. Water the patch the day before you sow, with a fine spray watering can. Sprinkle seeds thinly and rake a light covering of soil over them. When the seedlings are about 2 cm (1 inch) high, thin them out, to give the others room to grow. Later you may need to support the taller plants with sticks, and by early summer you should have a special and colourful patch to be proud of. The best kinds of seeds for this are hardy annuals such as cornflowers, marigolds, love-in-a-mist, candytuft and nasturtiums (you can eat the leaves, flowers **and** seeds from nasturtiums in salads – use the younger leaves, as the older ones tend to be bitter). Forget-me-nots, primulas and primroses only need planting once, if you think the gardening bug may not last until next year!

FILLING THE CRACKS: If you have a paved bit of garden with cracks where there is soil, or the edge of a wall that looks a bit bare, plant some Alyssum seeds in March, which will produce a pretty carpet of tiny white flowers. Keep watered while the seedlings are forming and once they have four leaves, pull some out to leave room for others to grow.

AN INDIAN WIGWAM: Make a frame from three beansticks and tie together at the top to get a wigwam shape. Plant a runner bean seed on each side of each stick in early summer. Encourage the plants to twine around the sticks and spray the flowers with water when they appear. Pick the beans often to encourage more to grow and when the plants reach the top of the sticks, pinch off the tips of the new shoots. Water frequently and pull out any weeds that grow around the bottom.

WHAT ABOUT A PUMPKIN?: Plant the seeds in the spring or early summer. First dig over a patch of garden and mix in some manure (when the children are not around, if they are very young), since pumpkins take a lot of feeding. Make a low hump with the soil and push

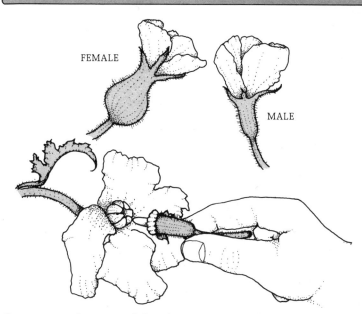

FEMALE

MALE

five or six seeds in around the edge. Water every day and you should see seedlings in a couple of weeks. When the flowers form, nip off any new bits of tendril, or the plant will take over the garden; nipping the new bits also makes the plant stronger. You will find the majority of the flowers will be male, but some will be female with the beginnings of a pumpkin just below the flower petals. You may see bees taking the pollen from the males to the females. If you do not see any bees, do the job yourselves – break off a male flower and show your child how to rub its stamen gently into the centre of the female flower (the stamen of the male flower is covered in pollen – so I hope neither of you suffers from hay fever). After a while, you will see the female petals withering and the pumpkin starting to grow. Water the roots every day and break off the rest of the flowers, so that all the food goes to the pumpkins. When the stalk begins to wither, the pumpkin can be picked for Halloween, or pumpkin pie.

OTHER OUTDOOR GARDEN POSSIBILITIES: Try radishes and lettuce. If you have a rabbit or guinea pig, they will love the lettuces that are going to seed. Start some lettuce from seed in early spring, then sow a few seeds every two weeks till July to provide a continuous crop, thinning them out as necessary.

COLLECT YOUR OWN SEEDS: Collect seeds from lupins, sunflowers, wallflowers, beans, pumpkin and peas. Keep in a labelled envelope in a cool dry place and sow the following spring.

THE TALLEST OF THE LOT: Sunflowers grow very fast indeed so are excellent for maintaining children's interest. You will need some tall sticks to support the plants. Sow the seeds in spring in a sunny place about 60 cm (2 feet) apart, keep well watered and measure their progress. Keep some of the seeds for next year – they are tasty on their own, or sprinkled on cereals. To gather the seeds, cut off the flower head and rub the seeds out with a garden fork. Keep in a bag for next year, or dry in the oven if you are going to eat them – they are delicious in the crunchy cereal on page 140. Alternatively, feed them to the birds in winter when the other food is scarce.

BACK INDOORS: Grow a bean wigwam indoors by pushing three sticks into a bucket sized pot, then continue as on page 124.

BABY TOMATOES: Buy a packet of dwarf bush tomato seeds and plant several in a pot of compost in spring. Once the plants are about 5 cm (2 inches) high, transplant each into its own pot and let them all grow on a window sill without draughts, feeding and watering regularly (you can buy small jars of plant food which will last ages). Soon you will get a delicious crop of tiny sweet tomatoes – yummy.

Nature ideas

BIRD CAKE: Make a hole in the bottom of a plastic margarine or yogurt tub. Thread a length of string through the hole and tie a knot on the end. Hang it up and put some odds and ends like peanuts (unsalted), bits of bread crusts, apple peel, broken biscuits, scraps of bacon into the pot. Melt about 100 g (4 oz) of lard, cool a little (so that the pot will not melt too) and pour over the ingredients in the pot. Leave to set in a cool place, hung up so that the string stays in the centre. When set put in the fridge for a couple of hours then turn out of the pot. You will probably have to cut down the sides of the pot to do this. Hang the bird cake up somewhere outside where you can see it.

AN INSTANT GARDEN: Find some moss and put on an aluminium foil plate to make a miniature garden with twigs, pools and bridges, sprigs of leaves or flowers.

SEE WHAT HAPPENS: Fill a jar with water and add red (or any other) food colouring. Red ink is more dramatic, but can also have nasty dramatic consequences when sent flying. Cut the bottom off a carrot, slice the bottom off a white carnation or daisy stem, and a stalk of celery and stick all three in the jar. You will be able to see the flower change colour. To see what effects the colouring has had on the carrot and celery, cut them open.

SOMETHING ELSE FOR THE BIRDS: Make a necklace of peanuts to hang up for the birds. Leave the shells on and thread by pushing a needle and cotton through the middle of each nut. (They will split if you do it lengthways.) It will attract blue-tits, which are beautiful to watch.

SOMETHING ELSE FOR CHRISTMAS: Collect some fir cones and paint them for Christmas, or keep some of the seeds from inside to sow in the summer.

DAISY CHAINS: Can **you** still remember how to make them?

11. Sorting and Threading

Useful things to have

Containers[1]
Things to thread on to[2]
Things to sort and thread[3]
Coloured card
‖ Glue (P.V.A. or water-based)
‖ Enamel paints (non-toxic type)

‖ Thin card with holes punched in, or commercial peg board (from D.I.Y. shops) knitter's needle (from wool shops, intended for sewing up knitted garments – these have no sharp point)

Notes

1. You can use any containers with or without lids, such as small boxes, plastic containers, bowls, margarine/yogurt/cream cartons, egg boxes, foil dishes, toy stacking cups, small tins (such as 100 g yeast tins), cylindrical film containers, baking tins or saucepans.

2. Things to thread on to could include long laces (intended for skating boots), strong cotton, string, wool, hollow green plastic tubing (sold in electrical shops as sleeving for electric wiring) or shirring elastic.

3. Items for sorting and threading include buttons (from your old clothes, jumble sales, Grandma or haberdashery sales in big department stores), caps (from spray cans, bottles, toothpaste, deodorant, cosmetics, perfume, etc.), stones, paperclips, cut-up straws, large beads (from old necklaces), macaroni, any shaped pasta, milk bottle tops, tin foil, small bells (from pet shops), squares of fabric in groups of different colours and textures, cotton reels, cutlery (without sharp knives), groups of cut-out magazine pictures (for example different pictures of birds, in cartoon form, photos, black and white, colour), screws (for example, ½ inch, 1 inch, 1½ inch), coloured card cut in different shapes, commercial toys that have 'bits' that can be sorted (for example, bricks, wooden balls, little people or animals, toy money, coloured plastic letters and numbers). You can buy sets of counting toys (usually animals and vehicles, in sets of about 72) which would make a useful addition to any sorting box.

General hints

'Sorting and Threading': The title of this activity may sound somewhat mundane and boring, but if it is not an activity you have tried before, you may be pleasantly surprised by its entertainment value.

The 'sorting' phase: Sorting is often a phase two to three year olds go through, and older children love sorting too. If yours is keen on this activity, it is worth finding lots of items and containers to keep the interest alive. It can provide quite a time of peace and quiet, as well as laying the foundations for maths at school.

Early maths: Sorting and grouping objects into sets is a major element of early maths nowadays, and if children show an interest early on, they will benefit from all the practical experience of recognising common features to form categories, and identifying odd ones out, although they may classify in what appears to you to be a random way.

 Early classification: You may find that, given a number of objects, your child will start by grouping items according to colour, then get distracted by the shape, or some other feature, and continue classifying according to this new scheme.

Lots of choice: The more objects you can collect, the more ways of grouping your children can use, such as colour, size, pairs, what they do, 'whether I like them', how many holes in them etc., and (most important!) the longer the activity will keep them amused.

Safety: !! At the age at which children begin to enjoy sorting and threading, they have usually gone past the stage of putting things in their mouths, up their noses or in their ears, but you need to keep a watchful eye, anyway, particularly if they are using a knitter's needle. Even if they value their own bodies, they may put things up the baby's nose. Apart from the safety angle, you will need to be close at hand if they are threading buttons on to strong cotton, because the cotton has an annoying tendency to get itself in tangles every so often. You will

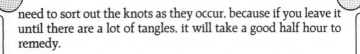

need to sort out the knots as they occur, because if you leave it until there are a lot of tangles, it will take a good half hour to remedy.

Making suggestions: Ideas for sorting, suitable classifications and so on, will obviously depend on what you have available. Some children just do not like suggestions, and even if you say something on the lines of 'see if you can find all the red ones' or 'are there any more the same as this one?', they will probably do what they want anyway. Others welcome ideas, and participation, from adults so the best strategy (as is often the case) is to see how things go. It is quite possible that the whole lot will end up on the floor, and you will be the one who does the sorting today, in which case have a rude mutter about ungrateful, uncooperative children, and try another day.

Ideas: Sorting

STARTING OFF: Provide a selection of the sorting ingredients and a selection of containers (but not too many at first) and see what happens. Younger children will just have great fun playing with the items, but for older ones you can be more organized. For example, put some buttons, large beads, and some different caps in an ice-cream container with about 15-20 of each, so that they can be sorted into four or five different groups, depending of course on what you have available. Give the box of items to your child, with half a dozen small foil dishes, or a couple of egg boxes. You may like to suggest a few ways of grouping things if nothing happens (although this is unlikely), or your child may prefer to be left to his/her own devices.

NOISY SORTING: Provide a noisy set of containers (bun tins, other small tins, saucepans) and some small items which will 'ping' when dropped into the container (stones, paper clips, large beads, macaroni, milk bottle tops).

***ARE* THEY ALL THE SAME?:** Provide items to sort that are all one colour and watch to see what criteria your child uses for sorting them out when she cannot use colour. When these have been sorted to your child's satisfaction, replace them with items all of a **different** colour from the first set, and see if your child uses the same system as the first time, or if she invents a new one.

LOTTO GAME: If you are feeling industrious, why not make a fabric 'lotto' game. Stick six to eight squares of different types of fabric or paper (fur, velvet, sandpaper, P.V.C., lace, foam, textured wallpaper, pretty cottons, plain paper) on to card, and provide matching squares on small separate cards. This is a good game to make as a present too. If this type of game seems to catch your child's interest significantly, make some different ones . . .

TACTILE LOTTO: Use fabrics and wallpaper with obvious textures, and play the game blindfolded. Choosing a texture difference makes this a particularly apt activity for children with sight difficulties, especially since they will often be much better at it than sighted children of a similar age. Younger partially-sighted or blind children will probably use their mouths more than sighted children, so you will have to make sure the squares are safe and you will not be able to use paper, because it will get soggy.

OBJECT LOTTO: Stick eight different small objects in each of eight squares on a piece of card and use identical objects for matching. There is no need to stick the matching objects on cards this time.

'NATURAL' SORTING: If you are a patient person, 'natural' sorting activities, such as sorting the washing, or cutlery (!! minus sharp knives) may be enjoyed. Be careful what you choose though, which is why it is better for patient mothers – I have tried getting my children to put the ironed washing into piles according to whom the items belong, but they always manage to unfold everything; perhaps yours are tidier!

ANIMAL SORTING: Collect sets of the same animal represented in different ways (such as a line drawing, a photograph, a coloured picture, a black and white picture, a cut-out fabric shape, a play-dough model, a collage picture (there is a cat on page 44), or a painting). You do not need all these of course, just pick a few and try to get a number of animals in each type of picture/representation. Then your child can sort out all the cats/dogs/birds etc. You could display them on a table if you like, as is done in playgroups.

TIDYING UP: Putting the toys away is a good sorting activity – you will probably be very good at it by now! It **is** possible to teach children where things go and if you start off fairly realistically by suggesting that they put two things away and tell you where to put the rest, the message might eventually sink in.

Threading

STARTING OFF: The size of the hole in the object and the type of threader will depend on your child's age and experience. Whatever you use, you need to thread the first object, and secure it, to stop the rest falling off; if you are using plastic tubing, you will need to glue something on the end, or tie a knot in it, if it is supple enough but does not immediately unravel. If you are using string, or some other threader with a wiggly end, a piece of sticky tape around the end makes it firmer for pushing through holes. If you use a knitter's needle, you need to tie the cotton to the needle after threading.

BUTTONS: !! Thread a knitter's needle with strong thread or shirring elastic and tie the thread in a knot by the eye. Thread one large button on to it and let it slide to the bottom, then tie the cotton around it so that all the other buttons will not fall off – a knot on its own will not work, because some buttons have particularly large holes, which would slip over a knot. Then simply provide a box of buttons and leave your child to it. Each button makes a satisfying 'click' as it lands on the others, which appears to be an important part of the fascination for this activity. Sort out any tangles before they get serious, and you should get a quiet half hour or so, apart from the 'clicks' which are actually strangely soothing.

COTTON REELS: Use string (with taped ends), or hollow plastic tubing; laces are never long enough for cotton reels. Either provide plain cotton reels, bought coloured ones, or paint your own: stick the cotton reel on the end of a pencil, paint with non-toxic enamel paint, then stand the pencil in a jam jar for the cotton reels to dry. You could get your child to decorate some (with glue, glitter and sequins) to make hanging Christmas decorations, or to make necklaces or snakes.

FOR THE BIRDS: Thread milk bottle tops, tin foil squares and a few small bells on to strong cotton to scare away (or amuse!) the birds. You could also thread some squares of toast to hang up for the birds to eat.

BRACELETS: ‼ Use shirring elastic, thread and secure into a knitter's needle, then thread through beads or macaroni. Necklaces and head-bands can be made to match.

PEGBOARD PICTURES: Draw an outline on a piece of pegboard. This can then be threaded with a lace or pretty coloured wool. Tape the thread at one end to make threading easier, and put a bead at the other to stop the whole lot being pulled right through.

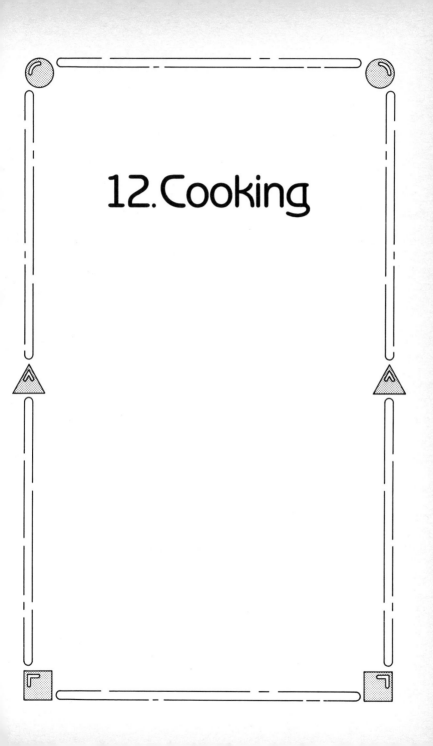

12. Cooking

General hints

Ingredients: See individual recipes

Cooking with children: There are many children's cook books available, but in my experience with children of this young age, you still end up doing all the organizing and a large portion of the cooking yourself. It seems to work better if you simply involve your child in the sort of things you always cook, but (a very important but), it will probably be unrewarding if you see it as a cooking session for yourself.

Play or cooking?: The major difference between your cooking on your own and cooking with children is that with children it is fairly essential not to be in a hurry. 'Let's make some cakes' often ends up meaning 'I'll make some cakes quickly while you put the paper cases in the tins and lick the bowl'. If you cook the same sorts of things as you normally cook, but change the emphasis to 'children's time', many of your and your child's favourite recipes are adaptable to provide a pleasant morning in the kitchen. It is all very well being able to make butterfly cakes, star biscuits, chocolate logs and cheese footballs, but it is also useful and satisfying for children to help make the main course of a dinner and the pudding. This does not mean, of course, that they cannot ice and stick cherries, smarties and hundreds and thousands all over small cakes and biscuits, rather that it can be just as much fun helping with the day-to-day cooking.

Something else?: Many of children's desires for kneading, cutting and shaping are fulfilled much more happily with play-dough (see chapter 4), than with a biscuit mixture, which is not always so cooperative, so you may prefer to consider one of the other activities first.

Your participation: It should be emphasised that cooking with children of this age is something that does require your participation (rather than just your supervision, as with water play for example) all the time, and as such is a different kind of activity from many of the others in this book. **!!** You need to direct, and many of the skills required are either too difficult or

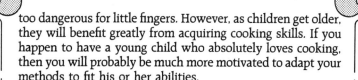

too dangerous for little fingers. However, as children get older, they will benefit greatly from acquiring cooking skills. If you happen to have a young child who absolutely loves cooking, then you will probably be much more motivated to adapt your methods to fit his or her abilities.

The art of watching: Many children are quite happy just to watch you making cakes, soups, etc., which is very useful, and they are picking up a lot of information, which will stand them in good stead when they start to do it on their own. They usually require a bit of entertainment by way of the odd cherry, sultana, carrot or bowl to lick (and see 'Passing time in the kitchen'). Do not despise watching as an activity, or feel guilty because your child seems not to be experiencing anything – it is very pleasant just to sit and watch now and again.

Adapting the recipes: !! The recipes in the ideas section are given in the traditional form. You are the best person to decide how much of each recipe your own child will be able to manage, although none of them are complicated. Some (such as the cereals) can only involve children at the beginning and the end, since the middle bit is hot, so the decision about which parts children can do is easy. Others (such as the egg mice) depend on particular abilities, so just see how it goes.

A few rules of the game: !! Start off by insisting on a few rules and you should find things much tidier and easier when children are older and begin cooking more or less on their own.
1. **Always** wash hands before a cooking session.
2. Wear an apron.
3. Get out all the ingredients and utensils before you start.
4. Wash up afterwards (well, you can always try!)
5. Understand that cookers and sharp knives need to be treated with respect.

One extra ingredient: One item that you may not already have in your kitchen but which would be a great help for children, is a plastic icing syringe with different screw-on nozzles. They are not too expensive and are much easier than using separate nozzles and bags.

Ideas: Starting off

PASSING TIME IN THE KITCHEN: Provide a bowl of fairly warm water and a few pieces of spaghetti to dip in and see what happens. Alternatively, provide a small jug of water, a dish of flour, a saucepan or large bowl and a fork and spoon. It will be a bit messy but will keep younger children happily occupied for a while. Less messily, they could soak a few oats in milk, or stir some raisins into cold tea (lovely in a cake after a few hours' soaking).

MAKING CEREALS: Making up cereals such as muesli is much more fun and cheaper than buying made up varieties and you can limit the amount of sugar or omit it altogether. If your children are still very young, or if you have already restricted sweet things, they will not miss it at all. Try some of the following. Children will enjoy helping to measure the ingredients, leaving you to do the cooking.

CRUNCHY CEREAL: Mix about 450 g (1 lb) of rolled oats and one tablespoon of bran with about 100 g (4 oz) each (or a selection) of sesame seeds, sunflower seeds, wheatgerm, desiccated coconut (or a tablespoon of demerara sugar if liked), flaked almonds or any other small-chopped nut mixture, in a large baking tray. Add a cup of half water and half oil (vegetable or any other variety) and bake in the oven at 190°C, 375°F, Gas Mark 5 for 30-45 minutes, stirring every 10 minutes or so to break up lumps. Add raisins (as many as you like) and when cool keep in an airtight container. Serve with milk, natural yogurt and chopped banana or any other fruit.

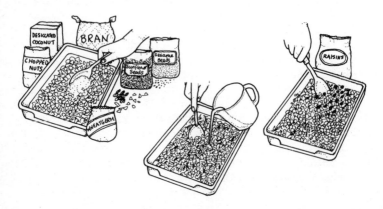

MUESLI: Use the same ingredients as for the crunchy cereal, but use muesli base (usually oats, rye and barley flakes) instead of the rolled oats and leave out the oil and water. It does not have to be cooked. You can add chopped dates, dried apple flakes, any other dried fruit (apricot, figs, banana) or soak these in freshly boiled water overnight and serve separately. Leave out the sesame seeds and sunflower seeds if you like – they are not traditional ingredients, although they make it tastier.

TOASTED OATS AND RAISINS: Toast 450 g (1 lb) of jumbo oats in a cup of half oil and half water in the oven, exactly as for the crunchy cereal. When cooled a bit, add as many raisins as you like. This can then be eaten as a standard cereal but it is also nice sprinkled on bought cereals, such as bran flakes or wheat flakes, for a bit of added interest and crunch. To provide a lovely crunchy chewy change, try sprinkling this on natural yogurt or even chocolate mousse. As children mix these cereals and watch as you stir them every ten minutes, they are getting the idea that cereals do not have to come in packets and, of course, these cereals are very adaptable – you can put in or leave out all sorts of different grains and fruits, according to taste. Barley flakes cooked like this in the oven have a wonderful taste and you can experiment with other sorts to your heart's content.

Savoury snacks

FACE BISCUITS: Mix 50 g (2 oz) of smooth pâté with a little milk, then put in a plastic icing syringe. Pipe the outline of a face and some hair on water biscuits or digestive biscuits, then squeeze some tomato purée straight from its tube for eyes, nose and mouth.

CHEESE STRAWS: You will need 100 g (4 oz) plain flour, a pinch of salt, 50 g (2 oz) butter or margarine, 50 g (2 oz) strong cheese and an egg. Sift the flour and salt into a plastic bowl, cut the butter or margarine into pieces and add to the flour. Rub all the ingredients together with the fingers until it is nice and crumbly. Grate the cheese and add to the mixture (with a teaspoon of mixed herbs if liked), then add the egg and mix very well. Leave to stand in the fridge for half an hour, then roll out on to a floured surface. First of all cut a few circles, then use a smaller cutter to make a hole in the middle of these. Cut the rest of the pastry into straws, and cook altogether on baking trays at 200°C, 400°F, Gas Mark 6 for about 15 minutes, depending on their thickness. To serve, push the straws through the pastry rings like bundles of firewood.

CHEESE-CRUSTED WHOLEWHEAT SCONES: Mix 75 g (3 oz) wholewheat flour and 75 g (3 oz) self-raising flour with 1 teaspoon of baking powder, then rub in 25 g (1 oz) butter. Add a pinch of cayenne pepper and ½ teaspoon of mustard powder plus 50 g (2 oz) strong grated cheese. Finally, mix in a large egg beaten with 2 tablespoons of milk and roll out at least 2 cm (¾ inch) thick. Cut into rings, brush with milk, sprinkle with a mixture of grated cheese and another pinch of cayenne pepper and cook in the oven at 220°C, 425°F, Gas Mark 7 for 15-20 minutes.

CHEESE SAVOURY SLICE: The ingredients are 100 g (4 oz) grated cheese, 125 g (5 oz) rolled oats, 1 small onion (grated), 1 egg, 50 g (2 oz) butter or margarine, salt, pepper and a teaspoon of mixed dried herbs if liked. Mix the cheese, oats and onion and beat in the egg. Melt the margarine/butter and stir until well blended. Season to taste with the salt, pepper and herbs. Put in a greased Swiss Roll tin and press down. Bake at 190°C, 375°F, Gas Mark 5 for about 30 minutes. This recipe is also extremely nice with a couple of large grated carrots added to the cheese mixture at the beginning.

CHEESE TARTS: Line tart tins with any pastry, then mix up 1 egg, 150 ml (¾ pint) of milk, 100 g (4 oz) strong cheese and a pinch of salt. Pour the mixture into the pastry cases and bake at 190°C, 375°F, Gas Mark 5 for 10-15 minutes. You can add chopped onion, mushrooms or tomatoes for a change, or pieces of left over cooked ham or any other cold meat.

CHEESECAKE BARS: Knead together 100 g (4 oz) each of lowfat (curd) cheese, any flour and margarine/butter. Roll about ½ cm (¼ inch) thick, brush with milk, sprinkle with sesame seeds, cut into bars or any shape you fancy, then bake at 180°C, 350°F, Gas Mark 4 until it looks pale brown.

EGG MICE: You will need hardboiled eggs (1 each), sliced cold meat (garlic sausage or salami or luncheon meat), currants and a blob of tomato sauce or brown sauce. Cut a slice off the side of each egg, so that the mice don't run away, and stand this cut side on a plate. From the meat, cut as many long thin 'tails' as you have eggs, and twice as many little triangles for ears. Cut two slits in each egg where the ears go, and stick the triangles in, then make another slit for each tail. Use the currants for eyes and a blob of sauce for the nose.

Spreads

FISH PASTE: You will need a small can of sardines in tomato sauce, 75 g (3 oz) cream cheese or curd cheese, a tablespoon of lemon juice, salt and pepper. Tip the sardines into a bowl, sprinkle with salt and pepper and mash with a fork. Add the cream/curd cheese and lemon juice and mash again. Spread in sandwiches or on toast, decorated with mustard and cress (see page 117 for how to grow your own mustard and cress).

CHEESE AND WALNUT SPREAD: Blend 100 g (4 oz) of blue or other cheese with 50 g (2 oz) melted butter or margarine, a pinch of cayenne pepper and 3 tablespoons of mayonnaise. Stir in a handful of finely chopped walnuts and refrigerate until firm.

Meals

SWEET AND SOUR CHICKEN: Mix together 4 tablespoons soy sauce, a tin of tomatoes (the size depends on how many chicken pieces you need), 2 tablespoons malt vinegar and one large chopped onion. Add 150 ml (¼ pint) water or stock and pour over the chicken pieces in a greased dish. Cook in a moderate oven, 180°C, 350°F, Gas Mark 4, for approximately an hour and a half.

SAUSAGE SURPRISE: Grease a shallow dish and spread 450 g (1 lb) sausage meat over the base. Press four hollows in the sausage meat with the back of a spoon and break an egg into each one (depending, of course, on how many people require an egg!). Lay four rashers of bacon and some tomato slices over the top, season, and bake for 20-25 minutes at 200°C, 400°F, Gas Mark 6.

CHEESE, ONION AND POTATO PIE: Slice 1 kg (2 lb) potatoes and 2 onions thinly, grate over 100 g (4 oz) cheese and put in layers in a greased dish, beginning with potatoes and finishing with cheese, sprinkling with salt and pepper between the layers. Pour on 300 ml (½ pint) milk and place the dish on a baking tray. Bake at 190°C, 375°F, Gas Mark 5 for one hour.

BEANSPROUT SALAD: Mash 100 g (4 oz) blue cheese and mix with 6 tablespoons of French dressing. Using home grown beansprouts (see page 118) and a bunch of watercress, chopped, pour over the blue cheese dressing and sprinkle with chopped walnuts. Serve with wholemeal rolls and butter.

Puddings

TERRIFIC TOPPINGS: Here are some toppings that can be used to cover any fruit before cooking in a moderate oven (180°C, 350°F, Gas Mark 4) for about half an hour.

▲ Basic crumble: Mix together 150 g (6 oz) flour, 75 g (3 oz) margarine/ butter, and a heaped tablespoon of sugar.

■ Oat crumble: Replace 50 g (2 oz) of flour in the basic crumble with rolled oats.

● Crunchy crumble: Use granary flour instead of the plain or self-raising in the basic recipe.

▲ Sponge topping: Beat 2 eggs with 50 g (2 oz) of any type of sugar, then fold in 40 g (1½ oz) plain flour.

■ Cobbler topping: Rub together 25 g (1 oz) margarine or butter, and 100 g (4 oz) self-raising flour, then add 50 g (2 oz) sugar and a little milk. Roll about 1 cm (½ inch) thick and cut out circles. Lay these in overlapping circles on top of the fruit.

● Crunchy cobbler: For an attractively crunchy version of the above, rub together 50 g (2 oz) margarine or butter and 225 g (8 oz) self-raising flour. Bind together with a little cold water and roll out on a floured surface. Spread with 25 g (1 oz) softened butter and sprinkle on 50 g (2 oz) of any type of brown sugar. Roll up like a Swiss roll and cut into thin slices. Lay these over the fruit again in overlapping circles and cook at 210°C, 425°F, Gas Mark 7 for about 20 minutes.

CRUMBLY CREATION: Make a sponge mixture with 75 g (3 oz) margarine or butter, 75 g (3 oz) sugar and 75 g (3 oz) self-raising flour with one egg. Use as a base by spreading in a greased dish. Lay any stewed fruit (blackberries, apples, strawberry and apple) over the sponge, then add any crumble topping. Bake in a moderate oven for about 45 minutes.

STRAWBERRY AND BANANA CREAM ICE: Blend 450 g (1 lb) strawberries with 2 tablespoons clear honey, 2 tablespoons soft brown sugar and 2 ripe bananas. Fold in 300 ml (½ pint) lightly whipped whipping cream or thick natural yogurt and freeze. Remove the container after half an hour and stir to break down the ice crystals, freeze, then stir again after another half hour.

MERINGUES: Whisk 2 egg whites until stiff, then whisk in 2 heaped tablespoons white sugar. Fold in another 2 heaped tablespoons sugar then, using a teaspoon put in blobs on a greased baking tray. Bake in a very low oven 120°C, 250°F, Gas Mark ½ for about an hour, then turn off the heat and leave the meringues in the oven until the meringues are cold. Serve as they are, or sandwich together with whipped cream, or whipped cream mixed with chopped nuts.

ICE CREAM SANDWICHES: You will need a block of ice cream, a packet of wafers, chocolate vermicelli, hundreds and thousands, and a tube of sugar-coated chocolate drops or a packet of chocolate buttons. Cut the wafers in half. Find three plates and put a layer of chocolate drops or buttons on one, hundreds and thousands on another and chocolate vermicelli on the last. Cut the ice cream into chunks to fit the wafer halves and make sandwiches. Dip some sandwiches into vermicelli around all four edges, some into hundreds and thousands and press chocolate drops/buttons around the sides of the remaining sandwiches. If you are making lots of these, you could press different sides of the same sandwich into different coatings.

Sweet treats

FLAPJACKS: Melt 175 g (6 oz) margarine with 100 g (4 oz) sugar and 1 tablespoon of syrup. Stir in 225 g (8 oz) rolled oats, spread in a baking tray and cook for 20 minutes at 180°C, 350°F, Gas Mark 4. If you have a large baking tray, double the quantities – this will be right for the size of tray that just fits into most ovens. Cut into fingers while still warm, but leave in the tin until cold.

FRUITY FLAPJACKS: To the above recipe add 4 level tablespoons of marmalade and 50 g (2 oz) raisins.

CRUNCHY CHOCOLATE BARS: Crush 275 g (10 oz) broken biscuits in a polythene bag with a rolling pin. Melt 125 g (5 oz) margarine, 25 g (1 oz) sugar, 40 g (1½ oz) cocoa and 2-3 tablespoons of golden syrup, and stir in the crumbs from the biscuits. Press the mixture into a shallow baking tin and cool. You could eat them like this, cut into slices, or for a treat melt 175 g (6 oz) cooking chocolate and spread over the set chocolate mixture. Cool then cut into bars.

EASTER EGG NESTS: Melt 225 g (8 oz) cooking chocolate in a bowl over a saucepan of hot water. Break up some shredded wheat cereal and stir in – make sure it is all coated and put enough in to make a fairly stiff mixture. Put dollops of the mixture into paper cake cases and make a hollow in the centre for some tiny chocolate or sugar eggs.

SCONES: Rub 50 g (2 oz) butter into 225 g (8 oz) self-raising flour and add 50 g (2 oz) sugar. Stir in 150 ml (¼ pint) milk, natural yogurt or soured cream and roll the mixture out about 1 cm (½ inch) thick. Cut into circles, place on a baking tray and brush the tops with milk. Bake at 210°C, 425°F, Gas Mark 7 for 10-15 minutes until golden brown. Serve still warm, with strawberry jam and, for a treat, a dollop of fresh whipped cream. A slice or two of banana is usually appreciated too!

FANCY BISCUITS: Choose a simple biscuit recipe such as 100 g (4 oz) each of butter and sugar creamed together, then add 175 g (6 oz) plain flour and an egg. Divide the mixture into four portions and experiment with variations, for example add some melted chocolate to one portion, sultanas and a teaspoon of mixed spice to another, cherries stuck in the top of another after rolling out, and the last one decorated with sugar and cinnamon mixed, or coloured sugar, or chopped nuts. Roll out, cut into shapes and cook at 180°C, 350°F, Gas Mark 4 for 10-15 minutes depending on thickness. Alternatively, cook them plain and ice them after cooling with glacé icing in a plastic icing syringe. These iced ones tend to go soft, so they have to be eaten fairly soon after icing.

ICED BUNS: Make some plain buns with a white bread recipe plus 2 tablespoons of sugar and an egg. Ice them after they have cooled, with glacé icing in white or different colours.

MALT LOAF: For a delicious malt loaf you will need 50 g (2 oz) margarine, 75 g (3 oz) sugar, 3 level tablespoons of golden syrup (or 2 of syrup and 1 of malt extract if you have any), 175 ml (7 fl oz) milk, 40 g (1½ oz) malted drink powder, 275 g (10 oz) self-raising flour, ¼ level teaspoon of bicarbonate of soda and 75 g (3 oz) sultanas. Melt the margarine with the sugar and syrup over a low heat, then stir in the milk and malted drink powder. Sift the flour into a bowl with the bicarbonate of soda, stir in the sultanas and mix in the melted mixture. Spoon the mixture into a greased 1 kg (2 lb) loaf tin and bake at 180°C, 350°F, Gas Mark 4 for 1-1¼ hours. Serve buttered.

GINGER MARMALADE TEABREAD: You will need 40 g (1½ oz) margarine, 175 g (7 oz) plain flour, 1 level teaspoon of ground ginger and one of baking powder, 65 g (2½ oz) light soft brown sugar, 4 table-spoons marmalade (ginger, if you have some), 1 beaten egg, 4 table-spoons milk. Rub the fat into the dry ingredients, stir in the sugar. Mix together the marmalade, egg and milk, then stir into the flour mixture. Spoon into a 1 kg (2 lb) greased loaf tin and bake for one hour at 170°C, 325°F, Gas Mark 3.

BRAN FRUIT LOAF: Soak together 100 g (4 oz) bran cereal, 125 g (5 oz) sugar, 275 g (10 oz) mixed dried fruit and 300 ml (½ pint) of milk. After an hour add 100 g (4 oz) sieved self-raising flour and pour into a greased 1 kg (2 lb) loaf tin. Bake at 180°C, 350°F, Gas Mark 4 for about an hour. Serve sliced with butter.

YOUR OWN FAVOURITES: This chapter just contains a few suggestions, but it is much nicer to choose recipes that your family likes and that you often cook. It is very interesting for a child to see how food that he or she already knows and likes is actually cooked, and to discover that it still tastes as delicious even when he or she has been involved in cooking it!

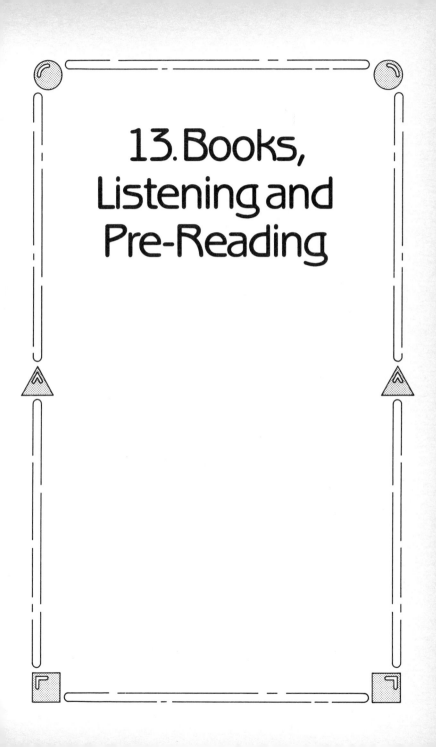

13. Books,
Listening and
Pre-Reading

General hints

All children are different: Young children vary a great deal in their attitude towards books, according to their age, their experience and their predominant interests. Nearly all children will enjoy *some* form of contact with books, whether it is cosy and cuddly listening to parents telling a story, making their own colourful books, singing and dancing to rhymes or making their first tentative progress towards reading themselves. Some children are only too happy to sit quietly listening to a half-understood story, enjoying the gentle rhythm of the voice and the full attention of an adult; others, although still apparently enjoying the situation, ask questions, turn pages continuously and generally fidget throughout. Some children see the whole thing as an unwelcome and unnecessary restriction, although they may come to enjoy it later on.

Age differences: Before the age of about 18 months, nursery rhymes usually command the best attention, followed closely by a constant delight in naming pictures of objects and animals as soon as they can say a few words. Later they will be more able to follow a story, particularly if there is much raising and lowering of the voice, suspense ('and what do you think happened next?), sound effects (Splat! Splosh! Splish! Grr! etc) and repetition. Traditional stories like The Three Bears and The Three Little Pigs have phrases that keep occurring (I'll huff and I'll puff and I'll BLOW your house down), which appeal greatly to young children, partly because the stories become predictable, something they can look forward to and understand. When choosing a book therefore, it is worth considering what scope there is for sound effects, and, at first anyway, buying or borrowing books with plenty of repetition. Children of all ages often like to make their own books, and there are some suggestions for these in the ideas section.

Preparation for 'proper' reading: So-called 'pre-reading' activities are often suggested in educational books written for parents. The main ingredient of these activities is to encourage children to notice detail; it is essential in reading to be aware of very fine distinctions between letters, since many look very similar to each other. Children of two or so have learnt that

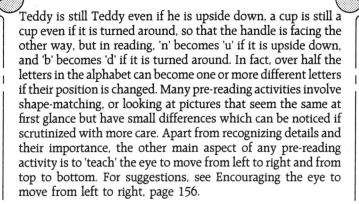

Teddy is still Teddy even if he is upside down, a cup is still a cup even if it is turned around, so that the handle is facing the other way, but in reading, 'n' becomes 'u' if it is upside down, and 'b' becomes 'd' if it is turned around. In fact, over half the letters in the alphabet can become one or more different letters if their position is changed. Many pre-reading activities involve shape-matching, or looking at pictures that seem the same at first glance but have small differences which can be noticed if scrutinized with more care. Apart from recognizing details and their importance, the other main aspect of any pre-reading activity is to 'teach' the eye to move from left to right and from top to bottom. For suggestions, see Encouraging the eye to move from left to right, page 156.

But what's reading for?: Young children, quite naturally, are often very unsure what reading is, and it is a useful activity to point out all the situations where you use your own reading skills, so that they gradually discover the relationship between a lot of squiggly lines and some practical end result. For example, you read something in the paper that tells you when a favourite programme is on television, you read a recipe and produce something scrumptious to eat, you read a knitting pattern and produce a bobble hat for Action-Man or Teddy, you read your shopping list, so you do not forget your child's favourite cereal, the postman reads addresses, so that children get their birthday cards. Bus and train timetables, instructions on toys, names in a telephone directory – all these help a child to appreciate exactly what is going on with these funny letters, once they are pointed out.

To teach or not to teach?: Many of the skills required for reading can be picked up very easily in play by a young child. She does not realise she is being taught and you will probably not even realise you are teaching, but then that is the way pre-school children learn most of their skills, and very effectively too. Many children (but not all) will show such an interest in letters that they soon move on to proper reading. Others will not seem so keen at the time, but the abilities they have picked up will stand them in very good stead when they get to school, and they will find themselves reading with very little effort.

In the mood: Since one of the aims of the activities in this chapter is to encourage attention and concentration, it is even more important that they are not suggested when children are either too grumpily tired or too excitedly active. To prevent any pressure, stop all games while they are still being thoroughly enjoyed rather than waiting until boredom sets in. Generally, with any activity which demands a certain amount of concentration, little and often is the best rule. To encourage initial interest, try sitting down and playing the games on your own – this nearly always attracts attention and participation.

Using a library: There are three good reasons for using a local library –

1. You will be able to provide a much greater selection of books.

2. You are introducing the idea of libraries as a source of enjoyment, which will be very useful later when your child may want to use the library's reference section and he will be already familiar with the procedures and the atmosphere there.

3. Perhaps the most useful advantage at this stage is that borrowed books can give you an excellent idea of what sort of books your child likes at the moment, without having to spend any money. You can use this informatin to guide you when buying books, or suggesting particular books as presents.

Ideas

A COSY CORNER: If you have a spare corner somewhere warm, why not establish a book corner, such as can be found in good playgroups? The main aim is that both you and your child(ren) should find this place inviting – a large comfy armchair or a few cushions, a soft rug and a few shelves or similar to provide a changing display of favourite books make a cosy retreat for those moments when you all feel like exploding. It need not take up much space – next to a cupboard, behind a settee, anywhere that can be made comfortable and welcoming. You could always call it 'the QUIET CORNER' in the hope that the message may get through.

HOME-MADE BOOKS: There are various ways to produce your own books – here are a couple: punch holes in the left hand side of sheets of paper, reinforce with linen rings, and secure with some wool, string or ribbon; fold large sheets of paper in half and tie through 2 holes down the centre-fold, then leave under a heavy book to crease properly.

ABOUT-ME BOOKS: Children are usually much intrigued by books about themselves. You can use a home-made book, or a purchased scrapbook or notebook. Collect photographs of babyhood (in the bath, feeding, sleeping, cuddling), holidays, birthdays and other high points of a little one's life, then write a story beginning (for example) 'Once upon a time there was a lady called ------ and a man called ------. They had a baby whom they called ------. Here is his/her picture . . .'

'MY' BOOKS: Using pictures cut from catalogues and magazines, or photos or drawings, make a personal catalogue of 'MY TOYS' or 'THINGS I LIKE TO PLAY WITH', or 'BETHAN'S BOOK OF BLUE THINGS' by Bethan or 'HANNAH'S BOOK OF HORRIBLE MONSTERS', or whatever the passion of the moment is.

LETTER BOOK: If your child is showing a particular interest in letters, you could get a scrapbook, or make your own, and put a letter at the top of each page, including the more widely used 2-letter combinations such as 'th', 'sh' and 'ch'. Then collect pictures of objects, people or animals beginning with the sound at the top of the page.

Encouraging children to notice detail

LOOK AROUND YOU: When you are out together encourage observation of the things in the environment – colours, sizes and shapes of things, what people are wearing (did they have glasses? what colour was their coat/hair/dress? were they smiling?). This is a good game and the habit of good observation which it encourages will be very helpful in recognizing individual letters and words later on.

WHAT IS IT?: Try covering a picture with a piece of paper, or put it in a wide envelope, then gradually reveal it to your child until he or she can guess what it is. You could also use the activity suggested in the chapter on painting and drawing, page 32, where a piece of tissue paper is laid over a picture and 'painted' with water until it can be recognized.

ARE THEY ALL THE SAME?: Draw three pictures, the first the same as the second and third except for one or two details and ask your child which is different. Alternatively draw a row of letters all the same except for one. A blackboard is useful here – you can paint the shiny side of hardboard with blackboard paint for a very passable blackboard, and later on it can be used for practising letters.

WHAT'S GOING ON HERE?: Have a look at a picture with your child and ask for the story 'What's happening in this picture', prompting when your child appears to be running out of ideas, by pointing out a detail that has not been mentioned yet.

JIGSAWS: Jigsaws require careful observation of detail in order to be completed successfully, and if you sit with your child, pointing out the important details on each piece, he or she will come to realise how useful it is to be closely observant. If you have trouble sorting the various jigsaws out after a play session, try colour coding the backs of each piece with a felt-tipped pen. Later on, your child will be able to sort them out alone, although if the details on the fronts have really been noticed, the colour coding will not be necessary!

COLOUR GAMES: Collect objects all the same colour for a 'colour table', or use pictures of (for example) red things, to stick in a home-made book. When you go anywhere, you can tell your child 'Today we are looking for red things, I wonder if you will spot some?'.

SHAPE GAMES: Cut out triangles, squares and circles from card, which can then be coloured by your child. You can use these to sort by colour, shape or size. Alternatively, you could use play-dough shapes, or any of the items in the sorting and threading chapter, page 130.

PLASTIC LETTERS: A set of plastic letters and a moulded tray provide a useful introduction to the observation of detail required in reading. If you run your fingers around the letters (in the direction they should be written), saying 'Up down around' or whatever, then get your child to do the same, it helps encourage appreciation of the nature of the shapes involved. Fitting the letters in to the board, matching letters ('see if you can find another like this'), turning them round to make a different letter, all give a basic grounding which will come in useful later.

WHAT HAPPENED TODAY?: Towards the end of the afternoon, tell a story together about your day – what was for breakfast? where did you go? who did you see? what were they wearing? who came to the door? were there any letters this morning? was the man/woman next door cross and how do you know he/she was (or wasn't)?

SILLY RHYMES: There are a number of activities for encouraging children to **listen** to detail in the chapter on sounds and music, page 107, but an amusing and simple one can be played when your child is familiar with a few nursery rhymes. Once they know the words, they are often tickled by silly variations such as:

> Hey Diddle Diddle, the cat in the middle
> The Cow jumped over the moon
> The little dog burped to see such fun
> And the dish ran away with the banana

Or: Baa Baa Black Sheep have you any sausages
　　 Yes sir, yes sir three bags full
　　 One for my dad and one for my mum
　　 And one for my sister who's sitting on her bottom

These are not difficult to think up, especially since you know so well what will amuse your own child, and it certainly makes them attend to what you are saying, in spite of all the giggling.

I SPY: To encourage children to notice the initial sounds of words, play phonic I spy, that is, make the sounds of the letters (buh) rather than giving the names of letters (bee). At first the starter 'I spy with my little eye' may be too hard, so you will have to add extra clues 'I spy with my little eye something that you eat for breakfast beginning with 't'.

Encouraging the eye to move from left to right

POINTING: As you are reading a book, point to each of the words as you are reading. Then say that your pointing finger is getting most awfully tired and can you use his/her finger instead? At the end of each line, the finger must fly back to the beginning of the next line without touching the page; some children get the idea that reading goes from left to right and then back from right to left on the next line and so on, so the finger must not slide along the paper.

POOR KITTEN: Draw a sad kitten on one side of the paper (the left) and a plate of food on the right, so the child can join them up with a finger or a crayon. A smile can then be drawn on the kitten's face. Any two objects that go together can be used and at first you could draw a wiggly line between them for your child to trace.

STARTING WORDS: If your child seems particularly interested in words, make some word cards using white card (all the same size, about 10 cm by 7 cm (4 inches × 3 inches), red or black felt-tipped pen and lower case letters except for the first letter of a name. Write one word on each card. It seems to work best to start with the child's own name. Show the card, point from left to right as you say 'This word is . . .' two or three times, then ask your child what it is. You can then add another name (Mummy, or Daddy) and do the same, then see if he/she knows which is which. Make enough cards for the family (and pets if you like). Your children can use these to label their rooms, or you could tell a story about the family, using the cards instead of pictures. Once the family names have been learned, important things in your child's everyday environment could come next – table teddy, chair, crisps, door, cup, etc. You could arrange the cards on the floor as an imaginary house where your child arranges the furniture and people and food as he or she would like it, or so that one of the toys can have a nice time throwing crisps at Aunty Mary or whatever. Other words that will soon be needed are prepositions such as in, on, under, behind, by, on top of – some could be stuck in the appropriate positions on a box, to help learning.

GAMES WITH STARTING WORDS: Action words such as run, walk, hop, sing, cry, jump, once learned, can each be put on a card, then stacked in a pile; 2 players then take one at a time and have to do the action on the card. It will take a long time to reach this stage, but games can be played with the cards as a means of teaching them, not just when the word is thoroughly learnt.

OTHER PRE-READING ACTIVITIES: Many of the skills needed for reading will be automatically learned through other activities in this book. For example, see Sorting and Threading (for matching activities such as Lotto, page 133), Music (for listening practice, page 107) and Play-dough (for shape recognition, page 57).

14. Play Ideas For Particular Occasions

Introduction

This chapter gives hints and ideas for particular sorts of play. Parties are looked at first, followed by television, which although not a particular occasion, is a particular entertainment that is widespread. Suggestions are also given for entertaining children who are not feeling very well, ideas for travelling with young children, places to take them out, and, finally, a list of '4.30 pm' ideas, which are suggestions that take little or no preparation and can be used to fill up the odd half-hour at the end of a long day, or while you are all waiting for visitors who are unexpectedly late.

Parties

WHAT DAY?: Try to have the party on the birthday itself, since younger ones find it hard to understand the connection otherwise. If it must be on another day (such as a Saturday) make it the Saturday **after** the actual birthday, or the birthday itself comes as a bit of a disappointment. Make sure first that it is a day when best friends can come.

INVITATIONS: If there is one thing all children love, it is receiving their own personal letters. You can buy invitation cards (at a price) but it is much more fun to make your own. Cut them out of plain card, or buy some plain postcards, then decorate with stick-on stars, glitter, or tiny dried flowers (see the chapter on collage page 40). You could paint your child's name on the card with P.V.A. glue, then he or she could sprinkle glitter over it, shaking the surplus into a saucer to be used again. Alternatively, cut some coloured card into fancy shapes, decorate and fill in the details:

Whose party, and age (for example, Daniel's 5th birthday party)
Name of guest
Place of party
Times of start and finish
Telephone number or address for reply, or include a reply slip with the invitation. Make sure the invitations are given out in time for any preparations to be made on the part of the invited child's parents.

HOW LONG?: For children under 7, two hours is ample, for them and you. The plan is usually opening presents and a few games or play with toys before tea, tea, then a few more games, finishing off with something relaxing such as a sing-song or a special story. For children under 3, an hour is probably quite enough. If quite a few children come, you may prefer to label presents as they arrive, so that you can thank the child's parents personally at a later date.

DECORATIONS: Balloons are usually popular, (although a few children are a little nervous of a potential 'pop') and can be tied around in bunches, including one on the gate or front door; they can be given out at going home time rather than left to wither in your own house. Christmas streamers could be brought out for a treat in the middle of the year. You could also make some hats or crowns (see page 88).

WHERE'S MY MUM/DAD?: Under threes will need their mothers or fathers with them. For older children, make sure you have a telephone number where their parents can be reached – if you cannot contact someone to help, you could be left cuddling and consoling one child instead of entertaining the others. Whatever the ages of the children, you will need more than one adult, firstly in case of emergencies, and secondly to share the load! If there are going to be a number of mothers present, don't forget that they will appreciate a cup of tea (or something stronger) and a bite to eat too.

PRIZES: Again, small prizes are all you need, and try to arrange for all the children to get one. But keep competitive games to a minimum for under fives, as they cannot understand being 'out'.

GOING HOME PRESENTS: Once children have been to a few parties, they come to see going-home presents as their incontestable right. It is probably best just to accept this, and provide something small for them to take home in a bag with a piece of birthday cake and something small to nibble – an apple, a tangerine or a packet of crisps. Depending on age, small presents include a pencil, notebook, small packet of crayons, colouring book, badge, balloon, pencil sharpener, pencil top, pack of cards, plastic toy, toy jewellery, packet of seeds and any amusements from a joke shop, such as false noses, lips or ears. Put the items in a bag with the child's name on, and don't forget your own children will expect a 'going home' bag too!

PROTECTION – OF CHILDREN: !! If you have gas or electric fires, turn the fires off when the children arrive, if possible; they will make their own warmth! If you have to leave a fire on, make sure it is very well guarded. Make sure the children cannot get out into the road. If you have a garden with a pond, cover the water securely and lock any sheds or garages which may contain dangerous substances. If the party is to stay in the house, lock the door to the garden. Keep pets out of the way, both for their sake and for the children's. Remove any keys from doors, locked if you want children to stay out, and unlocked if you don't want them to lock themselves in – children have this remarkable knack for turning keys one way very adeptly, then, despite all cajoling, not being able to turn them the other.

PROTECTION – OF YOUR HOUSE: Remove all small objects you care about and cover good chairs with a sheet. Cover floors too, if they are going to have food and drink anywhere near them. If you have toddlers coming, provide potties, and have polythene bags available for damp clothes to be taken home. It is probably a good idea with young children, to suggest a break for trips to the toilet two or three times during the party.

Games

BE PREPARED: Make a list of games in the order of play beforehand both to ensure you have the necessary ingredients, and to use as a reference during the party.

THE MAIN ATTRACTION: For younger children up to about four, the most interesting part of a party is the food and the other children, so the games suggested here are mainly for the older ones, although three-year-olds often join in with great enthusiasm, if not with great understanding.

UNDER THREES: Just provide a supply of toys (see the chapter on babies, page 13, for some ideas). Organized games just will not work. If you have space for small bikes and other sit-on wheeled toys, try to borrow a few from other people, to minimize fighting. Some action rhymes may be popular, such as Here We Go Round The Mulberry Bush (see page 109), Ring a Ring of Roses or **Here we go looby loo:**

Here we go looby loo
Here we go looby li
Here we go looby loo
All on a Saturday night

You put your right arm in
You put your right arm out
You shake it a little a little

And turn yourself about
(and so on, with your left arm, both your arms, your right foot, your left foot, both your feet, your whole self)

In the main, parties for the under threes involve just doing what they normally like doing, only with more food and more little friends.

Children over three

The old favourites come into their own for this age group –

MUSICAL CUSHIONS: Place enough cushions for all but one of the children in a circle on the floor. Play some music while the children dance about. When the music stops, each child finds a cushion and plonks down on to it, the one without a cushion being 'out'. Take away a cushion and start the music again, taking a cushion away between each go. When there are only a few children left, they must dance around two adults rather than hovering over the remaining few cushions.

PASS THE PARCEL: Wrap a small toy or book in lots of layers of paper, with a chocolate miniature or other little treat between each layer. Sit the children in a circle on the floor. Play some music as they pass round the parcel and when it stops, the child holding the parcel unwraps a layer and gets the treat. Then the music starts again. If you can, wrap up two parcels, since this is a useful game to quieten down the children between two more energetic ones. If there is a big group of children, you could have two parcels and two rings at the same time.

MUSICAL HATS: Sit the children on the floor in a circle and give one child a hat to wear. Play some music and the hat is put on the head of the next child who passes it to the head of the next and so on. When the music stops, whoever is wearing the hat is 'out'. The winner is the last child left.

MUSICAL STATUES: The children all dance round to some music, and when it stops they have to try to stand still. Anyone moving is 'out' (but you will need to be tolerant in your 'judging' since **all** the younger ones will be wobbling!)

WHAT'S THE *TIME* MR. WOLF?: An adult is Mr. Wolf and a settee or rug is declared 'home'. The children stalk around the house (keep to one floor) following Mr. Wolf and asking 'What's the **TIME** Mr. Wolf'. Mr. Wolf replies with various times, and the children are quite safe unless he says 'TWELVE O'CLOCK, DINNER TIME' in which case they have to run 'home'. Anyone caught by Mr. Wolf for his dinner is 'out', although older children can then take a turn at being Mr. Wolf.

PIN THE TAIL ON THE DONKEY: Before the party, draw the outline of a donkey (or a pig, or whatever you can draw) and fix this on to a piece of chipboard. Make a drawing of the tail on stiff paper and put a small piece of non sticky adhesive on the back of the tail at the top. Then make as many more tails as there will be children and write their names on. When you are ready to play the game, give each child a tail and show him or her the animal, then blindfold him (provided he's willing) and point him towards the donkey (or whatever). The child then has to stick the tail on wherever he or she thinks the bottom is. The one nearest the right place wins.

THE FARMER'S IN HIS DEN: All the children except one hold hands and walk around in a circle with the last child in the middle (the farmer), singing –

The farmer's in his den, The farmer's in his den,
EE, aye, ee, aye, the farmer's in his den
The farmer wants a wife, the farmer wants a wife
EE, aye, ee, aye, the farmer wants a wife.
(At this point the farmer chooses a wife to stand in the middle of the circle with him, and the singing starts again)
The wife wants a child etc.
The child wants a nurse etc.
The nurse wants a dog etc.
(then the last verse is reached, sing –
We all pat the dog, We all pat the dog
EE, aye, ee, aye, we all pat the dog

(where everyone playing pats the dog on the head as he crouches down, usually with his hands over his head for protection!)
(Note – in some of the following games, you may find that some children do not like being blindfolded.)

SQUEAK PIGGY SQUEAK: All the children except one sit in a circle. The standing one is blindfolded, and given a cushion to hold. He or she is led around the circle and after a bit says 'Stop', and is then taken to the nearest child on the floor where he or she puts the cushion on the child's lap, sits down on it and says 'Squeak, Piggy, Squeak'. The child sitting underneath has to make a noise, and the blindfolded child has to guess whose lap is being sat on. If correct, they change places and the second child is blindfolded. If wrong 'Squeak Piggy Squeak' must be said again before another squeak and another guess.

GRANDMA'S FOOTSTEPS: One child is 'Grandma', standing at one end of the room with her back to the others, who stand at the opposite end of the room, in a line. The aim is to creep up on Grandma before she turns round. If she spins round and sees a child moving, that child must go back to the start. The one who manages to touch Grandma first changes places with her and the game starts again.

BLIND MAN'S BUFF: This is for the over-fives. One child is blind-folded and has to catch one of the others and then try to guess who has been caught by feeling face and hair. If the guess is correct, the children change places.

PING-PONG RACE: This is for the seven year olds. You can either organize teams, or let the children play individually. Give each child a ping-pong ball and a drinking straw. Place the children at some distance away from a finishing line, marked with string or ribbon. The ball must be got to the finishing line by blowing through the straw. If the straw touches the ball, the child must go back to the beginning.

Other ideas

VIDEO BREAK: Nowadays, over fives often sit and watch a video for some of the time at parties, and younger ones will often enjoy a quietish half hour of cartoons during or at the end of a boisterous party, if you have the facilities.

MUSICAL INTERLUDE: If you play an instrument, or know some-one who would be willing to bring along a guitar or other portable instrument, children of all ages will usually enjoy a sing-song to live music at some stage during the party.

HIRED ENTERTAINERS: There are usually children's entertainers (magicians or people who can do puppet shows) in every district, but since they are quite expensive, you would probably need to 'share' a party with another parent and perhaps hire a hall. If there are not many entertainers in your area, the children may have seen the act before, especially if they go to a lot of parties, but younger ones probably will not mind. If you cannot face entertaining a group of boisterous young children, this is definitely an alternative worth considering. You can get names from the Yellow Pages or from the local paper.

FANCY DRESS PARTIES: If you decide to hold a fancy dress party, be prepared for groans from the invited children's parents (who usually have to do all the work for the costume!). Have a theme (such as a particular television programme or a fairy story) and keep it simple. An alternative is to invite a small group of children and let them loose on a dressing-up box when they arrive (see the chapter on dressing up and fantasy play, page 76).

FEEDING TIME: Set the table with paper plates, cups and the food **before** the children arrive and cover with a sheet, shutting off the room if you can. You can find plenty of ideas for party food in cookery books, but apart from the cake, be warned that home cooking is largely wasted on children this young, who tend to stick to the familiar; they are usually much too excited to try anything remotely different at a party. You'll be sure to make them happy with crisps, cubes of cheese, savoury sandwiches, fruit (grapes and satsumas are particularly popular), cut-up sausages and fancy biscuits, plus individual jellies with hundreds and thousands or grated chocolate sprinkled liberally over, or ice cream in cornets, again with something interesting sprinkled on, or a chocolate flake stuck into the ice cream. Keep everything in small portions. One nice idea is to put a bit of everything at each place on the table, either on a largish plate or in a cake box – it makes for a much quieter teatime and children feel very important having their own personal box of party food – they can always swap what they don't fancy, or put it on a large plate in the centre of the table. You could label places with name badges (plain ones can be bought fairly cheaply in stationers) which they can wear at the party and take home afterwards. !! By the way, do **not** include peanuts in your list of food – although they are often extremely popular, they are dangerous if a child chokes on one, and at parties children are often encouraged by their friends to do silly things with their food.

Television

TELEVISION AS ENTERTAINMENT: Generally, television has been given a bad press as a means of entertaining young children at home. The major objections are that television stops children doing more useful things, that they see 'unsuitable' events, and that they will get into the habit of passing many hours in passive and unproductive inactivity in front of the screens. None of these criticisms applies directly to younger children, however. Television does not stop them from doing more useful things, rather it provides a quieter activity in an energetic day. 'Unsuitable' events are not normally shown during the hours when such young children are awake, apart from the News, which can be turned off, although in fact most young children find the News eminently uninteresting and switch **themselves** off first. There is a possibility that they will get into 'bad' habits, although again, most little ones are very choosy about the programmes they will watch; this period could be seen as a time to encourage selectivity, to turn off at the end of a chosen programme, to comment on what they have been watching, and to select in advance.

WHAT DO THEY WATCH?: Generally, children begin with a fascination for cartoons (soon after the second birthday, normally), and other programmes with plenty of action and noise. Theme tunes are often the first aspect of television to attract their attention, but by three, many children come to know and look forward to their favourite programmes. Older children often enjoy schools programmes, cookery lessons, and musical items too.

SHOULD YOU WATCH TOO?: At first you will need to sit with your child, putting the programmes into words he or she understands. If you are there too, this encourages whole-hearted attention rather than half-watching while playing with something else. This habit of attention will be a useful one in all sorts of later learning situations, even though the span of attention will be short.

YES, BUT . . .: Parents are often encouraged to watch with their children, and perhaps this would be the ideal situation and an excellent excuse for a sit down. However, for many of us, half an hour of children's programmes gives a welcome chance to get on with other tasks that are much easier without little hands round your legs and toys all over the floor just where you want to walk. A bit of quiet reading would be nice, although I suspect that many a dinner is prepared during afternoon television. It is very easy to preach about good and bad habits where television and children are concerned, but many adults enjoy an inane half hour in front of the television where the only obvious benefit is a rest after a hard day. Perhaps we should not deny this to our children. Once past the under-five stage, problems with 'too much' television are likely to arise whatever the experience in the first five years, as children hear about programmes from friends who are allowed to stay up later than they are, so just tell yourself you will deal with them when they arise. While the children are little, let them watch some children's programmes, relax, and enjoy the reviving effect they have on you.

MAKING THINGS FROM TELEVISION: If there is a programme coming up on which you know from experience things are often constructed, you will need to watch, with a pencil and paper in hand, since it is impossible to recreate objects from a young child's instructions as he or she heard and interpreted them.

BUYING THE TRIMMINGS: Many T.V. programmes have books connected with them, either stories about the characters, activity books or reading books. Most children love these, and if you can afford to buy one or two or ask for them as presents, it will be much appreciated. Again, make sure you have a pencil and paper to take down titles, addresses and prices so that you can order or buy the book. An added bonus is that you can use the pictures in them to copy and make a collage of the characters or their homes (see page 45).

BEYOND TELEVISION: Apart from the relaxing entertainment television can provide, you can go beyond the programme itself by doing activities suggested on it, using the characters in various ways (telling stories or making pictures, models or soft toy versions), purchasing accompanying texts or annuals and so on, so that the amusement from the programme is only a small proportion of the overall entertainment time provided.

Amusing children who are not feeling very well

ALWAYS SOMETHING TO DO: A general bonus of collecting useful bits and pieces as advocated in this book is that you can be sure of something available if your child becomes ill. Illness nearly always comes as a surprise, so to be on the safe side, you may like to keep a shiny new pack of felt-tipped pens (perhaps some special brush-tipped ones) and a new notepad somewhere just for this sort of situation, particularly as your opportunities for shopping trips are restricted with a child in bed.

MAKE IT TEMPTING: In the same way that people often prepare and present food in a tempting way for 'invalids', it is worth making little bits of play activities tempting. Make a specific change in the normal routine – paper to draw on cut in circles or triangles instead of rectangles, presented on a tray with some bright pens in a pot and perhaps a flower stencil, for example.

ADAPTING IDEAS: A number of activities in this book can be adapted for a child who is not feeling his or her normal energetic self, although you need to bear in mind two general points about play ideas for ill or convalescing children. Firstly, it is best to provide just one activity at a time, particularly if your child is confined to bed. Secondly, provide activities that would have amused your child a year or so ago; when we are feeling off-colour we often want undemanding activities, watching programmes on television that we would not normally watch, or reading books or magazines that normally would not interest us. Children are the same if they are tired, or getting over an illness, and for them 'undemanding' usually means the types of activities they enjoyed last year. Here are some suggestions for uncomplicated and quiet activities from this book:

CHAPTER 2

(Painting and Drawing)	Squiggles (page 34)
	Colouring books and stencils (page 35)
	A sampler (page 35)

CHAPTER 11

(Sorting and Threading)	Animal sorting (page 133)
	Cotton reels (page 134)
	Threading buttons (page 134)
	For the birds (page 134)
	Bracelets (page 135)
	Pegboard pictures (page 135)

CHAPTER 14

Other possible toys include picture dominoes, a toy telephone, musical toys, small plastic people and animals, puppets and fit-together toys.

THE BEST OF THE LOT: If a child is just feeling like lying in bed but cannot sleep, a cassette tape recorder with a few tapes can do wonders to relieve boredom. A tape recording of nursery rhymes, songs, stories or music played softly nearby will soothe and comfort them.

Travelling with young children

CAREFUL PLANNING: Travelling longish distances with young children can be an infuriating experience for everyone in the car, so it is worth thinking ahead and packing a box of entertainments to be distributed one by one as necessary.

BAG OF GOODIES: The first essentials are snacks and drinks – more drinks than you think you will need, particularly if you are travelling on a warm day. Crisps are popular, although you will have to brush out the car after the journey, and they are greasy, so do not give them if your child is prone to travel sickness. Other possibilities include satsumas, apples, plain biscuits and seedless grapes. If you have time beforehand, prepare a selection of items to put in a small plastic lidded pot – raisins, sunflower seeds, banana chips, toasted coconut, pieces of satsuma, anything small that will take a long time to eat and which cannot cause choking (!! therefore not peanuts).

THINGS TO DO: If your child does not suffer from travel sickness (since trying to 'read' makes them feel worse) books, pencils, paper and a few toy cars, with a tray to rest on, will be appreciated. All children will be likely to enjoy listening to tapes of nursery rhymes, music or stories, so if you have a portable cassette recorder this will be an invaluable help on a journey. Your own sing-song would be nice too.

SIMPLE GAMES: Games that involve spotting pub signs or car number plates are too advanced for this age group, although you can point out things that you think may interest them. Unfortunately, what usually happens with younger children is that by the time you have their attention and they have looked in the right place, the object of interest is a few miles back! Simpler spotting games may be enjoyed. If you're driving in built-up areas, look for a certain colour; if in the country look for different animals.

BREAKS: If a child is not sleeping, you will need frequent breaks every hour or so to stretch legs and visit toilets. (It's also a good idea to carry a potty in the car for emergencies.) You may be able to collect some treasures for a scrapbook, or at each break ask your child to tell you what is around; write it down, add the name of the place or the nearest town, and at the end of the journey you will have a 'diary' to keep and illustrate later on.

Trips out

A BREATH OF FRESH AIR: It often seems to be so much trouble getting everyone ready to go out, particularly in winter, but it really is worth it. The one rule is not to be in a hurry, particularly with a toddler who wants to explore everything.

LOCAL FACILITIES: To a great extent, your trips out will be limited by your local attractions, unless you have access to a car and can afford the petrol to travel, or have an efficient bus or train service nearby. Make sure you know of all the available attractions near you by asking neighbours or enquiring at the library.

EXTEND THE TRIP: Wherever you go, prepare for the trip by talking about it, getting suitable clothes ready, and a bag to keep treasures in. When you get home, 'write up' the trip and illustrate with pictures, postcards, items collected while out, bus tickets and so on.

WHERE TO GO: Possible trips out include visits to a local church (different from your normal one), a bridge, the park, the shops (perhaps different ones from the places you do your every-day shopping), doctors, dentist, on a train or a bus (particularly if you rarely use buses and trains to travel), roadworks, building site (from a safe distance), a petshop, fruit and vegetable picking, a zoo, a farm, riding stables, a pub with a family room for a lunch treat, watching the postman emptying the postbox (check the collection times first), watching the roadsweeper or dustman (again from a distance if the rubbish is a bit 'strong'!), or someone moving house, the outside of a police station or a fire-station, a picnic in the local park, preceded of course by lots of fun **preparing** the picnic, often enjoyed as much as the trip itself.

COLLECTING THINGS: Use the time you have out in the fresh air to collect items like bark and leaves to be used for rubbing or printing (see the chapter on painting and drawing, page 33), stones for miniature gardens and sand and water play, or fircones for Christmas decorations. In the autumn, acorns and conkers can be picked, and in late autumn, when all the leaves have fallen, interesting twigs can be collected.

NIGHT EXCITEMENT: Younger children very often do not have much experience of being outside when it is dark. A trip out after five o'clock, well wrapped up, to look at the lights, the moon and the stars will cause much excitement, particularly if you come back to some delicious warm soup and crusty bread.

FEEDING THE BIRDS: If you are visiting a park where there are ducks on a pond or a town square where pigeons congregate, take some bread and/or broken biscuits for your child to feed them – if you can get him or her to throw the bits rather than eat them.

4.30 p.m. ideas

GO FISHING: Cut out fish shapes from a cereal packet. Put a paper clip on the 'head' end and go fishing over the edge of a table or chair with a magnet on a piece of string. When the children are tired of this, the magnet could be used to find out what else is metal.

JIGSAWS: Glue pictures on to card and cut them up to make jigsaws. You could use photos (enlarged if possible) of people your child knows, or of familiar toys. An enlarged photo would still be cheaper than a new jigsaw. When you have more time and if you have an actual jig-saw (a saw which enables the user to follow wiggly lines with a fair amount of accuracy), you could make a more permanent toy by pasting the pictures on to thin plywood rather than on card.

KIM'S GAME: Put a number of objects on a tray (what, and how many will depend on the child's interests and abilities, try starting with just six objects). Talk about them and make sure the child has a good look. Put a tea towel or other cloth over the tray, and get him to shut his eyes while you remove one object. He then has to guess what is missing.

A NEW BIN: Decorate a box with paper or foil or paintings, and then use it as a wastepaper bin, toy box, etc.

SKITTLES: Collect some plastic bottles (washing up liquid, squash bottles) and use to play a quick game of skittles.

USEFUL INVENTIONS: If you have a set of interlocking construction pieces, get it out and make something you can use at tea-time – a basket with wheels for the bread and butter, so your child can 'drive' it to whoever wants some, or if your table is small, perhaps a transporter for the salt and pepper would create less chaos.

BE CREATIVE: Many of the bought toys that children acquire and tire of quickly can be made more interesting if an adult sits down with the child and thinks of novel ways of using them, and once into the swing of things, children will often be extremely inventive. When they realise there are more ways of using many toys than the one originally intended, they may start on their own next time. This comes more naturally to some children than to others, and you will know how much prompting your child(ren)'s imagination needs.

GRAND PRIX: Put the end of a plank on a box to make a ramp for racing toy cars.

PICNIC TIME: Have a mini picnic, a packed lunch in the bedroom, or in a tent made from a blanket over a line weighted with stones outside, or over a table inside.

VOLLEY BALLOON: Tie some string between the backs of two chairs, then blow up a balloon and pat it backwards and forwards over the string.

KEEP THEM BUSY: Keep some pipecleaners handy for odd empty half hours (such as in waiting rooms, or when visitors you are expecting are late). Make people, animals, glasses, spiders or trees, or get some tissues as well, and make some flowers with a pipe cleaner stalk.

WHERE'S IT GONE?: For the younger ones, cut a hole in the top of a container (ice cream container, ground coffee tin) to use as a posting box for buttons, pebbles, bits of Lego, small bells etc.

WHAT DO WE NEED?: Sort out the shopping list together before you go out. Involving young children in the preparation helps them to understand why you go shopping, and gives them more of an interest once in the shop.

FUN WITH A DUSTER: Do some housework, children will love to 'help'. It is perhaps a good idea not to let children grow up with the word 'chores' – look on housework as lots of little achievements. For that matter, looking after children is often not valued as much as it should be – I hope the ideas in this book will help make it more restful and enjoyable too.

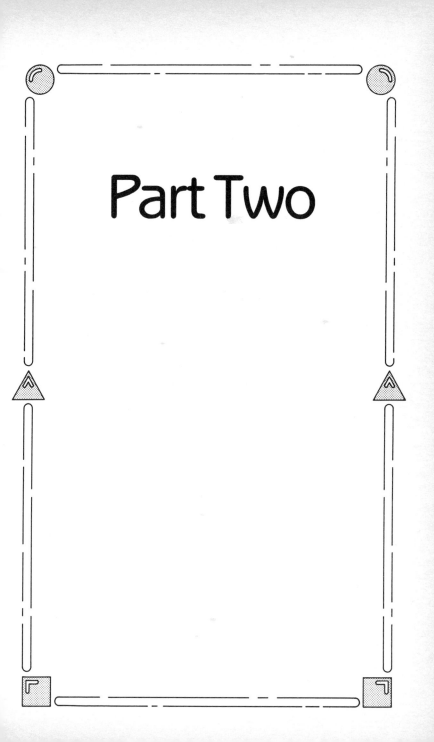

Part Two

Safety Note

Always be very safety conscious when your child is working his or her way through the things in this book. However accustomed he or she may be to using even a simple thing like a pencil, remember that it has a pointed end that could easily cause damage to soft parts of the body, and that it is for holding in the hand and not in the mouth! Here are a few more tips to be aware of – and you obviously will have more ideas of your own to add to this list.

1) Never let your child run or jump about with anything other than soft unbreakable things.

2) Only things which are edible should go in the mouth.

3) Try to make sure that your child uses scissors with blunt not sharpened points.

4) Look at the labels on all paints and crayons to make sure they are non-toxic. If this is not displayed please ask the shop assistant – and if in doubt, don't buy them.

5) Make sure any glue used is a safe type with no fumes that could affect your child. Use P.V.A. adhesive or water-based glues. (If you have other types for your own household use, please keep them locked away.)

6) Never leave your child unattended when cooking any-thing that needs heating in any way (see also page 291).

7) If your child is using anything that is powered by mains electricity, make sure it is fitted correctly and that you personally switch it off and on.

Introduction

Although this book is divided into two sections as an age guide, you will probably find that the first part is also useful for some 7-11 year olds. As Pam Harris says in her introduction, children vary so much in their rate of development that it is impossible to stipulate at which age your child should move from one aspect of this book to another. Don't be worried if your 8 year old child shows interest in something that is in the first part, it may be that he or she has no experience of the particular subject, and if so, then it's always best to start from the beginning. I think that this is of paramount importance when working with your children; there is no set time to help to introduce them to new subjects. Some of the ideas in this part may have been covered by the teachers at your child's school. In fact, find out what he or she has enjoyed doing at school and use some of the activities in this book to help take your child one step further.

Again, as with the first part of the book, do try to let children do as much as possible by themselves. You can provide the materials and the initial ideas but then let your children see what they can make out of them with *their* minds, which at this age are so uncluttered, you will often be surprised at the originality of their approach. This does not mean, however, that you leave your child totally alone – try to be there physically but not verbally, and always be prepared to help with anything should your child request it. The question may not be resolved instantly, but may lead you both to the local library, as described in Chapter 8. When using this book let your child have fun while he or she is learning new experiences. Praise every stage of development, and if your child begins to get bored with an activity, don't push him or her into continuing, but suggest he or she has a rest and starts again later.

I would like to thank the people who have helped me with the research and development of this book: Sally Angel; Paul Kears; David Arthur, Jonathan and Timothy Arthur and Chris Manger; also, the expert nanny and teacher whose comments on the manuscript were invaluable.

1. Painting And Drawing

Useful things to have

Soft pencils
Crayons (all colours including
    black)
Felt-tipped pens
Coloured chalks
Water colours
Poster paints
Charcoal[1]
Paper[2]
Tracing paper
Magazines

Printing materials
Lino or lino tiles[3]
!! Lino cutting tools[4]
Oil-based paints for lino
    printing[5]
Roller or large brush
!! Knife (not too sharp)
Washing-up bowl
Washing-up liquid
Cooking oil
Straws
Blunt pencil or pen nib
Stencils

Notes

1. Charcoal can be especially effective when the edges of the outlines are rubbed with the fingers or a soft cloth. In this way shading starts to take place and suddenly the drawing looks much more lifelike.

2. The paper to be used for pencil drawings could be any scraps of the following:
▲ Writing paper – backs of typewritten letters.
■ Art paper – but be aware of cost.
● Note pads.
▲ Computer paper – possibly scraps brought home from work.
■ Scrap books bought from any stationers – these are really quite cheap.

When using charcoal the surface used could be:
● Reverse side of remains of wallpaper rolls.
▲ Insides of cereal packets.
■ Insides of large envelopes slit around the edges to open out into large surface.
● Sugar paper.
▲ Reverse side of pictures brought home from school.

Do go and ask local offices if they have any scrap or waste paper that you may have to use for this purpose. It is often easier than you think. Mostly, as long as you don't 'hassle' them too much, people will be only too pleased to help. Anyway – nothing ventured nothing gained, as the saying goes. They can only say 'no': they won't bite your head off.

Paper for lino printing is the same as for charcoal. Bubble pictures should be done on any type of matt paper. 'What's in a scribble?' can be done on any notepaper – preferably unlined, and potato printing is on plain matt paper.

3. If you have off-cuts of lino, cut them into a manageable shape before giving them to a child. Plain lino is best but a patterned one will work.

4. Anything that has a sharp edge to cut into the lino. Obviously, safety is of the essence here. You could buy lino cutting tools for this from an art shop, but potato peelers and apple corers will do. Make sure that whatever your child uses has a handle to grip with and show him or her how to work with the tool. Cutting movements should be made away from the body and the fingers of the other hand must be kept clear.

5. Water colours are not suitable for lino printing, as the oily surface of the lino rejects them.

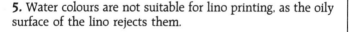

General hints

Improving the technique: For this part of the book, designed for older children, it is a good idea to try to lay the foundation for proper painting and drawing techniques. Watch the way children hold the brush, pencil or crayon. Only too often this is held as near the tip as possible and gripped really tightly. Demonstrate that by holding the brush, pencil or crayon about one inch from the tip, and pressing lightly, in fact more control can be achieved. Also show that a dark or thick line can be built up with lots of thin strokes rather than one stroke made by heavy pressure.

Two budding artists: If you don't consider yourself an artist, this may be the time for you to have more confidence in drawing. There is nothing like trying to make someone else think about painting and drawing for giving yourself a new perspective on art. Have a go with your child, and learn from each other.

Increasing awareness: The main thing at this age is to increase your children's powers of observation by helping them to be aware of what they know is there (see 'What's in a face?', below).

Drawing the face and body

WHAT'S IN A FACE?: Before your child starts a portrait get him/her to list everything he/she sees when looking at a face. Ask yourself the same question. So often the reply is simply – two eyes, two ears, a nose, a mouth and a chin. If that is all you see that is all you will draw. Encourage the child to get more than these in his/her list. The following is a list of most of the things that will have to be drawn. How many did you leave out?

Forehead	Pupil	Lower lip
Eyebrows	Ears	Tongue
Upper eye lid	Ear lobes	Jaw
Lower eye lid	Neck	Chin
Upper lashes	Nose	Teeth
Lower lashes	Two nostrils	Dimples
White of eye	Cheeks	Laughter lines
Iris	Upper lip	Folds of skin under
Wrinkles		eyes

SHAPELY FACE: Ask your child to draw an outline of a face – say your face – and tell him/her that not all faces are the same shape, some are round, some are heart-shaped, thin, fat, square, lopsided, pear shaped and so on. Ask him/her to decide what shape your face is, then watch as he/she draws it.

FURTHER FIGURES: Later on try to show what a face looks like in profile, and try to draw that.

A HAIR'S BREADTH: The addition of hair to the drawing is always the fun bit of a portrait as far as children are concerned. Try to get them to see hair as a moving many stranded thing rather than a blob stuck on the top of the head.

TRACING THE SHAPE: For children who find free drawing a little difficult, get some tracing paper and let them draw round the shape of models' faces in magazines. They could either add features to this or copy the resulting tracing and work on that.

KEEPING YOUR HAND IN: Draw round the outline of your child's hand on a piece of paper (or he/she can do this). Then, just as you helped him/her observe all the different parts of the face, do the same with the hands – measuring if need be. Fill in the hand drawing, using this information.

FOOTSTEPS: Draw, observe, measure and fill in the outline of a bare foot as well.

BODY SHAPE: Teach the child to list the important parts of the body as for the face. So many times shoulders, elbows, knees, wrists and ankles are forgotten. Get him/her to draw a body first, then play a game or have a joke about how someone like their drawing would move. This is not meant to embarrass but as an aid to observation – so it should be a funny game.

WASTING AWAY?: I once read a horrifying piece of information that the circumference of the waist should be almost the same as that of the head! Try it out in a drawing – make the waist the same size as the head. Depending on your own particular physical make-up it's surprising how big/small the head/waist should be, isn't it?

Drawing other objects

PET SUBJECT: Suggest your child draws his or her favourite animal. This may well be the family pet, providing it will keep still for long enough. Sleeping cats and dogs are a safe bet. Make sure the proportions of the animal's body are drawn correctly. Quite often, to a child's mind, the head of any animal is larger than the rest of the body. This is because the face is the most interesting thing about almost all living things.

FILLING IN THE DETAIL: Start with the general outlines, concentrating on getting a realistic pose. If all this goes well, then get your child to draw in more detail. Gentle strokes all over the finished drawing will give the effect of fur. And don't forget – if it's a cat you are drawing – those lovely whiskers!

PICTURE GALLERY: If one of your child's drawings has been particularly good, pin it on a notice board or display area to show it off. The door of the refrigerator provides a good white background if the pictures would otherwise clash with the decor. If he or she is a prolific artist, you could change the display once a week. As a really special treat, you could mount and frame one of the pictures. Frame kits – the kind sold for photographs – are good for small pictures, otherwise you could try the poster hanging devices.

STILL LIFE: If animate objects still don't inspire, why not get your child to draw inanimate ones? A box would be a very good thing with which to start. It helps children to learn about perspective. To start with, they may just draw a square to represent the box, so point out to them that this is only one side of the box. Get them to try to draw the rest of the box, and then help them if it doesn't look quite right.

SQUARE ARTIST: Once the technique of drawing the three-dimensional box is mastered, suggest that your child constructs a

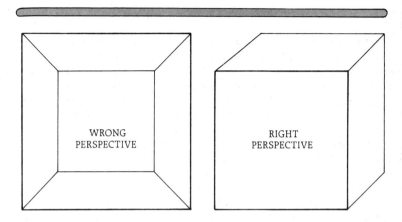

picture around it. It could be a kitchen scene, for instance, with the units and washing machine. Alternatively, you could go outside together and draw your house from different angles.

AT HOME: Suggest your child picks a small area in your house as a subject for a painting. It could be a part of his/her bedroom (and this may even encourage them to tidy up) or a vase of flowers on the mantlepiece, the telephone table, a bowl of fruit or even the biscuit tin (this often has a design which can be copied).

USES FOR THE FINISHED WORK: Any of the pictures that a child draws can be used in many different ways. It is better for children to see that they have created a useful piece of work rather than for you to put their work away in a drawer or – worse still – throw it away. So you could do any of these things:

1. Cover a book and paste the drawing on to the front cover.

2. Stick the drawings on to suitable boxes or tins.

3. Put them all in a scrap book.

4. Cut out the best bits of all the pictures and make them into another picture by using a collage technique.

5. Stick the picture on to a piece of cardboard (such as from the back of a cereal packet) cut it up into different shapes and make a jigsaw from it.

Colouring

FELT-TIPPED PENS: Here are some useful hints when using felt-tipped pens.

1. When using them to colour in a large section keep the strokes all going the same way.

2. Try to keep an even pressure on the pen – this gives a constant colour instead of lighter and darker variations.

3. Put one colour over another, then wet the area by dipping a paint-brush in some water and applying gentle brush strokes. This instantly mixes the colours on the pages.

4. Always put the lid back on the pens after using, otherwise they will dry up and cannot be used again. And this always happens to the favourite colours.

USING WATER COLOURS: Here are a few hints on painting with water colours:

1. Don't mix too much water with the paint. If the paint is in a block form just add a brushful of water at a time and mix in. The less water, the deeper the colour.

2. If the paint mixture is too runny, have some kitchen roll handy, so that any dribbles, which will ruin the picture, can be mopped up.

3. Use a saucer or a plate to act as a palate for mixing colours to the right shade if the desired colour is not already in the box. In fact this could be turned into quite a useful pastime in itself. You could write down a list of colours and how you obtained them.

4. Start by using light colours and build up to dark.

COLOUR CLUES: You do not need a vast range of paints to provide a good variety of colours. Red, yellow and blue are the basic colours which when mixed in different combinations will make lots of new colours. Remember that you will alter the depth of the new colour by how much of each of the mixtures you put in.

SKIN COLOUR: One of the most difficult colours to capture is the colour of skin. Try to get a more subtle colour than simply pink, brown or black: skin tones are much more varied than that. A good guide to a reasonable colour is to mix up a colour that is similar to the colour of the foundation creams you use.

POWDER PAINTS: Even if these are used with the greatest care in the world they can be very messy. On the market now there are various non-spill pots. They have wide bases but small tops – just big enough to get a brush in, and these cut down some risk of mess. There are also pots of pre-mixed paints – the powder paint having been already mixed with a liquid. Do bear these in mind when buying the materials for your child. They are a little more expensive, but cut down on accidents.

USING POWDER PAINTS: These can be used and mixed in the same fashion as the block water colours, but wet the brush before putting it into the pot – this saves a lot of the powder spraying all over the place.

CRAYONS AND COLOURED PENCILS: These can be used with the same effect as the felt-tipped pens but they will not mix with water. However, now that felt-tipped pens are so easily available, they can take second place.

COLOURED CHALKS: These are marvellous to use – the colours mix easily and any mistakes can easily be rubbed out with the fingers. I think they are well worth the dirty fingers, faces and surfaces. They are very easily cleaned up. Wetting the chalks or damping the paper makes an interesting alternative.

OIL PAINTS AND EMULSIONS: These are quite an advanced and difficult medium to use properly, but if your child finds painting an absorbing pastime let him have a go with oils. Have some turps ready to deal with spillages.

Lettering

LETTERS WITH A DIFFERENCE: At this age children will be making progress at school with their writing. Why don't you see how many different ways they can write the letters of the alphabet? Use type faces from different magazines and get your child to try to copy them.

WHAT TO WRITE WITH: You may also discover that you want to write with different sorts of implements other than pencils and biros. The old-fashioned school pens with changeable nibs are still quite cheap to buy. The different nibs give different thickness to the strokes and are fun for all the family to use. Ink is not too expensive either, but do buy the washable type. The following make unusual writing implements and should help to sustain a flagging interest.

1. Discarded birds feathers – as quills.
2. Paintbrushes.
3. Old make-up brushes once cleaned.
4. Forks – three or four lines to each stroke.
5. Slivers of wood – sand them down first to avoid splinters.
6. Ends of rulers for very large letters.

I'm sure you can think of many more things around the house that you could use. Keep experimenting. It helps make your child aware that writing is an art in itself and not just a way of putting words on paper.

BACK-TO-FRONT ADVICE: One extra tip I've learned is that after you've written on a piece of paper you should hold it up to the light with the reverse side facing you. It should look as pleasing to you that way as it does straight on.

ROYAL SIGNATURE: One extra thing to show your children is Elizabeth I's signature. See if they can copy that!

THE HOME CALLIGRAPHER: Good lettering is never wasted. Your child could find endless ways to make use of the newly-learned skill. Here are some ideas:

1. Labelling spice jars.
2. Labelling book jackets.
3. Writing on homemade Christmas and birthday cards.
4. Menus for special meals.
5. Making up advertisements – both lettering and drawings could be used.
6. Labelling drawers, boxes, bottles.
7. Party invitations.
8. Play programmes (see page 224).

STENCILS AND RUB-ON LETTERS: If, with all the encouragement in the world, your child finds lettering difficult, there is always an easy way out. You can buy stencil sets with letters and numbers of different sizes, so that he or she can make words using these stencil letters. The rub-on letters are more expensive, but also provide instant letters. Letters and numbers in varying type faces are sold on sheets of paper. When the letters are pressed or rubbed, they detach themselves from the plasticized paper and transfer themselves to the surface pressed on. It works like brass rubbing in reverse. But do make sure that your child presses all the letter out. Rather like transfers, it is very annoying to lift off the paper and find that only half the print has come out. It is virtually impossible to put the original top paper into the exact place and try to release the remainder of the letter or number.

Lino printing

STEADY
WITH
OTHER
HAND

CUTTING
MOVEMENTS
AWAY FROM
BODY

KEEP STEADYING HAND CLEAR

STARTING OFF: When using lino it is best to use the thicker, more old-fashioned kind of lino. Plain lino is also preferable. Use the side that would normally be walked on and mark out the design in pencil or felt tip. !! Cut away both sides of the outline to give a solid shape (see page 183 for safety note). Small feathery cuts across the solid shape will give a shading effect as in a pencil drawing.

PUTTING ON THE PAINT: When the design or picture has been cut out, cover a paint roller in paint and roll over the surface of the lino. (If you don't have a paint roller, brush the paint over the surface of the lino with light strokes, making sure that the cuts in the lino are not clogged up with paint. This would ruin the effect.) Also make sure that all the surface of the lino is covered.

MAKING THE PRINT: Press the paint-covered lino carefully face down on to a sheet of paper. Try to make sure that the lino doesn't move too much for that would smudge the end result. The result is really interesting for the child, for it works almost as a photographic negative. The child will soon learn that what is cut out of the lino will *not* be printed and that which is not cut out is printed.

PRINT PRODUCTION: Small lino cuts could be used over and over again and could, in fact, be used to print home made Christmas cards. A very suitable design for this would be a round or star-shaped piece of lino which has snowflake patterns cut out.

FABRIC PRINTING: Oil-based paints lead to interesting extensions of this method, for the design can then be printed on material. Plain handkerchiefs can be made quite pretty with a small design. The bottom of a plain skirt can also be decorated in this way, using prints of different colours. Once the design has been made there is no end to its uses. The fabric can be washed, though the design will fade in time.

LONG-LIFE LINO CUTS: Should the etches on the lino become full of paint, they can either be washed, or in the case of oil paints cleaned with white spirit or turpentine. (!! Keep these cleaners locked away when not in use and supervise your children when they are in use.)

LETTER HEADINGS: Make a lino cut featuring something to do with your child or the area you live in. Use this to print on the top of plain writing paper and on the back of a plain envelope. Below are some ideas for designs which reflect something about you:

1. Draw seven trees for Sevenoaks.
2. The Humber Bridge if you live in Hull.
3. A shepherd's crook if your surname is Shepherd.
4. A milk bottle if Dad is a milkman, or a dairy farmer.
5. A guitar if you or your child are musical.
6. A pair of scissors if your name is Taylor.
7. A church if you live in Church street.
8. A bath if you live in Bath.
9. A cathedral if you live in a Cathedral town, like Canterbury or York.

PARTY PIECES: Design your own party invitations. Make a lino cut of something relevant to your party. If it's a tea party, draw a large cup and saucer, if it's a birthday party, do a design of a huge cake. Print on to postcards, add the details of time and place and you have a really individual party invitation.

MAKE A CALENDAR: Your child could make twelve different lino cuts; one for each month of the year and print them on the top of twelve different pieces of card. Then he or she could practise the lettering, as mentioned on page 189 in this chapter, and write the name of the months and the days of the month underneath. Attach the tops of twelve sheets together with string and there you have a calendar. And if your child really enjoys the lettering, the lino cuts can be used again to make more of the same, to give as Christmas presents.

GRAPHIC DESIGNS: Once your child has become familiar with the technique of lino cutting, he or she may like to develop the printing side. Try to get him or her to do some graphic designs. By this I mean making a basic pattern shape cut out of lino. It is best to keep it simple to begin with, e.g. a zig zag or a semi-circle. Roll or brush on the paint, then make different patterns with the shape on a large piece of paper. The shapes can be printed in rows or circles, alternately the right way up and upside down or overlapping. Add interest by changing the colour used. If this is successful your child could carry on the design to decorate a larger surface and make more complicated shapes.

WRAPPING PAPER: Turn large sheets of plain brown wrapping paper into patterned wrapping paper with the repeated graphic design. Use bright primary colours so that they show up against the brown.

WALL ARTIST: If you are going to redecorate your child's room why not let him or her pattern one roll of plain paper. It will take quite a time, but once on the wall of his or her room, it will give a huge sense of achievement. Of course, if you and your child are confident, the pattern could be printed straight on to the already hanging wallpaper – providing of course that the original wallpaper is quite plain, and of course, providing that you help and supervise the whole operation.

MATERIAL DESIGN: The same graphic design printing operation could be performed with oil-based paints on to plain materials, so that when dry the material could be made up into something nice to wear.

WHERE TO GET THE IDEAS FOR GRAPHIC DESIGNS: The main secret of a graphic design is that the basic shape should be simple enough and flexible enough to look good when it is used over and over again to fill a large area. For inspiration begin by looking at your own wallpaper and material designs. Look also at curtains and carpets. If this becomes a long-term interest, you could keep a scrapbook of ideas taken from magazines or newspaper advertisements.

Random design printing

BUBBLE PICTURES: Fill a washing up bowl with water and add a little washing-up liquid. Get your child to froth up the suds either by hand, or by blowing through a straw. !! But do make sure that they blow down and don't suck up the straw. Next shake different coloured powder paints over the surface. Bubble up the water again. Don't agitate it too much and make sure if your child is using a straw that he/she doesn't blow too hard and get the paint all over his/her face – and your work surfaces. Then lay a piece of paper over the top of the bubbles. Lift it off very gently. The coloured bubbles will leave a pattern of blobs and specks. Leave the paper to dry. This will be an end result of its own but you could let the children take it one stage further by drawing round or over the resulting colours to make an over-printed picture. Perhaps the shape of the blobs is reminiscent of an animal or building and this could be drawn in.

OILY PICTURE: Fill a washing-up bowl with water and add one teaspoon of cooking oil. (This will demonstrate the fact that oil and water do not mix!) Sprinkle some different coloured poster paints on the surface. Put a sheet of paper on the surface and drag it off – this mixes the colours and makes the most interesting marbled effects. Leave the paper to dry. The water, oil and paints can be used as many times as wished but after a while, the colours all merge with one another and don't look so good.

PRETTY COVER-UP: Both the oily picture technique and the bubble pictures make very attractive wrapping paper. Use it for presents or for covering books (see page 197).

MORE MAGICAL PICTURES: In the first section of this book we showed how to make 'magic' pictures for younger children (page 32). Here is a step further for the older ones.

SCRATCH AND SEE: Cover the paper with almost a rainbow effect using coloured crayons. This could be:

a) Stripes going from one corner to the opposite diagonally, each stripe a different colour.
b) Zig-zag shapes across the paper again with each zig-zag a different colour.
c) Start from the centre of the paper and draw circles – each circle a different colour.

Then cover the whole page with black crayon, making sure that all the coloured crayon is covered. (This takes quite a time – do make sure that the end result is that of a black piece of paper.) Now, using a blunt pencil or pen nib, scratch off a design (for example a street scene, or a party dress) and watch how all the rainbow colours appear. Even if the scratches remove all the wax, the colour from the first layer of wax will stain the paper underneath and therefore show through.

UNDERLYING DESIGNS: Once your child has got used to this idea, get him to try to plan where he wants the colour underneath. He may be able to make simple designs which include real elements in them. For instance, by planning where to put green and brown, a tree could be etched out.

WHAT'S IN A SCRIBBLE?: This is something which has given considerable fun to our family. It not only stimulates the brain, but also is a great aid to concentration. It can be played as a kind of game between a few children, or be done quite successfully by one child as long as you are on hand to admire and comment on the results.

STARTING THE SCRIBBLE: If there is more than one child, get each to draw a scribble on to a piece of paper in pencil, then pass the piece of paper on to someone else, and in turn receive a piece of paper with another person's scribble on. (If there is just one child, perhaps you could draw the scribble or get him or her to scribble blindfolded. This is to ensure that there is no pre-planned design.) Obviously the scribble should not be too messy.

ORDER OUT OF CHAOS: When the scribble is completed, put away the pencil and use only coloured paints, crayons or pencils. The idea is to try to make a picture up from the scribbled pencil design. Plenty of time should be given to staring at the scribble to see exactly what the best result could be. From the most bizarre pencil marks the resulting picture could be quite interesting. See if the children can make dogs, cats, people, houses, bicycles or cars out of the design.

ADDED INSPIRATION: Children may need help to begin with. They may not be able to see anything in the scribble at first (you may not either) but by constant staring and a bit of concentration every scribble should be able to inspire something. It will make children aware of their surroundings. Don't just get them to think of everyday things: stretch their creativity by helping them to think of all sorts of things. It may be that some scribble reminds them of maps, sausages, swings, fires, curtains or even just a piece of rubbish left on a rubbish dump.

UNDERCOVER STORY: Covering a book is always a difficult job. Here are some hints you may find useful: Try to make sure that the material used is fairly firm. The popular use of cling film is more trouble than it's worth. Suggest your child uses paper that he or she has coloured, or wrapping paper, Christmas present paper, brown paper for parcels, or of course any leftovers from wallpaper.

Cut a shape that is approximately 2 to 3 cm (1 to 1½ inches) larger than the opened book.

Place the **closed** book so that its spine is in the centre of the paper and fold the paper over, so that the two right-hand edges and top and bottom edges are equidistant.

Lift the top cover of the book up slightly and fold the top surface of paper under the right hand edge only.

Hold the paper and book carefully and turn over so that the open end of the book now faces your left hand. Lift the bottom cover of the book and fold the paper under as before.

Cut a wedge shape from the centre of the top and bottom spine edges of the book. Fold wedge shapes from the four edges of the book where the paper is double thickness.

Open the book and turn the top and bottom four edges down.

Using sticky tape, stick only wrapping paper to wrapping paper. Do not stick down to the book jacket. This may cause the paper to tear if you haven't positioned it correctly.

The book is covered.

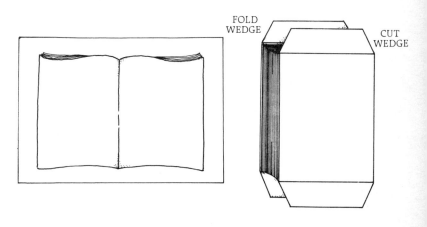

FOLD WEDGE

CUT WEDGE

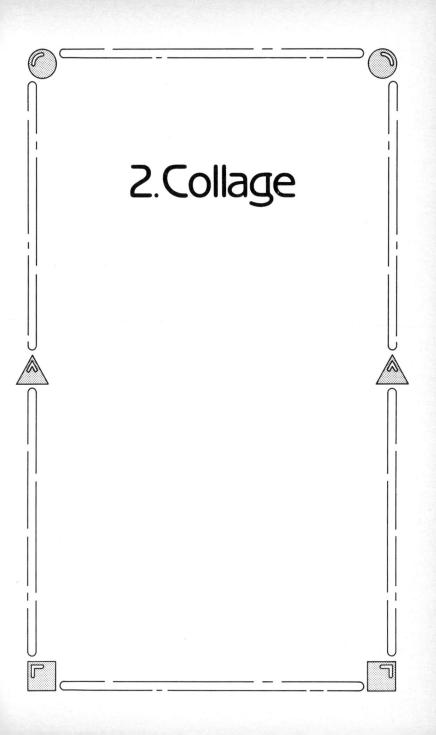

2.Collage

Useful things to have

Large sheet of paper or card[1]

Different cut-outs from old photographs, papers, magazines, Christmas and birthday cards or old tatty picture books that would otherwise be thrown away

Pieces of left-over wallpaper, used stamps, coloured paper, discarded Christmas decorations, coloured cellophane, bits of old jigsaw, silver foil

Letters or words from magazines to make into new sentences

Pressed and dried grasses and flowers (see flower pressing on page 202)

Seeds from flowers e.g. sunflower seeds, poppy seeds

Leaves, bark, feathers, shells

Kitchen food stuffs, such as rice, lentils, beans, tapioca, coffee granules, herbs, cornflakes, porridge oats, rock salt

Ribbons, wool, cotton, string, buttons and safety pins

Fabric scraps, especially velvet, silk and hessian

!! Paste or glue[2]

Pot for glue

Paint brush or small spoon. (The glue could be applied with the back of the spoon bowl, or handle.)

!! Scissors

Plenty of newspaper to protect working surface

Blotting paper[3]

Notes

1. Art card can be expensive, make your own pieces from the large sides of cereal packets. Trim these down to give two fair-sized rectangular surfaces at no cost at all. Either side could be used. The coloured, advertisement side could have plain paper patterns stuck on them. The plain cardboard side could be used for anything.

2. The easiest glue to make is a flour and water paste. This is made quite simply by mixing flour and water together into quite a thick paste. If it is too runny it will take far too long to dry and also it is more messy to use. See page 255 for full instructions on proportions. The flour and water paste can be used for all the ideas in this chapter, alternatively use a water-based or P.V.A. glue.

3. Blotting paper or any absorbent paper, such as kitchen roll, is needed for flower pressing, see page 202. Make sure that the paper is fairly strong though and will come clean away from the flower after it has been pressed. If it is too thin, like some loo papers and tissue papers, the moisture pressed out of the flower could cause the paper to stick to the flower and thus ruin the pressing.

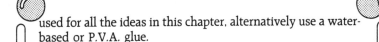

General hints

Make it lively: Collages used for this older age group should be quite exciting and very creative. Once the basic art has been mastered, there are many useful applications for it.

Suiting the materials to the subject matter: The general idea is for the children to make a thematic or artistic picture from the materials supplied. For example, round objects suggest eyes, wool is good for hair, corduroy would do for corrugated fencing or roofing.

Glue it first: When making a collage using small items it is best to put glue on the paper first, then add the material. For example, should you wish to put a lane made out of rice in a picture, paint on the glue in the shape you require, then pour on the rice, and leave to settle for a brief moment before shaking loose rice off the surface. This process really is like magic and providing there is a suitable surface to shake the loose bits of rice on to, everything will be all right.

Contain it: Put all seeds, rices, herbs, small stones, into empty, clean yogurt pots. This helps to pour them on to the glued surfaces. It also makes collecting spilled contents easier.

Bushy beards: When making a collage of a face old brushes (household type) that are no longer useful can give a very good imitation of a beard. First put some glue on the chin area of the face, then scatter small clippings from the brush over this area.

Mirror images: Silver foil can make mirrors.

Silky seas: Thin but silky material, folded in half and cut almost up to the edges in strips, placed in a crunched up position on the paper will give an excellent effect of waves on the sea or a lake.

Ideas

TO MAKE A FACE: Begin by outlining the general shape of the face with string. Add some wool in squiggles for hair (unravelled knitting wool is good for this). Stick on two buttons for eyes and some string for a nose. Then cut out two red circles to make the cheeks and a strip of felt or ribbon for the mouth.

PICTURE GALLERY: Using the same method described above, you could make clowns', witches', fairies' and even relations' faces, and have a great deal of fun with this.

IDENTIKIT PIC: Another way to make a collage face is to cut out pictures of famous people from magazines and make one face up from lots of different people's features. For example, you could put into a basic face shape Princess Diana's eyes, Tommy Cooper's nose, Mick Jagger's mouth, Prince Charles's ears and Telly Savalas's forehead and hair – or rather lack of hair. I wonder what that would look like? Incidentally, as a side game, you could try to find a name for this new character.

TO PRESS FLOWERS: You could buy a flower press for this which is really not a very expensive item. But if you don't have one, don't despair, you can press flowers very well without one. Apart from the flowers themselves and the absorbent paper mentioned on page 201, you will also need a large, heavy object, such as a block of wood or a pile of books, to act as a weight.

WHAT TO DO: Put the heavy book or block of wood flat on a table. Cover this with two sheets of newspaper to protect book or wood, and then place some blotting paper on top. Arrange the flowers in as attractive a position as possible. Try not to use buds of flowers – they don't press very well. Put some more blotting paper on top, making sure that the flowers aren't disturbed underneath. Depending on the number of flowers to be pressed, you could insert a piece of cardboard, then more blotting paper, more flowers, blotting paper, etc, but if only a few flowers are being pressed – just enough to fit the sheet of blotting paper without touching each other – place on the blotting paper, then some newspaper and put a heavy book or block of wood on top. Remove from the table very carefully and leave in an undisturbed dry area for about 3-5 days. The bottom of an airing cupboard is a good place. Then remove the press layer by layer and carefully lift out the pressed (dried and flattened) flowers. They are now ready to use for a collage.

TYPES OF FLOWERS TO USE: Any small, common wild flower, such as daisies, buttercups and poppies can be pressed. Only pick the very common ones and leave some stem behind. Don't pull them up by the roots. Be very careful not to pick the precious wild flowers that are protected by conservation laws. You can also press flowers from the garden that do not have very 'fat' heads, e.g. pansies, geraniums, daffodils, clematis, dog roses, lavender. Practically all kinds of herbs press well and make the resulting work smell good. Finally, heathers, most types of grasses and freshly fallen leaves are all interesting to press.

TO MAKE A FLOWER PICTURE: Pressed flower pictures were very popular in Victorian times and indeed are coming back into popularity now. Start by making just one picture or design on the back of a cereal packet. Use grasses to give the general shape, then fill in the picture with other flowers. Sometimes the flowers used sparingly are better than a clump that look a bit messy. Show children how to do this, then leave them to their own individual talents.

THEMATIC PICTURES: Make a collage from lots of cut out pictures all concerned with one subject. For instance, if the main interest is horses, use only pictures connected with horses: bridles, bits, saddles, horse racing, horses jumping and put a horse's head in the middle of the picture, then surround it with other relevant pictures. The same could be done with motor bikes, pop stars, houses – the list is endless. The main thing about a collage of this kind is that it could help in the understanding of basic values of perspective. A small item will look better at the top of the picture, making it look further away and the larger the object the further down the picture, but this really depends on whether or not the aim is to have a realistic picture.

LANDSCAPE COLLAGES: This is when the seeds and foodstuffs are useful. Rice could be made to look like a white, wide, winding path made of pebbles that weaves in and out of the countryside. Mixed dried herbs make splendid green/grey hills and other herbs of differing greens alter the colour of the hills. The sun could be a large round made out of lentils. Use leaves and twigs for trees, but most of all use your own and your child's initiative.

Uses for collages

MAKING A BIRTHDAY OR CHRISTMAS CARD WITH A PRESSED FLOWER COLLAGE: First cut out an oblong shape from thin cardboard or art paper. Fold it in half. Arrange some flowers and leaves sparingly in the centre of the front card. Mark their positions lightly in pencil, then remove them one by one. Add a little glue then re-position them and leave until dry. Next cut out a square of cellophane paper (clear) or cling film and glue over the pressed flower area. Use lettering as described on page 189 for the greeting inside the card.

SOUND SENSE: Why not get your child to design a record sleeve made from a collage of pictures cut from magazines? So often existing record sleeves get damaged. Just tape it up again, then cover the original with other pictures. If it is one of your child's favourite pop records, you could suggest that they make up a collage of pictures from magazines of the group concerned.

PAINTING AND COLLAGE COMBINED: Use collage techniques to highlight one part of a child's painting. For example if he or she has painted a scene with trees in, use a piece of real bark to glue to the trunk of the tree in the drawing. If the drawing is of a vase, use some pressed flowers to glue on, so that they look as if they are coming out of the vase, or if the scene involves costumes, curtains or bedspreads, this feature of the drawing could be picked out in a patchwork of fabrics.

TOUCH OF CLASS: Pressed flower or seed collages look very good mounted on a board covered with velvet or fine corduroy, then hung on the wall. This makes an ideal present.

PERSONALIZED COVERS: Collages of photographs or magazine cuttings make ideal and individual covers for exercise books, diaries or notebooks.

MAKE A WALL GAME: I have seen this done several times and it can be most effective if handled well. The object is to cover a wall or part of a wall with a collage. This is an ideal way of covering up an uneven surface, but make sure that you really have thought it out first.

Start by cutting out pictures that you think will all eventually go together. One wall game I saw was made out of landscape or garden pictures, but they were arranged in such a way that they made a rainbow effect. The pictures had to be stuck on according to colour. There are many ways of doing the wall game. In the kitchen it could be a wall of vegetables. In a child's bedroom – cars and football players, fashions and pop stars.

This could be a very good idea for convalescing children. While they are confined to bed they could sort and cut out pictures. Then as they get better, they can start to glue the pictures to the wall, using polycell glue (this is a permanent fixture). The wall remains a creative thing for a long time, for if you take a dislike to a certain picture you just cover it over with another one.

Visitors to the house will use it as a conversational piece, and it is a constant joy to the creator. But don't be ambitious with it – start small. It takes a great deal of time to do and a lot of working out.

3. Dressing Up And Other Fantasy Play

Useful things to have

Make up box[1]
Box of hair clipping from last
   hair cut[2]

Paper and pens
Props[3]
Thin card

Wardrobe items
Braces
Crash helmets
Evening dresses
Top hats
'Old Lady' felt hats
High-heeled shoes
Wellingtons
Cloaks – use old curtains
Scarves
Suits
Gloves
Canes
Belts
Wigs
Jewellery

Stockings and tights
Feather boas
Cloth caps
Hair nets
Ribbons
Elastic bands
Boots
Ties
Shirts
Pyjamas
Dresses
Skirts
Jumpers
Jackets
Net curtains
Old sheets and blankets

Stage set materials
4 old bed sheets (2 as
   backdrops, 2 as front
   curtains, see page 217)
Assorted cardboard boxes
Lights (see page 219)

Plain paper
Toilet paper
Poster paints
Glue (flour and water paste, see
   page 255, or water-based)
!! Scissors

Notes

1. A make-up box is essential and should include the following pieces from a reputable cosmetic firm to avoid the possibility of skin allergies:

Foundation cream of
   differing shades
Lipstick

Moisturising cream
Eyeliner pencils
Hair grips

Rouge
Powder
Eyeshadows
Mascara
Nail varnish

Make-up pencils or crayons
Cotton wool
Baby lotion or remover for
    make-up removal

2. Hair clippings will be of great use for making moustaches or beards. Flour and water paste will be safe to use as glue to stick hair in position.

3. Props will depend on the type of character your children are portraying. The following are used in this chapter. Suggestions are given for substitutes in the text.

Plastic bucket
Newspaper
Paper plates
Rubber balls
Skipping rope
Wooden skittles
Earrings

Sticks (not pointed) or broom
    handles
Radio or record player
Toilet roll inner
Cotton wool
Bin liner

General hints

Rainy day blues: The dressing-up box is one of the most useful things to have in the house for those cold wet days when your child has friends coming to visit and you have totally run out of ideas with which to amuse them. Hours of fantasy play can be successfully achieved with literally nothing more than a box of old clothes.

Big ideas: Adult clothes are best, for the child always sees himself as playing the role of someone in the grown up world. Grandparents are often one of the best sources for clothes.

Other uses: Not only can the contents of the box be used at home, but it can also be extremely useful for fancy dress parties or competitions.

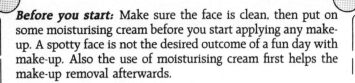

Before you start: Make sure the face is clean, then put on some moisturising cream before you start applying any make-up. A spotty face is not the desired outcome of a fun day with make-up. Also the use of moisturising cream first helps the make-up removal afterwards.

Make-up: If you don't mind spending money on this idea, special make-up crayons for children can be bought.

Pin up: Pin the hair back from the face – make up on the hair is not part of the process. Make-up which has found its way on to clothes should wash off. Any stubborn stain should come out with a little gentle soaking in warm, sudsy water.

Some favourite characters

BECOMING A CLOWN: Believe it or not, clown make-up is a skilled art which has been patented. Every clown has to register the design of his make-up and it has to be passed as an original design before he is allowed to use it. However, you will not have any trouble with the clowns' union when you are making up children's faces. It is possibly best to make them up yourself the first time to show them the general way to do it, afterwards they should be able to do it for themselves.

A CLOWN'S MAKE-UP: There are four stages to making a clown's face involving first foundation, then mouth, eyes and nose.

1. Put as light a foundation cream as possible over the face. Leave a circle round the eyes and about an inch around the mouth. The edges of the foundation should be as clear as possible, almost as if the foundation has been painted on.

2. The mouth. Draw a black or brown line around the outside area of the mouth at the edge of the foundation cream. Decide first whether you want your clown's face happy or sad and tilt the corners of the mouth up or down appropriately. The clown could of course have one side of his mouth happy and one side sad. It is up to you. Now fill in the whole

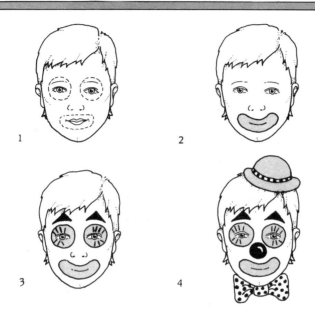

extended mouth area with whatever colour you wish. Obviously red is best, for you can use lipsticks, but coloured lips are fun – greasy eye shadows in lipstick type containers are best for this.

3. The eyes. Get the child to close his eyes and, again, as for the mouth, draw a black line round the edges of the foundation, then fill in the eye shape with colour, but don't go too near the eyes. Yellow, pink or orange are good colours. Draw lines for upper and lower eyelashes – really large lines – and just four or five on top and three or four for bottom lid. This should have covered the eyebrow area, so draw on eyebrows much higher up than normal. You can really have fun with this. They could be triangular, or like question marks. They could even be like enormous commas, with the tail part coming right down on the cheeks.

4. The nose. Either colour the tip of the nose red or black or cut a ping-pong ball in half and paint it with red nail varnish. (This is a bit tricky and should be done by an adult.) When it is dry stick it to the nose with a bit of flour and water paste or with some double-sided sticky tape or you could thread some string or elastic through two holes in either side and tie it to the back of the child's head. Perhaps you could even buy a clown's nose from a toy shop – they're not very expensive.

A CLOWN'S CLOTHES: This should be the easiest part – providing your dressing up box can cope. The following ideas should help.

▲ The trousers if possible should be brightly coloured and checked, but if resources don't run to that, just the baggiest trousers you can find. If you have some braces, attach them to the trousers to hold them up – but string will do. Hold the trousers in by using a belt and stop the child falling over by turning up the bottoms into large folds.

■ Brightly coloured socks pulled up over trouser bottoms could be fun.

● Big Wellington boots or any boots – the larger the better. Pack the toe with newspaper to stop it curling up where the child's feet don't reach. This also helps with walking.

▲ Shirt – this should be as bright as possible – but if you only have plain ones – glue or sew some bright patches on it.

■ Tie a ribbon or old tie in a bow shape around the neck but leave the shirt open.

● A jacket or cardigan with the sleeves rolled up could be an optional extra. Tie a belt or piece of string around the waist. Put a large flower made out of paper petals in the button hole or an old windmill will do.

▲ A large floppy hat, or cap, or bobble hat will complete the image.

A SUMMER CLOWN: In warm weather the clown could just wear the baggy trousers and belt and braces. Put on or paint on a black tie and put a pair of shirt cuffs on the wrist. No shoes are necessary and the bright socks should have the toes cut off.

PROPS FOR THE CLOWN: These will vary according to the act. Here are a few suggestions, most of which are from around the house:

■ A bucket filled with torn up newspaper (very small pieces). Looks like water, doesn't make quite the mess, but think that they all have to be picked up afterwards. Cut up pieces of foil look more realistic but are more expensive.

▲ Rubber balls to juggle with, or anything else, e.g. soft toys.

● Custard pies – this could be paper plates covered with shaving foam if you dare risk it.

■ Skipping ropes

● Wooden skittles

BECOMING A WITCH: The following are some ideas for making a truly awesome witch's make-up.

FOUNDATION CREAM

SHADED CHEEKS

BLACKENED TEETH

SCARF COVERING HAIR

▲ Put moisturiser on skin before starting (see page 210).

■ White or green foundation. The green could be greasy green eye shadow or mix powdered eye shadow with base. The compact powders will crumble easily if you poke them about a bit as most of us will know to our cost if we have ever man-handled our own make-up.

● Dark lines around and under eyes.

▲ Heavy dark eyebrows.

■ Get the child to suck in cheeks and fill the sucked in area with dark colours too – this gives a very gaunt look.

● Draw 'crows feet' around the corners of the eyes but avoiding the actual eye and dark lines around the nose.

▲ A red dot near the corner of the eyes nearest the nose will give a good effect.

■ Bright red lipstick also makes a ghoulish effect together with the greenish base.

● To black out a tooth, dry out the surface with a piece of cotton wool – make sure the lips stay clear of the tooth after you've done this then cover the tooth with black eyebrow pencil. One top tooth and/or one bottom tooth should be enough.

▲ Black wig or black scarf to hide light coloured hair.

THE WITCH'S CLOTHES: Anything black, long and ragged will do. Preferably a black dress, that you can cut a ragged hem on, with black tights and black high-heeled shoes or black boots. A black shirt will do as a jacket.

WITCHES' HATS: These are easily made by making a cone shape out of black paper or card. Stick some star and moon shapes on it, cut from silver looking foil.

COMPLETING THE PICTURE: Long black finger nails are always associated with witches. These can be easily achieved by cutting out long fingernail shapes from black card or paper. Then paint the child's nails with nail varnish and when it is nearly dry press the cut-out nails on to each nail. They don't last too long but are great fun.

PROPS FOR A WITCH: The following objects all help to set the scene for a spellbinding performance.

■ Broom stick – two long round-ended sticks with strips of paper tied round one end will do.

● Cauldron – a bucket, preserving pan or large bowl will suffice.

▲ Witch's cat – a soft toy.

■ Use anything else that could be described as witchy – if you have them. My children have a collection of rubber spiders, lizzards, bats and frogs. If you don't have any of these, get the children to draw frog, spider or bat shapes on to dark paper, then cut them out. These will then be ready to throw into the cauldron with some suitably awful spell.

A WITCH'S SPELL: Try this one:

Eye of newt (button)
Leg of toad (stick or pencil)
Squashed beetle from the road (Plasticine)
Mix them up and turn around
And you'll be lifted off the ground.

BECOMING A POP STAR: The theme of the make-up for a pop star can be copied from any of the popular heroes. It should be bold and bright. Start with a moisturiser base as before, then use any normal base make-up if the child wants it but it isn't absolutely necessary. Use a bright colour eye shadow, draw on eyelashes, put rouge on the cheeks and some lipstick. Stick on star and circle shapes made from silver foil using flour and water paste as glue.

THE HAIR STYLE: Try to copy whatever is the popular trend:

▲ To make the hair stand up, a little judicial back combing will usually be enough but if you want to go to extremes, use hair lacquer or a proprietary hair gel or mousse.

■ There are many spray-on hair colours on the market that are fun to use and will just wash out afterwards.

● Crumbled, powdered eyeshadow brushed into hair looks good.

▲ If the style is for 'slicked down' hair, just wet the hair.

EARRINGS: If you haven't any clip-on earrings, then thread beads or buttons on to a loop of cotton and hang them over the ears.

A POP STAR'S CLOTHES: Anything modern, trendy and bright with lots of scarves, bangles and belts. Wear high-heeled shoes or boots on the feet.

PROPS FOR THE POP STAR: Music makes the act so you will need a radio or record player with volume turned up as loud as you can bear it. Make a microphone out of a toilet roll inner and a ball of cotton wool or old rags, covered with a bit of black plastic bin liner. Push the end of the bin liner through the cardboard tube and trim off. Fix into place with sticky tape.

THE POP SONG: Those who get carried away with this dressing up idea and like to repeat it often may also enjoy writing their own pop song to go with the act, see page 270.

EXTRAS: For anyone not in on the act, there are two invaluable extras: good neighbours and cotton wool ear plugs.

Staging a play

GETTING THE ACT TOGETHER: This can be done with the minimum of expense, using items found throughout the house. The best way to illustrate how to stage a play is to run through an example: let's choose 'Jack and the Beanstalk'.

SETTING THE SCENE: Two backdrop sheets are needed, one for Jack's house and one for the Giant's house in the clouds. Paint the basic outline and colour each scene with pastel paint (copied from a fairy tale book). This is best done by laying the sheet out on the floor or if the weather is good in the garden and painting them. It doesn't have to be too detailed. Decorate the sheet with cut-out pieces of card and paper depicting the sun, moon, lanterns, birds, clouds and so on. These can either be stuck on with water-based glue or pinned on. Once decorated, the sheets can be hung from a picture rail, or, if you haven't one, tuck the top edge into a closed cupboard door. As long as the scene can hang from something the effect is achieved.

FILLING THE SET: Furnish the set with chairs and tables decorated with paper and card, preferably tied on to prevent any damage. For instance a large piece of cardboard painted gold will make an enormous throne, or the chair can be covered with some brightly coloured, silky material to make it look very rich. Cardboard boxes can also be painted to make tree stumps. The bean-stalk can be made by decorating a hat stand with coloured toilet paper and painted paper and card. If you haven't a hat stand, any tall object fixed from the bottom will do.

THE WARDROBE: For 'Jack and the Beanstalk' there need only be four characters, but the story can be expanded if more children are involved. The idea of costume is, like make-up, a way of making children think they are acting, so make the costumes as strident and colourful as possible.

For Jack, a big shirt and belt as a top, a pair of children's trousers and nice colourful long socks for the trousers to tuck into will do. Normal shoes can be transformed by making cardboard buckles painted silver, and attaching them with string to tie underneath.

Jack's cow can be portrayed by tying a brown rug or sheet round the body and wearing long brown stockings or tights. The simplest way to make a child look like a cow is to make a face mask, looped on with elastic. The tail can be an old dressing gown cord.

The giant will look big if he or she wears a big overcoat, baggy trousers and a big pair of shoes. If the giant is standing still, put him on a box and drape the overcoat round it, thus making him taller. A beard can be made by cutting out a beard shape on card and glueing on pieces of cotton wool. Make two holes in edge, thread string through and tie into place. A long walking stick is also helpful to create the character in children's minds.

Jack's mother can wear an old skirt and smock, with a blanket as a shawl. Again a walking stick helps to increase the character.

THE MAKE-UP: This is a very important part and is no end of a boost to children's imagination when they are acting. Use your own ideas as to what you do, together with some of the hints that are in the section on making-up a clown, a witch and a pop star.

LIGHTING: !! Lighting can be quite simply achieved by using two angle poise lights and a lamp without a shade. The two angle poise lights can shine in from each side, and will be very effective if all other lights are off and the curtains are drawn. The uncovered lamp can be placed behind the backing sheet, to create an illusion of light on the scene. With this in place, the performance can start.

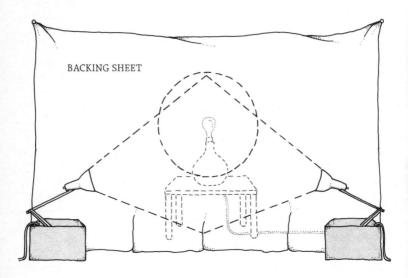

BACKING SHEET

OPTIONAL FRONT CURTAIN: The front curtain is the last part of making the play work for children. If you can fix two sheets in front of the set, they will feel more that they are performing when the set is revealed. The sheets could be tacked to the ceiling with four tacks, and the set would then be revealed by taking out the middle tacks or lifting the curtains back. However, if you want to keep a nice ceiling, then why don't you run a piece of rope or string across the room and drape the sheet over it. Alternatively, if you had something to use as a screen, this would be a very good idea and save all the problems.

THE STORY: Children will have their own idea of what the story is, so when telling them how to act it, keep to their basic idea of the plot. Very few words are really needed, children often take to miming a story far more quickly than telling it. Despite this, they will want some lines, so that they feel that they are acting. Keep to the famous lines like 'Fe Fi Foe Fum, I smell the blood of an Englishman' – children learn these very quickly. What also works is for the mother to tell the story whilst the children act it out. You will need to simplify the story, so that it fits into the two sets which you have made.

Sketches and plays

CHARACTER SKETCHES: Ideas will soon come forward if the children concentrate on any of their favourite television characters. This is a good time to get a group of children together, sit them down and get them to actually write out the words. First decide what the sketch will be about, then choose the characters. Let each character make up his own words, and write them down as the situation develops. Keep the sketches to about 5 minutes long and try to make sure that the characters in the sketch are very well known to all concerned. Use famous soap opera characters or famous situation comedy characters. Costume and make-up really aren't necessary for this, but a few household props might help. It might be good to show the finished results of this to the children's parents, when they arrive to take them home.

MUMMING PLAYS: One of the oldest plays to take place in the British Isles is the Mumming Play. These were plays designed to enact the struggle between good and evil and between light and dark. They usually take place at about Christmas time and are very good plays to let children act out. They make an interesting change from currently popular stories of space, superheroes and robots.

MATERIALS YOU NEED TO MAKE COSTUMES: You will need these from the play wardrobe. Old shirts or old pyjama jackets; long strips of ribbon, coloured paper or strips of brightly coloured material and large hats. Cover the hats in ribbons or make a sort of witch's hat (see page 214) and cover that in ribbons, or use a plastic flower pot that is painted and turned upside down. The holes at the end of the flower pot can be filled with rags or ribbons that hang down all around and will hang down over the face of the actor.

MATERIALS FOR THE PROPS: The hero and villain need sticks of wood (not too pointed) for use as swords to fight with and possibly a shield. The doctor needs a bag full of pretend medicines like a bottle of water, a toy frog, talcum powder and a mallet with which to tap the patients' knees.

TO MAKE THE COSTUMES: Stick or sew on to the pyjama jacket or old shirt strips of ribbon or paper or material about 1 cm wide and 14 cm long (¼ inch × 6 inches) in as many places as you wish, so that they're all over the costume. This, however, takes some time and there is a quicker and equally effective way of making a costume. Simply make a circle of ribbon which can be tied loosely around the shoulders of the actor, then tie long ribbons in the same colour or pieces of paper or indeed bits of material on the circle, so that they hang from it. The important thing is that the colour usually indicates what type of character the person is, for instance:

The villain will be dressed in black
The hero dressed in white
The doctor dressed in green
Father Christmas dressed in red
Jolly Jack Tar dressed in any colour

Any other character you wish can be in the play, and can wear their own distinctive colour.

THE SCRIPT: You can write your own script and give your villain and hero your own name. Here is a rough guide for you. It can be made as long or as short as you like.

JOLLY JACK TAR:

In come I, old Jolly Jack Tar.
I've come from near and I've come from far.
Come rain or shine I'll not stay away
I've come to see the Mummers Play.
Good mister and missus, give what you please
And give it to old Father Chrissymas please.
The players in their colours bright
Are here to tell their tale tonight.

FATHER CHRISTMAS:

In come I, old Father Christmas.
Welcome or welcome not,
I hope old Father Christmas
Will never be forgot.
We've come to show you such a sight
As was seen through history on many a night.
In comes our hero dressed in white
He's bold St. George – yes, George the Knight.

ST. GEORGE:

In come I, St. George your hero bold
And with this shining sword I've won three crowns of gold.
I've fought the fiery dragon and brought him to the slaughter
And that is how I won the King of Egypt's daughter.
I am the greatest hero of honour and renown
And now I'll fight the Black Knight that lives around this town.

BLACK KNIGHT:

In come I, the Black, Black Knight.
Methinks this day I fancy a fight.
I'll fight St. George – they say he's strong
But between you and me he won't last long.

My head is made of iron,
My body's made of steel,
My hands and feet are knuckle bones
And no one can make me yield.

ST. GEORGE:

If your head is made of iron
And if your body's made of steel
And your hands and feet are knuckle bones
I can still make you yield.
I'll swish him and I'll slash him
And I'll chop him small as flies
And send him back to where he came
Wrapped up as small mince pies.

(St. George and Black Knight take out wooden swords and fight. The Black Knight wins. St. George falls to the ground. The audience shouts 'Aaah!')

DOCTOR:

In come I, the good doctor Hammett.
I'll wake St. George with my strong mallett.
(Pretends to hit St. George with mallet but actually bangs floor to make loud sound.)
I'll sprinkle him with holy water
It'll make him better – at least it oughter.
I'll put some powder on his head
Rise up St. George you're not dead.

(Cheers from audience)

FATHER CHRISTMAS AND JOLLY JACK TAR:

Good people now our play is done,
Evil has lost and good has won.
We can no longer stay round here,
Merry Christmas, Happy New Year.

(Cheers from audience)

OTHER CHARACTERS: There are a lot more characters that can be put into a mumming play, if you have more would-be actors to cater for. You could make a dragon costume and have the hero, St. George, stage a fight between himself and the dragon before he goes on to fight the Black Knight. Other characters have been taken from popular characters of the times. Here are some from past and present that you might like to choose from: Nelson; Robin Hood; Maid Marion; Beelzebub; Adam Ant; Boy George; or even your own 'Auntie Flo'.

DESIGNING THE WHOLE PROGRAMME: If you do decide to help your children write and perform a play and you do manage to involve some of your and their friends to be an audience, then why not get your child to make a programme for them to remember the event by. It need not be an elaborate affair, one page will do. All you need to help your child do is to write out the title of the play, the characters in the play and the names of the people performing these characters. Decorate the borders and if there is enough room on the sheet, you could encourage him or her to put a bit of jokey advertising such as 'weak orange juice and mouldy buns supplied by old Mother (then your family's surname)'. If you can run to the expense have photostat copies made of the programmes to give to everyone – if not, they will have to be hand-copied: it will be more work for the actors, and more peace and quiet for you while they are doing it!

Drama ideas

THE ART OF ACTING: Quite often children have a great urge to take part in plays at school or to put on plays themselves. It's not until they start acting that they realize there is quite an art in it. Diction, projection and stage presence are the main stumbling blocks. As so many children today watch an enormous amount of television, not only can you try to teach your child some of the basic acting skills, but you can help them look at and admire or criticize the art of the professionals, watching for the above three skills in particular.

JUST FOR FUN: The ideas given next are intended just for your and your children's amusement. As an added attraction though, some of them might even prove to be a direct cause of your child being successful in a job application later on. Anyone who has confidence in himself and can show it to others is likely to impress. Good luck with this section.

EVERYDAY SITUATIONS: It's fun to re-enact the sort of situations that happen on ordinary days and most children have been through at one stage or other. Below are some suggestions to start you off. The children will soon come up with their own ideas.

1. Tell the child to imagine he is a Mother walking into a child's bedroom which is very untidy. Ask him what he thinks and what would he do – get him to say the thoughts out loud.

2. Tell her to imagine she is driving the children to school and suddenly gets a flat tyre – what would she do and say?

3. Tell him that he is in class at school in the middle of an examination and feels sick. What would he do and say?

4. Tell her to pretend that she is shopping for some clothes and trying to buy what she wants and not what the sales assistant wants to sell her.

THE OBJECT OF THE EXERCISE: The main objective is to watch carefully and observe anything that is not a typical action – in other words watch for over acting, which in general showbiz terms is called O.T.T. (Over the top). Here are some hints which may come in handy.

▲ Hands on hip stance – very good to cover the initial shock of state of room – but the action should only be held for a short time, too much posturing is O.T.T.

◼ Too many groans and 'Oh Dears!' are also O.T.T. The child should think of something constructive to say.

● Rushing around the room and slamming and banging things is a waste of energy.

▲ Clowning about especially in situation no. 3 where really the accident is far from funny should not be overdone.

DRIVING TO SCHOOL: Yes, there will be a few cross words when children act out the second scenario. Let's hope there are not too many expletives, certainly one wouldn't use them all the time. Make sure that the child who is acting the parent's role takes care of the children who may be frightened.

AN OPPORTUNITY FOR MIME: If you get the child to sit on a chair as if in the driver's seat of a car, there would be a lot of miming to do. For instance, he must mime turning off the engine, looking in the mirror to see if there is a car coming before opening the door. There could be quite a lot of fun and laughter to be had out of this, if the child just stands up from the chair and walks out pretending to inspect a tyre, because you could point out that he/she has just walked through a closed door. Get the child to go through the practicalities of changing a wheel if he knows them. If he doesn't, tell him about it.

TELL OTHERS WHO YOU ARE: This is a good drama school exercise and possibly one of the most useful. Get one of a group of children to enter the room from an outer door and stand fairly centrally placed and literally tell everyone in the room about himself. It should take about three minutes. Explain that in this exercise he is trying to describe to a person from another planet, or indeed to a future boss, all about himself.

IT'S NOT WHAT YOU SAY, IT'S THE WAY YOU SAY IT: Sometimes if an actor or a child cannot be understood it is not because of volume, speed or accent but enunciation. Lots of young people seem to have lazy mouths nowadays.

TONGUE TWISTERS: The old tongue twisters are best for this. They're fun to do as well – try some of these.

1. The rugged rascal ran around the rugged rock.

2. Peter Piper picked a peck of pickled peppers.
   If Peter Piper picked a peck of pickled peppers,
   Where's the peck of pickled peppers Peter Piper picked?

3. Red leather, yellow leather. (This is the worst and
   most difficult one I ever found.)

4. If you know the tune to this one you could sing it, but if not saying it will do just as well. This was an exercise used at the Central School of Speech and Drama.

   What I want is a proper cup of coffee
   Made in a proper copper coffee pot
   I may be off my dot
   But I want a cup of coffee from a proper coffee pot
   Tin coffee pots and iron coffee pots
   They're no use to me
   If I can't have a proper cup of coffee
   From a proper copper coffee pot
   I'll have a cup of tea.

5. She sells sea shells on the sea shore
   The shells she sells are sea shells I'm sure.

6. The fluttering butterfly flapped his wings and flew on by.

LOUD AND CLEAR: The tongue twisters can also be used to practise controlling the volume of the voice. Get the children to go through them again in a whisper but so that another child can hear them at the other end of the room. By speaking fairly slowly and by lifting the tone of the voice they should make themselves heard really clearly.

Fancy dress

SKELETON: First you need to cut out some bone shapes from white paper or material. Do a skull, upper and lower arm bones, ribs, the spine, the pelvis and upper and lower leg bones. Then give your child a complete outfit of black clothes, i.e. roll-neck sweater, tights, socks, gloves and balaclava. Next stick the bones in the appropriate positions, back and front, using a flour and water paste (see page 255). This works quite well and is easily washed out of the clothes afterwards. However, your child does need to stay still while the glue is drying. Alternatively, you could tack the material bones in position, being careful not to prick your child. Suggest that your child walks with jerky movements when wearing the costume.

ICE CREAM MAN: Wrap a large amount of corrugated brown paper around your child in a cone shape, and secure with sticky tape. Mark whereabouts the eyes are, take off the cone and cut a slit so that the ice cream man can see, then cut two more holes for his arms to come through. Cut a circle out for a 'lid', tape it on, then add a pile of 'scrunched' up kitchen paper stuck on to the top to make the ice cream.

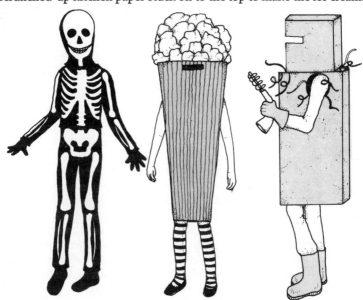

OXO MAN: You'll need a large cardboard box from a friendly supermarket. Carefully cut a large hole so that your child can see out of it and two arm holes. Either cover the box with red paper or paint it red, then cut out the letters OXO five times each in silver foil and put these on each side. The child could also hold an appropriate advertising slogan with this one to provide the original touch.

DALEK OR SPACE MAN: Cover two boxes (one small and square, one large and oblong) with silver foil. Carefully cut eye holes in the smaller box. Cut two arm holes in the larger box in two opposite long sides, then cut out and discard the smaller sides. Drape coloured string or wool from the bottom of the small box and around the arm holes to resemble stray wires.

MORE IDEAS: The above examples were all demonstrated in a fancy dress competition and were obviously great fun to do. See what else you can invent yourselves. And if you get really stuck, go to the library and get a book on fancy dress. One main point to remember is to try to get the children to act out the character of the costumes. If it's a red Indian costume, get them to do a mock war dance and make whooping noises. A 'belly dancer' ought to wriggle and wiggle and dance, rather than just walk around. Don't worry about your child being shy, once inside the costume, she'll be only too delighted to act out the part.

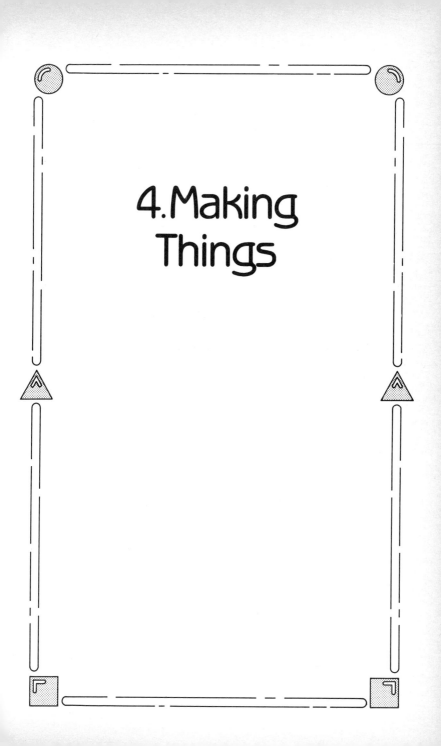

4. Making Things

Useful things to have

Old socks
Scraps of felt
Fabric remnants (including velvet)
Paper (thin and thick, crêpe and tissue, paper bags)
Newspaper
Cardboard (from cereal packets or postcards)
Boxes (shoe box, matchboxes, cardboard boxes)
Felt-tipped pens
Pencils
Paints
Paintbrush
Crayons
Edible food colouring
!! Sewing needle
!! Pins
Cotton thread
Wool
String
Ribbon
Cotton reel

Glue (water-based)
Flour and water paste
!! Drawing pins
Old wooden spoons
!! Scissors
!! Pipe cleaners
Orange stick
Marbles
Ping pong balls
Plastic or paper cups
Toilet roll inners

Extras
Soap
Potato
Pebbles
Potato peeler
Apple corer
Clear nail varnish
Bucket (for papier mâché)
For the naily picture:
!! Hammer
!! Nails
Block of wood

General hints

A helping hand: It is very important that the things children make are well within their capabilities. If not, you must be prepared to help them. Sometimes the setting up will have to be left to you but the actual making can be done by the child. In this section you will find puppets, flowers, pictures and games to make as well as traditional pastimes, simple cosmetics and some fashion tips for things to do with clothes.

Now read on: Start with the things shown in this book, then if one thing particularly interests your child, go to your local library and ask them to suggest further reading.

Starting off: Whatever it is that you make with your child, consider the following points:

Make sure there will be enough time to complete the item.

Provide enough space in which to do it.

Prepare the surfaces and your child with protective covering to minimize the mess.

Prepare all the things you need to make the project with, before you start.

Make sure you will have enough space to store or display the finished item.

Sock puppets

ODD ANIMALS: Here's something for your children to make that will solve an age old problem: the problem of the single sock. If your family is like any other there will probably be drawers of odd socks. They can be made into all sorts of different puppet characters.

MAKING A DOG PUPPET: Put the sock on the hand with the fingers where the toes should be, and the thumb where the heel should be, with the rest of the foot of the sock folded into the palm of the hand. With the hand turned towards you, bend the fingers a bit. In the gap between the first and second finger close to the second joint on the finger make a mark with a felt-tipped pen. Do the same thing between the 3rd and 4th finger. Now take the sock off and get the children to sew buttons on to the marks. (This might need a bit of help from you, to make sure that one side of the sock isn't sewn to the other, or the hand will not be able to get into the sock to operate it properly.) Alternatively, you could stick a circle of light-coloured material or paper on to the marks.

Or you could stick a large circle with a small darker circle inside on to the eyes. Consider the placing of the darker circle, the puppet could be made to look cross-eyed.

Or you could stick a large circle on the mark and sew a small button on to the centre.

Next cut a red, oval shape out of felt or paper for the tongue, and stick or sew it halfway between the toe and the heel of the sock.

Cut two more oval shapes from material or paper for ears. Stick or sew

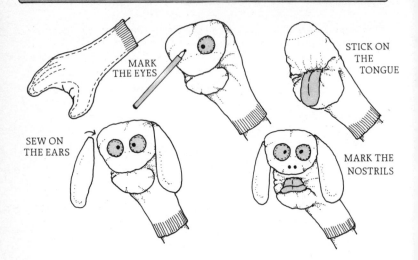

them on either side of the sock and slightly higher up than the eyes. If you want floppy, spaniel-type ears make the ovals long and cut them from fairly thin fabric.

Finally, below the eyes and closer together two circles could be fitted in to represent nostrils.

OPERATING THE PUPPET: If you bend the thumb, the dog's mouth will appear to close. When his mouth is open he can make lots of panting noises. If you angle his tongue, it looks comically as though it's hanging out to one side.

CAT PUPPET: Make it the same way as the dog puppet, but cut the ears out of triangular pieces of paper or material and put a pleat in the centre of the wide base before sewing or sticking down, so that the ears are rounded just like a cat's. The nose should be just one large felt-tipped pen mark, placed lower down but centrally between the eyes. Either side of the nose stick six pieces of strong strips of paper for whiskers; alternatively three bristles from an old broom could be threaded through the socks.

ELEPHANT PUPPET: For this you need two old or odd grey socks. One sock is to be put on the hand with eyes sewn or stuck on as for the dog. This is the puppet sock. From the other sock, cut off the toe and cut it in two round the curved part. This will make two grey ears – sew them on as before. Now comes the tricky bit: the trunk! Cut a hole in the toe of the puppet sock and push your middle finger through. Cut the foot from the spare sock and push the long part through the hole in the puppet sock. Sew into place. Move the trunk by wiggling the middle finger.

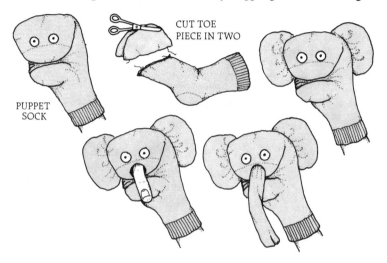

CUT TOE PIECE IN TWO

PUPPET SOCK

SNAKE PUPPET: To make a snake, use a green, yellow or striped sock. The method is basically the same as for the dog, but you won't need the ears. Make the tongue longer and thinner and cut a forked shape in the end.

A COMPLETE MENAGERIE: Many more puppets can be made – just using as many ideas as possible. Pack the ears with cardboard and you can make them stand up – this could be useful if you are making rabbits for instance. Use a variety of small, medium or large socks in lots of different colours to make an endless number of animals. A plain sock for instance could have stripes painted on to them to make a zebra. Spots and splodges painted on could make a giraffe.

STAGING THE SHOW: The stage for these puppets is simple. A table with a cloth that touches the ground when seen from the front would hide all the performers sitting behind the table. Each person could have two puppets one on each arm and the puppet slowly appears above the table and takes his part in the play. Help the children write a play for the animals to be spoken with suitable animal voices.

Finger puppets

THE ELEPHANT: Draw the outline of an elephant on a piece of cardboard as if he were facing you. He should have two thick legs, a big wide body and huge ears. Cut around the shape, then paint all of the card grey. When the paint is dry, paint eyes, tusks, toes, ears and wrinkles in black or darker grey. Cut a hole where the nose should be. The hole should be large enough to put your first finger through.

WALKING THE ELEPHANT: Put the first finger through the hole – this is the elephant's trunk and the finger can be painted grey, too, if you wish. The elephant can walk along by rocking the hand from side to side and moving it forward. The trunk can be lifted or swung around when wished.

CHARACTER PUPPET: Draw an outline of a person on cardboard, without the legs. Cut this out and paint in features on the face and some clothes. Stick some wool on for the hair. Cut two holes near the bottom of the body. These holes are for the first and second fingers to look like legs. For shoes, make two tubes to fit the fingers out of paper and glue. Then cut four triangles out of the same paper. Glue one to the outside of the tube and one to another and join the tip together with glue. Do exactly the same for the other shoe. Alternatively, the tops from two tubes of toothpaste may fit the bottom of the tubes to act as shoes.

FAMOUS FINGERS: You can make any character you wish like this. It could be fun to cut the faces of famous people from magazines and use them for the faces of your finger puppets.

A WOODEN SPOON PUPPET: Here's a quick and easy way of bringing a discarded wooden spoon to life. Turn the spoon round so that the back of the spoon is facing you: the bowl of the spoon will become the face of the puppet. Draw on some features with a felt-tipped pen. Stick some strands of wool around the edge of the spoon for hair. Cut an oblong piece of material long enough to cover the handle of the spoon by about 25 cm (10 inches) wide. Sew some gathering stitches across the top of the width. Pull all the gathers together and wrap the material around the handle of the spoon. Put some glue around the handle to help keep the material in place. As a final touch tie a piece of ribbon around the top of the material in a bow.

TO WORK THE PUPPET: Hold the handle of the spoon (underneath the skirt, so that it is hidden) and move the puppet up and down or twist the 'face' from side to side.

FAMILY GET-TOGETHER: A whole family of wooden spoon dolls could be made using different sized spoons. Male puppets of this kind need to have short hair and moustaches drawn on.

POTATO HEAD PUPPET: !! Scrub the potato first, then using an apple corer, take out a portion of the potato from the middle, about half way through the potato. This is for the first finger to go in to make the

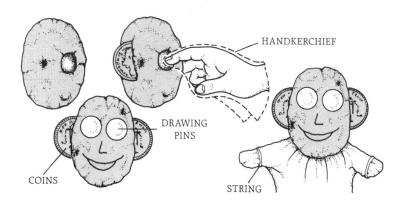

HANDKERCHIEF

DRAWING
PINS

COINS

STRING

head of the puppet. Stick two drawing pins in the potato for eyes. Draw a nose and mouth using a felt-tip pen. Press a coin in each side of the head to make the ears. Using a torn handkerchief, or a square of material cut from a remnant, place it over the first finger so that the finger is in the centre, then poke the handkerchief and finger into the hole in the potato. Finally get someone else to tie bits of string around the handkerchief and your thumb and finger. This will make the arms of the puppet. You are now ready to play with Mr. Potatohead. Again a whole family can be made using different sizes of potato.

FURTHER FEATURES: The eyes can also be made by cutting small paper circles and pinning these into position with dressmaking pins. Different sorts of eyes could be made from buttons that are also kept in place by the use of dressmaking pins provided the pinhead is larger than the buttonholes. Hair could be made by glueing on cotton wool or arranging knitting wool down the sides of the face and glueing it on the top of the potato. The glue used could be flour and water paste.

PAPER BAG PUPPET: This is a very cheap and fun puppet to make. It would be ideal for a sick or convalescing child to do.

WHAT TO DO: Fold both of the bottom corners of a paper bag to the back and glue them into position. Paint a face on to the top of the pointed bit of the bag. It might be useful to make it look as if the puppet had a pointed hat on, like a witch or a clown. Paint on a patterned costume. Cut two holes at the front of the bag for thumb and second finger to come through.

HOW TO WORK THE PUPPET: Put your hand inside the bag. The first finger sticks up to the head of the puppet to make it nod its head and move a little. Put thumb and second finger through the two holes in the front of the bag to make the puppet's arms. The other fingers remain tucked away in the palm of the hand.

PUPPET PLAYS: How to perform plays is explained in the previous chapter (page 220). One of the easiest types of plays to write, or help your child to write, is one of the fairy tales, such as 'The three little pigs' or 'Goldilocks and the three bears', or perhaps you could make up a play about all the members of your family going to the seaside and make the finger puppets as described on page 236 to act out the play. Suggest the children make some small props for the puppets – for example the bucket and spade could be cut-out pictures from a magazine. Children love to enter a fantasy world with their parents. You could get them to act out the parents' roles and you could be the children. But be aware that your own favourite expressions of admonishment sound rather funny coming from your child. They won't be taking the mickey out of you, just literally imitating you.

VENTRILOQUIST'S MATE: Your child could make a very good ventriloquist's dummy by using a large head made from papier mâché (see page 257). Sew or stick a child's jumper to its neck, then sew long trousers on to the front of the jumper and pad them both out with old stockings or tissues. Your child's hand goes up the back of the jumper – the trousers resting or 'sitting' on the lap and his or her hand moving the head of the dummy.

SEW UP SLEEVE ENDS

SEW JUMPER TO TROUSERS AT FRONT

WHAT TO DO: The art of ventriloquism is for the dummy and its operator to look as if they are talking to each other. When the dummy is supposed to be talking to the operator, it should look at him or her and move or nod its head as if it were having a proper conversation. This makes the audience look at the dummy rather than at the operator, then it won't be so obvious if the operator's lips move when it is supposed to be the doll talking.

HINTS ON VENTRILOQUISM: This is a very difficult art to master but here are some useful tips for the beginner.

1. Make sure that the dummy's 'voice' is not like your own – give it an accent, or a higher or lower pitch and make sure you don't get yours and his tone mixed up. Ventriloquism is the art of making one voice sound like two different people talking to each other. So make sure that **you** don't say something in the dummy's voice – who'll be the dummy then?

2. Most people who try to 'throw their voices' fix a silly grin on their face and clench their teeth, which is how to get the well known 'GOTTLE OF GEER' sound, when really you are trying to get the dummy to say 'BOTTLE OF BEER'.

3. The mouth should be relaxed and lips and teeth gently parted.

4. The tongue works very hard, and by placing it in different positions on the palate and teeth, it is surprising how nearly accurate sounds can be made without moving the lips.

5. It is a good idea to practise this art without the ventriloquist's dummy for a while. Get children to stand in front of the mirror and watch their own mouths as they try to say the letters of the alphabet without moving their lips.

6. Suggest your child writes down the letters that are difficult to say and practises them, experimenting with all sorts of tongue movements until he finds out that which fits most closely to the letter attempted. In case he forgets how to do it later on, get him to write down the result of the experiment and where he found was the best place to put the tongue.

7. The most difficult letters are:
B, F, P, V, W.

So whenever it is possible your child should try to avoid words with these letters in. The dummy should say, for example:
not 'Hello boys and girls' but 'Hello children'
'Bye Bye' could be 'Tat-Tah!'
and don't let the dummy talk about balloons, balls, teddy bears or bunny rabbits.

Making flowers

BREAD FLOWERS: This original idea is not only decorative but has some sales potential as well. It is the kind of thing that makes an old pot or bottle much more attractive and appealing. How many times have we seen at the end of the day at the school jumble sale, sad and lonely pots and jugs waiting for their final resting place in the rubbish bin? But if they were decorated with flowers and leaves I'm sure they would sell very quickly.

WHAT TO DO: Start with clean hands and a piece of fresh white sliced bread. You'll need to work quite quickly, so get another pair of helping hands to assist if necessary. Cut a piece of bread from the centre of the slice – about the size of a 50p coin – and put it in the palm of the left hand. Knead it with the thumb of the right hand. Quite quickly – after about 2 minutes – the texture will become almost like Plasticine. Keep on kneading until the texture is very smooth. When the texture is right, break off a small piece of bread, about the size of a very small pea. Press this piece flat between the thumb and first finger, using thumb and first finger of other hand to help apply pressure. This should flatten out to be about the size of a 5p piece.

Now you are ready to make the centre of a rose. Tear off approximately a third of the flattened dough. Smooth it out by pressing with thumb and finger, so that you get rid of the jagged edges. Then, with thumb and finger again, roll it up from one side to the other. Because of the curved edges, this will form a cone, which resembles the centre of a rose. Squeeze the bottom of the cone together to hold it in place, then put to one side.

To make the first petal, you work on another piece of dough from the original lump with thumb and first finger pressure, moulding it roughly into a quarter circle shape. Try not to let the dough crack – but don't worry if it does – it will in fact make the petal look realistically weathered. The curved outer edge can be tapped gently with the forefinger to bend it over slightly – just the same way as a rose petal

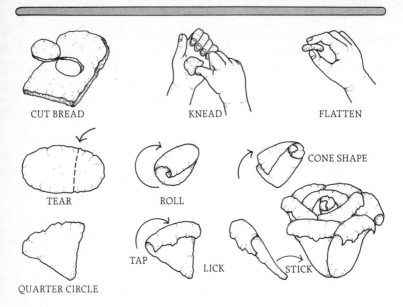

CUT BREAD KNEAD FLATTEN

TEAR ROLL CONE SHAPE

QUARTER CIRCLE TAP LICK STICK

curls at the outside. Pick up the centre of the rose that you have already made and lick – yes, lick (that's why the hands should be clean) – the bottom of the petal and fold it round the centre. Ideally it should come three quarters of the way round – not all the way round. It should also now be giving you a general idea of how the rest of the flower should work. Turn out the top of the petal away from the central cone until it looks realistic. Make another petal in the same way as before, lick the base and this time wrap it round the opposite way to the first petal.

Carry on until the rose is of the size of your choice. Provided the bread is fresh, it should not go dry while you are working with it, as it picks up moisture from the hands. However, you can add a drop or two of water if necessary. If the base of the flower looks too long or thick – bearing in mind that it will be stuck on a surface, this is the time to trim it down by slicing off a section with a knife. This could cause the whole flower to collapse, so be careful. Leave the finished flower to harden in a dry place for 2 to 3 hours.

MAKING A WHOLE BUNCH: While you are waiting for the first flower to dry you could make some more. One slice of bread usually makes three or four roses. You can also make leaves by cutting leaf shapes out of the flattened dough. Leaves are really useful as they can be used as a background filler to the shapes created by the flowers.

FINISHING TOUCHES: Once the leaves and flowers are rock hard, give them all a fine coating of nail varnish. When the varnish is dry, the flowers and leaves can be glued to whatever surface you wish to decorate. They will last for about two years, but see 'After care' below.

ADDING COLOUR: The fresh bread could have food colouring, inks or paint added to it, drop by drop when kneading into the palm of hand. This is only a little messy – and is great fun. The best colours are reds, yellows and oranges and obviously green for leaves. But the choice is the child's really.

DISPLAYING THE WORK: Glue the flowers to the side of an attractive coloured glass bottle: small Victorian ones are often to be found on stalls at a jumble sale.

FLOWER POTS: White salmon and meat paste pots are often in pretty shapes. Once the flowers are glued to the lids, the maker's advertisement is covered and you have a useful storage pot for buttons, pen nibs, tiddlywinks, etc.

SURROUNDED BY FLOWERS: Glued to odd make-up pots on a dressing table and the backs of brushes or even a round mirror, these really make everything look matched and very attractive.

DRESSING UP JEWELLERY: If the inside 'jewel' has come out of a brooch or pendant fill it with bread flowers and broken earrings can be treated the same way.

AFTER CARE: These ornaments should be dusted – not washed. Water is inclined to make them go soggy and spoil.

MAKING PAPER FLOWERS: Cut some petal shapes out of crêpe paper or coloured tissue. Arrange them in a circle, slightly overlapping: six petals should make one flower. Glue the bottoms together. Next cut a small circle from a piece of black card. Stick this in the centre of the petals with glue. Get a matchstick or a pencil and roll the edges of the petals over the pencil – away from the centre of the flower – this makes the petals bend over and look realistic. Push a pipe cleaner up through the centre of the flower, then bend the pipe cleaner into a loop to stop it falling out of the flower. Paint the looped end of the pipe cleaner yellow and the stem green.

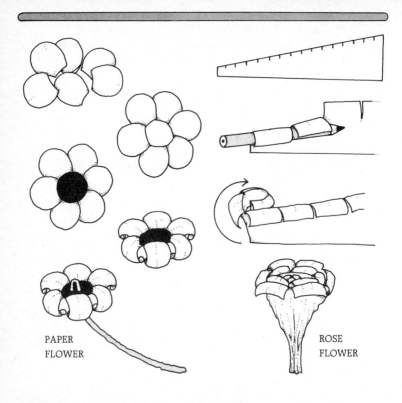

PAPER
FLOWER

ROSE
FLOWER

DISPLAY SHAPED PAPER FLOWERS: Cut three circles – small, medium and large – out of the crêpe paper and cut halfway into the centre at 3 mm (⅛ inch) intervals all the way round all three circles. Stick the centres together, then proceed as for previous flower.

ROSE FLOWER: Cut a strip of crêpe paper, making it about 30 cm (12 inches) long with one end 1 cm (½ inch) wide and the other 7 cm (3 inches) wide. Make a small cut approximately ½ cm (¼ inch) deep about every 1½ cm (¾ inch) along the tapering edge. Roll each section over a pencil to make the paper curve out a bit. Now gather up the paper from the smallest edge working towards the 7 cm (3 inch) end, turning out the petal shapes. Make sure that you have a tight grip on the straight edge and allow the top edge with the petals to curve out a little. When you have finished this, tie or sew the base together. Another way to keep the flower together is to paint about 1 cm (½ inch) glue to the bottom of the strip – but this could become rather messy, while the rolling process is going on. Poke a pipe cleaner through the centre of the flower and proceed as for the paper flower on page 243.

FLOWERY EFFECTS: These flowers have all sorts of uses. They can decorate costumes, look pretty in vases or even look quite good in the hair, but one of the best things to make with them is a table decoration.

TABLE CENTREPIECE: Next time you are out for a walk, look for a piece of wood that has an unusual shape. Along the sea-shore or in a wood or a park sometimes small but quite chunky branches fall from the trees. The more twisted and knotty the shape, the better. If the branch has been collected from the sea-shore it usually has been washed and almost bleached by the action of sea water over it, but if your child has collected it from a wood or park make sure that all the dirt and loose earth is rubbed free. Fill a flower pot, or any suitable container to fit the size of the branch, so that it won't fall over, with earth or sand. Stick the branch into the filling, so that it is well secure. Arrange some of the paper flowers in the soil, then wrap some flowers around the branch or just glue flower heads to the knots in the branch. This can be an attractive table or room decoration which will be especially useful at Christmas time. If you are helping your child to make this as a Christmas decoration, use gold or silver-coloured tinsel or spangled dust as an added decorative feature.

Pictures to make

PIN PICTURE: Start by making the background. You need a piece of thick cardboard about 20 × 15 cm (8 × 6 inches). Cover this with a piece of plain dark material, preferably velvet, glueing it at the back. !! Then, using sewing pins, either you or your child can mark out a design or picture in outline by pressing the pins into the surface. Now take a piece of coloured cotton, string, thread or wool. Knot one end securely to any of the pins then trim off the loose end with a pair of scissors. Wind the string or cotton round the pins, linking them up to make an interesting shape. Secure as you go by wrapping once round each pin. Tie the string/cotton off with a neat knot and trim the loose end off. The completed picture makes a good present or a personalized decoration for your child's bedroom.

FOR OLDER CHILDREN: !! A pin picture can also be done using wood for the base and nails. The larger the nail or pin, the coarser the material for winding can be. Even heavy jute can be used if large nails are used.

NAILY PICTURE: !! Be sure to supervise this activity and make certain that your child knows how to handle hammer and nails safely. Start with a block of wood about 30 × 25 cm (12 × 10 inches). Draw the outline of a picture with a pencil on the wood. Keep the shape fairly simple, for instance, a cat, a face, a boat or a bicycle. Use large headed nails for the outline and smaller headed nails for the details. It takes some time to work it out initially, and needs careful planning but a good end result is very effective.

A NEW PERSPECTIVE: !! This idea can help a child develop his/her idea of the perspective in the subject chosen as well as the outline. For things that are further away use the small headed shorter nails and show up the closer parts of the picture by using larger headed nails.

PROFESSIONAL GUIDANCE: Pictures made by this method do exist in some art galleries and are very expensive to buy. Try to find somewhere that has one of these pictures professionally executed to give you further ideas. The child who is not necessarily gifted with pen and ink may be able to express otherwise hidden artistic talents by using his skill with hammer and nails (but see safety note on 'Naily picture' above first).

Games to make

BALL CATCHING GAME: Take a yogurt carton and make sure it is empty and clean. !! Glue an empty cotton reel to the bottom underneath as near to the centre as possible, then with either a skewer or a pair of scissors carefully punch a hole through the bottom of the cup through to the hole in the middle of the cotton reel. Thread a piece of string about 35 cm (14 inches) long through the cup and cotton reel and knot it inside the cup, so that it cannot be pulled through from underneath. The string should now be dangling about 30 cm (12 inches) out of the carton. Next tape a ping-pong ball to the unknotted end. If you don't have a ping-pong ball, you can have a ball made of kitchen foil instead. To do this you tie a large knot in the string and twist the foil around it to form a ball. Decorate the yogurt carton and reel with oil paints or stickers.

To play the game, you have to hold the cotton reel and swing the ball high into the air, then try to catch it in the cup. Although this seems quite easy it is fairly tricky and takes some practice.

TRAVEL THROUGH THE TUNNELS: From the rim of each of four paper or plastic cups cut an arched shape, just large enough for a marble to go through. Using glue, stick the four cups upside down in alternating patterns to the underside of a shoebox lid. The game is played with four marbles. The rim of the lid will make sure that the marbles don't roll too far away. Leave the glue to dry. The game is to get the four marbles into the four plastic cups without any of them rolling out again.

As with the Ball Catching Game you could paint this and decorate it and it would make a very nice present.

INDOOR CRAZY GOLF: This is a very easy game to set up that can give hours of fun. You will need a number of 'obstacles' made from paper cups, small boxes and toilet roll inners and one pencil and one small matchbox and one marble per player. (The number of players really depends on the space available.) Tape the matchbox to the end of the pencil to make a golf club. Place the five cups either on their sides or with a bit cut out of the side, as with the travel through the tunnel game, on the floor. Mark the start of the course, for example the bedroom door, then with the boxes and toilet roll tubes make tunnels and obstacles through which you have to hit the marble with your club, until reaching a cup. At each cup you must try to get the marble inside. The winner is the person who has completed the course with the fewest hits of the marble. Once one course has been mastered you can make them harder and harder.

Fashion

NEW LIFE FOR OLD CLOTHES: Children at this age become very interested in the clothes that they wear, but they also grow at a tremendous rate, making it a costly job to keep buying new clothes. Below are a few hints for helping them make new clothes from old. This not only keeps them amused but is also much more practical than just showing them how to sew dolls' clothes.

MAKING THE BEST OF OLD T SHIRTS: Children quite often fill out sideways before they do an upward burst of growth. This is illustrated only too well by the tightness of T shirts. Here's a way of solving this and amusing your child at the same time. You need two old, tight T shirts. Get your child to do as much of this as possible but help them with the difficult parts, such as the cutting, pinning and machine-stitching. Cut both the T shirts into two pieces as shown in the diagram at the top of the next page, then turn them inside out. Unfold the hemming for a short distance at both the neck and the bottom of both T shirts. Pin the back of one T shirt to the back of the other. Do the same in front. Tack the two together, then remove the pins. Help your child either to machine stitch the two together or show them how to use backstitch (see page 252) and hand sew them together. Press the seams flat. To finish, fold over and sew the hems at the neck and bottom of the T shirt, using the catch stitch illustrated on page 252.

If you have two T shirts of different colours your child could have quite a lot of fun with these. The end result is a quite baggy T shirt, which could be tucked into trousers or skirts or belted, or worn loose over another jumper or shirt.

CUT THROUGH BOTH SIDES

HEM UNPICKER

SKIRTS: Exactly the same thing can be done with two skirts as with the two T shirts, provided they are of similar length and material. Sometimes, however, skirts become too short, but otherwise fit perfectly. They just need lengthening. So why don't you either take your child to a shop and let her choose some length of remnant material that will match the skirt or look through some old scraps of material that you may have at home. Maybe you could even cut up an old dress or skirt of your own to help in this instance.

WHAT TO DO: Show your child how to unpick the hem of the old skirt. The best method is to buy a 'hem unpicker', as shown in the diagram. They are not expensive. Press the hem flat. Either do this yourself or help your child to do it, depending on which end of the 7-11 age group she is. Take the new pieces of material. Cut them to twice the length of the new hem of the old skirt, plus about another 5 cm (2 inches) to allow for the new hem. Join any short pieces together and then join again to make a circle. Show your child how to turn the material over to make a hem along one long edge. Pin up the hem, then show your child how to do a catch stitch to hold the hem down (see page 252). Next demonstrate a 'gather' stitch and let them do the gather stitch all along the opposite side of the strip of material to the hem. Pull the gathers up evenly, then adjust until the 'frill' fits the hem of the old skirt. Pin the frill to the old skirt making sure that the seam is facing the inside of the skirt. Tack into position and then backstitch to hold firm. Press before wearing.

LACE IT UP: Your child could add to the skirt frill by putting a border of lace at the join of the skirt or at the bottom of the added hem. Also you could help your children make a pocket out of the same material as the fake hem and sew it on the front of the skirt.

TROUSERS OR JEANS: If trousers have become too tight then there is not much to be done with them – but if they have just become too short in the leg or frayed at the bottom, why not turn them into shorts? Boys and girls will find this not only easy but quite fun! Simply cut the trousers across the leg part to the desired length for shorts or bermudas. Hem the bottoms to make them look neat. Alternatively, cut them with pinking shears for a neat zig-zag or you could even cut large zig-zags in them. Another possibility is to show your child how to fringe or fray the edges. This is really easy – all you have to do (providing the material is suitable) is tease out with a needle and throw away five or six horizontal lines of weaving at the edge of the material, leaving the vertical ones hanging down in a fringe.

PATCHES AND DESIGNS: Many good, well-fitting clothes for children are often made unwearable by a stain or a small tear. By making something to cover the offending mark or tear, the garment can be made serviceable again. Here is the easiest and most fun way to conceal the error. Get your child to draw something on a piece of paper big enough to cover the stain or tear. This could be the outline of a rabbit, cat, witch, guitar, train or a flower, whatever you and your child decide is a suitable fun thing to have on the garment. If your child does not want to do this, he or she could cut a shape from a magazine. Place the cut-out on to a piece of coloured felt and draw round it with a felt-tip pen. You could even draw round a piece of large jig-saw or around some of those flat wooden animals left over in the toy box from when they were very young. Cut this shape out of the felt. Cut some wonder webbing (bought from most large chain stores) to fit the felt, then put the wonder webbing over the stain or tear. Cover it up with the felt, then (and perhaps you should really help quite a lot here) press with a damp cloth and hot iron. The wonder webbing instantly seals the felt to the fabric of the garment. For extra firmness you could oversew the edges. However, I have found that a patch will stay on through countless washings – providing your child doesn't pick it off.

SOFT TOY OWL: Soft toys can be made from patterns from knitting and dressmaking shops, or from various books in the local library. But

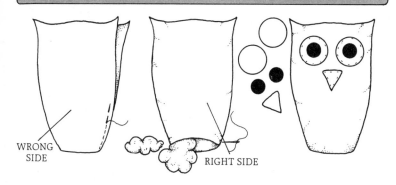

WRONG SIDE

RIGHT SIDE

why not start by helping your child to make a very simple toy, such as this owl.

First cut out two shapes (see above) from felt or thick material. Place the pieces with right sides together. Sew around the edges with tacking or back stitches but leave the base open. Turn the material so that right side is now on the outside and the hem is on the inside. Stuff with soft material, such as kapok, cotton wool or old tights (which you have boiled first). Sew up the open end neatly. Cut four circles for the eyes, two large and two small in contrasting colours. Cut a triangle for the beak. Sew these in position. Your child could make a family of owls of different sizes and if he or she gets really good at making them, they will make great gifts at Christmas time.

KNITTING: Teach your child to knit by making something useful. You don't have to use new wool. Unpick an old jumper that your child has outgrown. Children find this an enjoyable thing to do in itself. Wind the wool tightly round a piece of wood or stiff cardboard, then dip it in lukewarm water. Leave it to dry naturally and it will lose its kinks. Get your child to knit in squares of say 20 stitches across and 20 rows deep. Do try to start with the thickest wool and knitting needles for this gives quicker results and also means it is easier to correct any mistakes. The squares can then be sewn together to form a patchwork. But don't make the first item too large. Suggest they make a blanket for a doll's pram or cot, or even a blanket to line a cat/dog basket. Try also to make the squares out of as many different colours as possible. If you don't have any old wool, try your local wool shop, who often have odd balls of wool for sale quite cheaply. And again do remember that grannies or neighbours may have the odd ball of wool left over from some knitting project that they will let you have.

Stitches

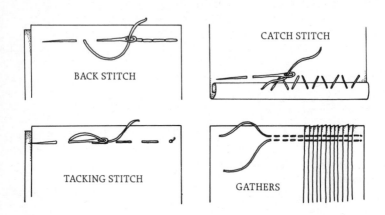

BACK STITCH

CATCH STITCH

TACKING STITCH

GATHERS

BACK STITCH: Working from right to left. Bring the thread through on the line to be stitched a little to the left of the point where you wish the stitching to begin. Take a small stitch backwards, bringing the needle out again the same distance ahead of the starting point. Continue until the line is complete. It looks a bit like machine stitching and should be as even as possible.

CATCH STITCH: This is the easiest stitch to use for hemming. First of all turn up the length of hem required and fold in about ½ cm (¼ inch) to tidy the edge. Pin into place. Press flat with an iron, then very lightly – without pulling the thread too tight otherwise the hem will pucker – catch the hem to the main garment using a single thread and sewing by hand. Pick up just a few threads from the hem and if possible just a single thread from the garment. Space the stitches about 1 cm (½ inch) apart. Be sure to make certain that the thread used is as close to the colour of the garment as possible.

TACKING: This is just a stitch to hold the material down in place. A handy tip is to make sure that the cotton used is obviously different from the material, so that it is easy to remove later on. You can in fact buy special tacking thread which is not very strong but is very cheap. Don't let the length of thread used be too long, otherwise it may get knots in it. Knot the end of the tacking cotton and just use large stitches about 1 cm (½ inch) long with 1 cm (½ inch) gap in between each stitch.

GATHERS: To make these you just sew two lines of tacking stitches identically spaced one underneath the other. Do not sew down the ends of the cotton. These are pulled up to gather the material and are fastened, but do not cut the surplus thread until you are sure the gather is the length you want it to be.

Macramé

WHAT IT IS: Macramé is the craft in which threads, cords or ropes are knotted together in a variety of different ways to form different designs and patterns. It originated in the Middle East many centuries ago. Macramé can be used to fashion anything from dog leads and collars to hanging baskets for potted plants. Getting a child interested in this will not only provide a useful way for him or her to make presents, but it will keep them quiet for hours. It is a good idea to involve a sick child in as well, for it doesn't take much effort but needs a lot of time and concentration to do and the end result is quite rewarding.

STARTING OFF: All of the equipment for macramé is inexpensive and easily obtainable from needlework shops, craft shops or department stores. All you need to begin with is a selection of cords, string or jute and a wooden or metal ring. Then you're ready to practise.

WHAT TO DO: Cut two lengths of string about 60 cm (24 inches) long. Fold each piece of string in half and attach to a wooden or metal ring with a larks head knot (as shown on the following page). Put the ring on to a hook or nail on the wall. Now you are ready to do the first piece of macramé.

The hanging cords – four in all – I will call 1, 2, 3, 4, from left to right.

Cords 2 and 3 are filler cords. You don't use them, in fact you just wrap the other two cords (1 and 4) around them. In other words the two outside cords are the knotting cords and the two inside cords are the knot bearers.

Now to make a flat knot, which is one of the most used knots in macramé. The knot is tied in 2 stages. Begin by taking cord 1 **over** cords 2 and 3 and **under** cord 4. Now bring cord 4 **under** cords 3 and 2 and **over** cord 1. Pull gently into place. This is half the knot. Finish the flat knot by bringing cord 1 back **over** 3 and 2 and **under** 4 and bringing cord 4 **under** 2 and 3 and **over** 1. Pull into place under the first half of the knot.

Continue with as many complete flat knots as you can make out of

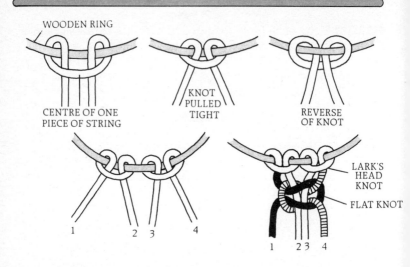

WOODEN RING

CENTRE OF ONE
PIECE OF STRING

KNOT
PULLED
TIGHT

REVERSE
OF KNOT

1   2 3   4

LARK'S
HEAD
KNOT

FLAT KNOT

1   2 3   4

your string. When about 5 cm (2 inches) of string remain on cords 1 and 4, cut all the strings level.

PENCIL HOLDER: Start by threading the cords on to a key ring, then tie the ends of the finished work around a pencil. Put a rubber stopper at the end of the pencil and thread the key ring round the telephone wire. You will then have a pencil always at the ready for phone messages.

FURTHER IDEAS: There is very little else to learn about macramé. If this has inspired your children, they can get many macramé patterns from craft or needlework shops. There are complete kits sold, as well, which include rings, beads and correct size cords. They may also borrow excellent books on the subject from libraries. If the interest is developed, there are endless gift possibilities for children to make, from place mats to decorative wall hangings.

Papier mâché

WHAT IS IT?: Papier mâché comes from the French and it literally means 'chewed paper'. It is a technique of soaking paper in water and kneading the soaked paper into a pulp, which can then be moulded into different shapes. It's rather like working with clay. This is also a very good way of recycling the paper waste which tends to accumulate in every home to make something interesting.

WHAT TO DO: Tear some newspaper in inch-long strips – several thicknesses at a time. Place this in a bucket and cover with boiling water. (This is best done by parents rather than children.) Leave overnight, then press out the excess water. You can now either leave the paper in strip form and cover each strip liberally with paste, if you want to mould the papier mâché over an existing shape, or you can mash the paper with the glue in proportions of two cups of paper to one cup of glue, if you wish to shape the papier mâché by itself.

FLOUR AND WATER PASTE: Pour one cup of water into a bowl and slowly add ¼ to ½ cup of flour – I've always found plain flour to be the best but have also used self-raising flour. Stir it in thoroughly. Some schools of thought say that this mixture should then be boiled for a few minutes – constantly stirring – and then left to cool. But I have always found that unnecessary. I just mix them together until the consistency looks right. It should look like a white sauce or a fairly thick custard mixture. Remember that the runnier the mixture, the more mess it can make but, on the other hand, the more quickly it dries.

PAPIER MÂCHÉ ITEMS MADE FROM MOULDS: This is probably the easiest way to start. The mould should be a dish to begin with or something that can be removed easily from the papier mâché when

RUB WITH JELLY

GLUE

CUT

GLUE

PAINT

GLUE IN TUBE FOR NECK

dry. Put some sheets of newspaper down on the working surface to protect it. Place the dish bowl side downwards on the working surface, then cover the outside of the dish with a film of petroleum jelly. This will make it easier to remove later on. Next place strips of the pasted and soaked paper over the bowl. Start with a cross shape and slowly fill in until surface is covered. Use paper in strips of 2 or 3 strip thickness. Press each firmly to remove air bubbles. Don't worry if the edges of the bowl are a bit uneven – these can be trimmed later.

Leave to dry for about 24 hours. Add another layer of papier mâché to make the dish thicker and stronger. Leave to dry, as before.

Remove the dish mould and trim the edge of the papier mâché bowl with scissors. If the edge looks a little sharp or uneven use more glued strips to fold over the edges, pressing them into the bowl shape until smooth. Again leave to dry.

Paint with poster paints – either plain or with a coloured design. The bowl could be left like this or with your help, your child could varnish the surface, which adds to the general appearance of the dish and also to its durability. These little dishes could make really lovely Christmas presents and they have all sorts of uses – for trinkets, buttons, collar studs, cuff links or hair grips.

OTHER MOULDS TO USE: Yogurt cartons, plates, ash trays and flowerpots all make interesting moulds for papier mâché pieces. If you use jam jars, put the paper strips only over the bottom half to make beaker shapes, which become good pencil holders. Balloons are very useful to make a rounded shape as for the head of a puppet. To remove the mould – just burst the balloon!

MORE COMPLEX SHAPES: Sometimes if you wish to help your child make more complicated things – like vases, which have curved sides, the papier mâché will have to be cut in half by you with a sharp knife and the two halves then stuck together with an adhesive. Further strips of papier mâché can be placed and moulded over the joins to give extra strength.

PAPIER MÂCHÉ WITHOUT MOULDS: Mix the soaked paper and glue together, then knead until the whole mixture resembles a thick clay. Make this into shapes as you would with clay or Plasticine. Start with something simple like a circle which could become a bracelet. This method takes longer to dry – the drying time is dependent on the thickness of the papier mâché.

HEAD FOR PUPPET OR VENTRILOQUIST'S DOLL: There are many ways of doing this, but here is the one we have used in our family. You will need a balloon and a toilet roll inner as well as papier mâché (strips and pulp), scissors and paint. Cut the toilet roll tube in half across the roll, to make a shorter tube. This will act as the neck and allow the fingers to go into the head of the puppet.

Poke a balloon through the cardboard tube and blow up to the size required. Tie up the end of the balloon and stick it down to the edge of the tube with sticky tape.

Cover with strips of papier mâché – cover the tube as well, but not the end of the balloon.

Leave to dry, then burst the balloon and pull it out. Next build on facial features with pulped papier mâché.

Leave to dry, then paint and varnish. Stick on 'hair' made from strands of wool. Clothing can be attached to the neck by glueing material on to the neck of the head.

Other ideas

SOAP CARVING: Begin by drawing the shape you want to carve on a piece of cardboard. For instance, it could be a teddy bear, cat, robin, pear or an apple, but whatever the shape make sure that it is smaller than the tablet of soap. Cut round the shape, then place this on one large side of the soap and draw round it. Do the same with the underside of the soap making sure that both sides are the right way up.

‼ Put the soap down on a board and cut off most of the areas that are not needed carefully with a knife. You may need to help your child here. Pick up the soap, then use a potato peeler to shave off the rough edges of the soap until you have almost the right shape. Use a knife for the fine shaping.

When all the shaping has been done, put the carved soap into a bowl of warm water and smooth down edges with your finger. Don't push too hard on things sticking out like ears or beaks. Take it out and leave it to dry, then use an orange stick to make any final markings, for example the eyes. When the soap is thoroughly dry, put a drop of baby oil or cooking oil on to a dry cloth and gently polish the soap. Either use for yourself or put in tissue paper and give it for a present.

SOAP BAGS: These are an ideal way of using up the left-over soap carvings from the above idea or for dealing with the remains of larger cakes of soap. Cut two pieces of thin material 8 cm (3 inches) square. Sew along three sides then turn inside out. Fill the bag with the leftovers of soap. Turn in edges of remaining side of bag and over stitch. This is a very cheap scent bag to place in drawers and cupboards to make things smell nice. If the material used is very pretty it could be edged with lace and given as a present (or sold at fêtes).

PEBBLE COLLECTIONS: Many children like to collect stones or pebbles as keepsakes from their holidays or visits to various places. But so often one stone looks just like another so put the place name and the date it was collected on the back of the stone.

ARTFUL PEBBLE COLLECTIONS: When looking for the stone or pebble try to find a fairly flat stone. This will make it easier to paint or draw on the surface. Use a felt-tip pen and draw a picture reminiscent of the place where the stone was collected. For example, if the stone or pebble comes from:

France –	draw the Eiffel Tower
Blackpool –	draw the Blackpool Tower
Granny's garden –	draw Granny's House
Giant's Causeway –	draw a giant
Derby –	draw a Derby Ram
Lake District –	draw a lake with trees, etc.

Scotland –	draw a thistle
Wales –	draw a leek
Ireland –	draw a shamrock
Cornwall –	draw a pixie
Railway museum –	draw a railway train or engine

This should give you plenty of ideas but do impress on children that they should collect only stones and pebbles, not part of the structure that they have visited. When the drawing is finished, varnish the pebble with clear nail varnish or household varnish to protect the picture.

CHRISTMAS PAPER CHAIN: Most people buy Christmas decorations nowadays but children can have a lot of fun making their own. ‼ To make a chain, cut lots of strips of paper 15 × 3 cm (6 × 1 inch). Use different coloured papers. Begin by glueing one strip to itself to make a circle. Thread the second strip through the first, then glue it into a circle. Do the same with the third strip and so on until the chain is long enough. Mix up the colours and add an occasional strip of silver foil to catch the light.

CHRISTMAS FRIEZE: Crêpe paper is sold in folded sheets about 50 cm (20 inches) deep. Cut this into 3 crossways. Make cuts in each of these but only about halfway up the paper. Unfold the paper and hang it as a frieze around the walls of your room.

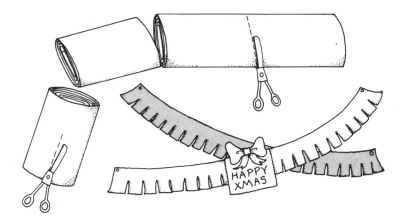

5. Sounds And Music

General hints

For useful things to have, see the following pages

Keeping a steady interest: Now that your child is a little older it's time for further development in music, providing of course both you and your child are really interested. Never force a child to participate in any form of the arts unless he or she is really keen to do so. The arts, especially music, have such therapeutic value that at an early age it is best to let any interest develop at its own pace. Of course, this pace may be alarmingly intense in some children and simply rush you off your feet, their enthusiasm being so great. But if it's not, just take it slowly and suggest the subject every once in a while. One day it will have a favourable reaction.

By popular request: The form of music which you use is all important. Use whatever kind of music appeals to your child – whether it be pop, folk, classical or country and western.

Sound development: Once your child has been through the simple sounds and songs described in the earlier part of this book, start being a little more adventurous and attack the rudiments of music. Here are some ideas.

Rhythm clapping

RHYTHM CLAPPING: Clap the notes that you would usually sing in a song and ask your child if he or she can guess what the song is that you are clapping. Start with nursery rhymes. Basically it's all a question of slow claps, medium-paced claps and fast claps. Let's take 'Baa Baa Black Sheep'. (X = clap)

BAA BAA BLACK SHEEP

Baa Baa Black Sheep have you any wool
 X   X   X   X   X   X XX   X

Yes Sir Yes Sir Three bags full
 X X   X X   X   X X

One for the master and one for the dame
 X X X X X X X X X X

And one for the little boy who lives down the lane
 X X X X XX X   X X   X   X X

QUICK, QUICK, SLOW: Most words have one clap to go with them but some words have two: 'any', 'master' and 'little'. Another thing is that if you give each clap the same time value it doesn't sound right. Some are much quicker than others and some, the ones at the end of each line, seem to take longer.

Understanding the notes

INSTRUMENTAL FUN: A good instrument to buy your child to help with learning to read music is called a MELODICA. It's an instrument that you blow, rather like a recorder, but instead of having holes to cover or uncover with your fingers it has a row of piano keys. You can also have great fun making up tunes for it.

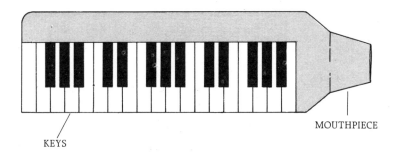

MOUTHPIECE

KEYS

TUNED IN: Another instrument which is not too expensive is the small computerized keyboard. This works on batteries and is easily portable. Some even have games to play and produce different sounds, such as the sound of a piano, an organ, a viola, a clarinet and a harpsichord, depending on which button is pressed. Some are even supplied with an earpiece, so that if your child is very inspired, you don't have to listen to all his or her creations. There are many different makes available and they make ideal Christmas or birthday presents. They look like this.

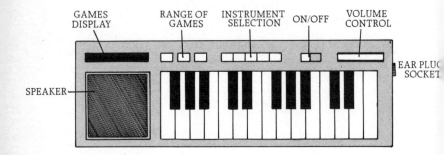

PIANO NOTES: The notes for music are not difficult, if your child knows the alphabet from A-G he or she is halfway there.

SEVEN LETTERS FOR SEVEN NOTES: On the piano they are placed like this:

The black notes are the ones that are called the sharps or flats. For example the black note above and to the right of the note C is called C sharp (or # for quickness) but it could also be called D flat if you think of it as the note below and to the left of the note D. The shorthand sign for a flat is ♭.

But don't worry about this to start with – for there is one set of notes, called a *scale*, which doesn't use any of them. This is the scale which is played from one note of C to the next. It's called the SCALE OF C.

THE FIRST SCALE: If you have a piano keyboard of any sort, use the diagram of the piano notes to get your child to play the following notes. Starting on one note C and going up to the next note C which I will mark C′ so that you know it is the one higher up the keyboard than the one with which you started. From C to C′ is called an octave.

C D E F G A B C′

This is called the SCALE OF C.

WHAT'S THIS?: Now get your child to play the following notes:

C C G G A B C′ A G
F F E E D D C
G G G F F F E G E D
D G G G F G A F E D D C

Do you both recognize the tune? Well maybe the time pattern was not quite right – but you **do** know it. It's 'Baa Baa Black Sheep'.

PLAY IT AND SEE: Try to find out what these tunes are. The answers are at the end of the chapter.

Tune One

G E F D G E C
C D E F E D G E C
G G E F E D G G E C
C D E F E D G E C

Tune Two
(The mark $_v$ means this note is below the first C you play)

C D E C
C D E C
E F G
E F G
G A G F E C
G A G F E C
C G_v C
C G_v C

Tune Three

E D C
E D C
G F F E
G F F E
G C' C' B A B C' G G
G C' C' C' B A B C' G G
G G C' C' B A B C' C' G G
F E D C

Musical notation

THE NEXT STEP: To convert the letters above into notes you need to know that the scale of C looks like this:

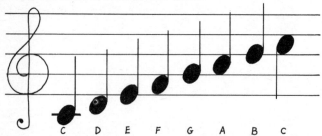

Just taking the notes of Frère Jacques they look like this:

and put together with its time pattern it looks like this:

ALTERNATIVES: Pianos do, of course, take up a lot of room. The numerous electronic pianos on the market take up less room but again are expensive. Before giving up the idea of piano lessons, however, why not look around the area you live in to see if some lonely old age pensioner still has a family piano. They might be only too delighted to have someone come into their home for half an hour a day to practise.

THE RECORDER: Your child can make a good start on learning to read and play music with a recorder. It is often not very highly thought of but it is both cheap and portable.

LEARNING WITHOUT AN INSTRUMENT: If you don't have any access to a musical instrument, you can still enjoy a sing-song with your child and even learn something at the same time. The brilliant 'Doe a Deer' from 'The Sound of Music' is a way of teaching children the sol-fa method of musical notation. Sol-fa is a way of giving a name to the notes of music regardless of key. Look at the key of C again.

C D E F G A B C'

Well in sol-fa this is simply:

doh – rey – me – fah – so – lah – te – doh

and if it were the key of G, which is

G A B C' D' E' F#' G'

the sol-fa names are still the same:

doh – rey – me – fah – so – lah – te – doh

Nothing could be simpler.
Here are the words that go with the song. You'll see that they are simply an aide-mémoire or a mnemonic.

Doh a deer a female deer
Rey a drop of golden sun
Me a name I call myself
Fah a long long way to run
So a needle pulling thread
Lah a note to follow so
Te a drink with jam and bread
And it takes you back to Doh

LEARNING AN INSTRUMENT: If your child really does want to learn an instrument, the next step is to choose which one. Obviously the piano is one of the best instruments to start with for it encompasses almost the entire range of notes that will be heard in any orchestra. However, although it is possible to buy a cheap secondhand piano, you may find that, in some cases, the 'touch' (that is the ease with which the notes can be played) may not be up to standard.

HIRING A PIANO: It is worth considering the hire of a piano, before going to the expense of buying something that may eventually be of little interest to your child. Pianos are usually rented for a twelve month period and an average cost of renting a piano is £30 per month starting with a three-month deposit. The value of the piano rented is approximately £1480 and ¾ of the first year's rental would be deducted from this overall price, if you finally decided to buy the instrument. Further information can be obtained from Morley Galleries, 4 Belmont Hill, Lewisham, London SE13, who deliver all over the country or will be able to give advice on the best kind of piano to rent and direct you to a more local stockist.

FINDING A TEACHER: Do make sure, before you select the instrument, that you can find a good teacher, that is, one who is suitably qualified. Ask for advice from your child's school or from the local educational authority. They usually have a list of recommended teachers for you to pick from.

HINTS FOR RECORDER BUYING: It really isn't worth buying a cheap recorder. The holes may all be in the right place but trying to produce an even sound without squeaks may be so difficult that it would put your child off from the beginning. Do also make sure that you buy a cleaning kit and suggest your child cleans the instrument after every practice session.

VIOLINS AND GUITARS: These, like pianos, can be rented for short terms, but do make sure, again, that you get advice on the type of instrument to hire. Some cheap violins and guitars have such high 'action' that the soft skin on children's fingers is damaged before they can really start to play. The 'action' is the colloquial term for the ease with which the strings are pressed on to the fret board to create the note. When a string is firmly trapped between the finger and the sound board a clear note is heard. If, however, the string stands a way off the board, harder pressure has to be used in order to get a clear note.

OTHER INSTRUMENTS: If you can find teachers for any other instrument remember that most instruments can be rented for a time either from your child's school or from your local music centre. Brass instruments seem to be gaining in popularity nowadays – I suppose mainly due to the fact that so many pop bands now include a brass section. They are also very portable and don't involve as much trouble with tuning as stringed instruments.

SCHOOL ORCHESTRAS: School Orchestras are very popular societies and even if your child is not terribly musical, he or she will have lots of fun taking part. Some school orchestras are made up solely of percussion instruments, like drums, triangles and tambourines together with tuned percussion – glockenspiels, chime bars and xylophones. (Glockenspiels are the ones with wooden bars – xylophones have metal bars.) Any child who can add another instrument to this line-up will be more than welcome. The tunes they play are usually quite simple at this age and also in the easier key range.

SCHOOL CHOIRS: Don't forget that the voice is one of the most useful and flexible of instruments. Should you not be able to afford a musical instrument or your child not wish to play one, the voice can be used instead. Joining the school choir not only teaches children the basic rudiments of music but also means they may get involved in out-of-school activities and competitions. This helps them build up a lot of confidence. Most children get very nervous when having to appear on a stage but doing so surrounded by friends in a choir helps them to overcome this.

IMPROMPTU CONCERTS: If your child plays an instrument and has friends who do the same, why don't you let them all practise together? Take it in turns to use each parent's house and at the end of each session be prepared for them to play some of their music to you. Invite some of the neighbours in, too. It will give them pleasure as well as making the children very proud of all their hard work.

WRITING POP MUSIC: So many children love pop music nowadays – why not suggest they write their own? They will probably start by copying the style of their favourite pop group and then branch out into a more individual style. Most pop songs have what is known as a 'hook'. That's the bit that everybody remembers; in fact it's the bit that makes or breaks the song. Pop songs usually have quite an ordinary verse, then this is followed by the 'hook'.

For example 'Yellow Submarine' by the Beatles has as its 'hook'

We all live in a yellow submarine
A yellow submarine
A yellow submarine
We all live in a yellow submarine
A yellow submarine
A yellow submarine

Or in the nursery rhyme 'Knick nack paddy wack', the three lines of chorus acts as the 'hook'.

Knick nack paddy wack
Give a dog a bone
This old man came rolling home

So suggest your child writes the best bit first. They should begin by thinking of the subject of the song, then consider the best things about it. Next comes the all-important phrase that can be made into a 'hook'.

Try these out first, then write the verses around the 'hook'.

For example: Subject: weather

Good things: pouring rain means splashy puddles

Hook: It's raining cats and dogs today
It's raining cats and dogs
It could have been bats and snakes and frogs
But it's raining cats and dogs

Musical appreciation

APPRECIATING CLASSICAL MUSIC: Apart from listening to classical music at home on the record player or television, one of the best ways of helping your children appreciate classical music is to take them to 'live' performances. Quite often during school holidays special classical performances are given in local civic centres or there are lunchtime recitals especially for children in local theatres. Information can be obtained by asking at the local library about local concerts for children. There are also lots of addresses on page 365 to help further this interest.

SOUND IT OUT: For a less active part in music, just try some musical appreciation. Your nearest music library will be able to advise you on the excellent records and tapes available for children to listen to. For instance 'Peter and the Wolf', 'The Sorcerer's Apprentice' and 'The Carnival of Animals' all help children to listen and be able to distinguish one orchestral instrument from another.

Songs and singing

A GOOD SING-SONG: If you feel like singing some songs with your child, first go to your local library and get out some song books. Use the books to help you and your child sing all the song all the way through. The following list contains just a few of the many songs that are very popular with this age group:

My Grandfather's clock;
Clementine;
Drunken sailor;

When I'm sixty four;
One man went to mow;
Halfway up the stairs;
Yellow submarine;
Lord of the dance.

SING AND WRITE: It would also be a good idea to ask your children to teach you some of the songs that they are learning at school and you could sing them all together. Get them to write down the words of the song for you to read – this will help with writing skills as well.

ROUNDSINGING: Roundsinging is where one person starts a song and then another person starts the same song, at the beginning but coming in a little later. For instance, the song LONDON'S BURNING –

1st person starts: London's burning, London's burning
2nd person: silence

1st person sings: Fetch the engine, Fetch the engine
2nd person sings: London's burning, London's burning

1st person sings: Fire! Fire! Fire! Fire!
2nd person sings: Fetch the engine, Fetch the engine

1st person sings: Pour on water, Pour on water
2nd person sings: Fire! Fire! Fire! Fire!

1st person sings: London's burning, London's burning
2nd person sings: Pour on water, Pour on water

and so on. This song may have four different people taking part, each one starting when the person singing before them has finished singing London's burning – London's burning.

'Three Blind Mice' and 'Frère Jacques' are two other very good rounds to sing. This is a good way of involving the whole family and it is also great fun, for sometimes it's not as easy as it seems to stay to your own part. Of course you don't have to have only one person to a part: you can have as many people as you wish, providing that they stay well balanced and one part isn't weaker or stronger than the others. This is a good activity for car journeys for everyone excluding the driver!

MAKING UP SONGS: If you have had something special happen in your lives it's a nice idea to suggest that the children write a song about it. They could write down the words to help them remember it or you could tape or cassette record it for them. They can either make up both the tune and the words or make up new words to an existing well-known tune.

ANSWER to Tune One is 'Boys and Girls Come out to Play'
ANSWER to Tune Two is 'Frère Jacques'
ANSWER to Tune Three is 'Three Blind Mice'

6. Growing Things

Useful things to have

Seeds
‼ Fertilizer[1]

Suggested tools[2]
‼ Spade – for digging
‼ Large fork – for breaking down lumps in the soil
Hoe – for removing weeds and further breaking up of soil
Hand trowel and fork – for planting seedlings and thinning
Dibber – for placing large seeds in ground
‼ Rake – to create fine texture for sowing after forking
Watering can

Notes

1. Store any fertilizers safely, out of reach of children.

2. Make sure that children know how to use all garden tools properly. Remind them about not leaving the tools lying around, especially rakes, which are particularly hazardous if stepped on. It is best to supervise the use of spades and forks.

General hints

Winter clothing: Wear as many old jumpers as the weather dictates. Jackets and coats are usually too bulky and only hinder the work. Scarves and trousers should be tucked in as flapping loose ends are a nuisance. ‼ Wear Wellington boots or heavy shoes to protect the feet and gloves to protect the hands from sharp stones or hidden pieces of glass.

Summer clothing: Wear old clothes again and as few as necessary for the weather conditions, but it is still important to protect hands and feet.

Know your plants: ‼ Remember that some leaves, flowers, fruits and seeds can be poisonous. Make sure that children know exactly which plants they can pick and eat and which they cannot.

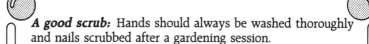

A good scrub: Hands should always be washed thoroughly and nails scrubbed after a gardening session.

Small can be beautiful: If you are lucky enough to have a garden or at least access to a strip of land, you already will have a head start for this section, but don't worry if you haven't, there are always flower pots and window boxes to grow an interesting variety of plants in.

A helping hand: You may have an elderly neighbour or grandparents living quite near who have a garden and would appreciate some help with it. If that is the case, then ask for a small plot to let your child grow something – but make sure that whatever he/she grows will fit into the general design of the garden.

Pride and produce: Very often when people plan a garden for children, they immediately think of flowers; but do remember that the not quite so attractive vegetable can have more appeal. Just imagine the child's pride when the family is served for dinner with vegetables that come from his/her own plot of garden.

Note it down: When children start gardening encourage them to keep a notebook and diary of the plants' progress. There don't need to be too many entries. Obviously when things are planted there should be quite a detailed entry – but after that a report should be written at fortnightly intervals, perhaps with measurements of the plant to work out what is the rate of growth.

Draw it: Alongside the report it is a good idea to get children to draw diagrams of what they see, to chart the progress of the plant. You can also encourage them to look up information about the plant in a gardening book, an encyclopedia or a detailed botanical study.

Developing study: Depending on how far your child's interest goes in this subject, it could be a good preparation for later biology studies at school. For instance you could just say the seed starts to grow when it is put in the soil – but why not use the word 'germinates' and explain what it means? As the plant progresses – which is a naturally slow process – suggest your child learns the proper name of every bit as it appears and labels the drawings accordingly.

Keep up the good work: If you do become actively involved in your children's gardening plot, give them a hand now and then to encourage them. We all know how back breaking some gardening chores can be and it is better to help the child with some of this than to let his/her enthusiasm be dampened by exhaustion. On the other hand don't help them too much. !! The best way would be to start them off by showing them the way to do the particular chore and how to handle the tools carefully (see safety note on page 276), then come back later to see how they've been getting on – and when you are sure that they fully understand just how hard some of the work is, give them a hand at the end.

Tea break: You will be doing all the preparatory work to get the plot of land ready in about October, so have a picnic with a flask of warm drink halfway through the session.

Accidents may happen: !! If a child does have an accident in the garden or a piece of nasty metal penetrates the skin in any way, go to your local doctor or the casualty department of the hospital and get a tetanus injection. Remember it is better to be safe than to be sorry.

Overexposed: !! One other thing to beware of when gardening in the summer is that quite often, if the child is gardening with only a pair of shorts on, the back is exposed to the sun. The child may not notice it at first for he/she will be absorbed in the garden, but it doesn't take long for a child's back to burn in the sun. It is a very good idea to protect children's backs with suntan cream and if you are still concerned, put a T shirt on them – just while they are gardening.

In the bleak midwinter: In the times when nothing seems to be happening in the garden take your child to a local garden centre to see the ordinary as well as the extraordinary plants that grow there.

Club together: Some schools may be interested in setting up a gardening club – especially if there is any spare land near the school, so if your child has become really interested in gardening as a hobby why don't you suggest that a group of parents get together with their children and run a school garden. Some of the produce could be make a valuable contribution to the Harvest Festival and it's always so much more appreciated if the produce is home grown.

Care of soil

GENERAL RULES: Once you have set aside a special area of the garden, then consider the site and care of soil. The ground must be prepared in October and the seeds sown in Spring. Vegetables should have as much air and light as possible – never under trees and not in drying north-east winds.

TO PREPARE THE SOIL: !! Clear all weeds and dig it with a spade to turn it over – you can mix heavy soil with lime to lighten it. You may need to help your children with this.

PREPARING FOR SEEDS: The top 10 cm (4 inches) of a seed bed should be forked over and raked before you sow, making sure there are no stones. You could help with the heavy work and let your child do the raking. Sow vegetable seeds from north to south if possible for maximum sunshine. Plant the seeds in a 'drill' – a tiny trench – put two sticks one at each end of a line and dig between them. Don't sow cabbage or salad crops too closely or too deeply. When sown cover lightly with soil and water gently with a watering can. Do not hose as the seeds only need a light sprinkling. Write on one of the sticks at the end of the row what you have planted. Keep a diary (see page 277).

Things to grow

WHAT AND WHEN?: Here are some ideas for growing useful vegetables. The time to start planting will be given on the seed packet or by the garden centre. The time will vary according to the type of seed.

BEANS: You will need a well-dug, well-drained, well-composted soil plus some potash fertilizer. Sow them in late April, 5 cm (2 inches) deep and 15 cm (6 inches) apart in double rows with 30 cm (12 inches) between each. Water well. When the beans begin to grow, erect bean poles between the rows to allow beans to climb. Harvest when the beans are between 7 to 10 cm (3 to 4 inches) long.

BEETROOT: You can have great fun with these for you can eat the leaves as well as the root when they are cooked. Dig a hole for each seed about 2.5 cm (1 inch) deep at intervals of 10 cm (4 inches), with 30 cm (1 foot) between the rows. As each beetroot seed is, in fact, a cluster of several, you will have to thin any extra growth after about 3 to 4 weeks. Water and hoe regularly. Harvest when they are the size of a golf ball – but be careful not to break their skins. Twist off the tops – don't cut them off as this causes them to 'bleed'. Boil them for half an hour and skin before eating.

CABBAGES: (See 'Caterpillars' page 284.) Always grow these in a lime-based soil for this is alkaline and cabbages do not like an acid soil. If you start from seeds, then sow them in 1.5 cm (½ inch) deep holes,

2.5 cm (1 inch) apart. Transplant the seedlings after 2 months into a level piece of ground, so that they are approximately 60 cm (2 feet) apart. Press them firmly into the soil with the leaves just above soil level. Feed regularly with nitrogen fertilizer.

CARROTS: Grow these in a light soil. Sow the seeds in drills 1 cm (½ inch) deep and 30 cm (1 foot) apart. Sprinkle the very tiny seeds evenly along the row. They sometimes take weeks or months to germinate, but when they do thin them out, throwing away the sickly ones, and plant the seedlings about 10 cm (4 inches) apart. Harvest when the tips of the leaves turn yellow – but try one for size before harvesting the lot.

Carrot tops – the feathery greenery – make excellent soup, or can be used as a poor man's parsley for any fish dishes.

LETTUCE: Sow the seeds ½ cm (¼ inch) deep and 30 cm (1 foot) apart. When the baby lettuces appear, thin them out to 15-25 cm (6-10 inches) apart. These can be grown successfully next to cabbage for they like the same kind of soil. Water and hoe regularly. Be careful not to let weeds grow round them for they are very delicate in the early stages and can easily be choked. Harvest throughout summertime, depending on the variety. This is a plant that you can grow in several batches, so your child can really use the diary he/she keeps to good effect and hopefully the crops will improve throughout the season.

MARROW: Try to enter prize-winning marrow contests with your crops. It is an added incentive for the child. If, however, you can't wait to taste the crop – pick them when they are small. Then they are called courgettes, which when sliced and fried in butter with a little garlic and salt are delicious! Buy seedlings, not seeds, from a garden centre. These are planted in May. They like heavily composted and manured soil. Plant in a warm sunny spot about 60 cm (2 feet) apart – and at least 60 cm (2 feet) away from any other vegetable. Female marrows are recognized by the baby marrows which sprout from behind the base of the petal. Marrows consist of 90% water, so do water regularly. If you are leaving them until they are fully grown, harvest at Hallowe'en or thereabouts. These are excellent vegetables for your child to take to the Harvest Fair at school.

ONIONS: These are bought in 'sets' from the gardening centre. They are planted in late March in well-composted soil in the top of the compost. The tips should be just above the surface – and planted 15 cm

(6 inches) apart. Extra fertilizer should be added in June. If they flower cut the flower off, for this would otherwise make the plant concentrate on the growth of the flower rather than the onion itself. Towards the end of the summer, the stalks will turn yellow and bend. They will then be fully grown.

Gently lift them out of the ground with a fork and leave them in the sun – on top of the soil – to dry (weather permitting!). Store by tying the stalks together.

WHICH TYPE OF FLOWERS?: Garden flowers fall into three groups.

Annuals – Which complete their life cycle in 12 months. Summer bedding plants and cut flower plants belong to this group.

Biennials – These take two years to complete life cycle from sowing to seed production, e.g. border plants and bedding plants.

Perennials – These live and grow for more than two years and include trees, shrubs, bulbs, corms, climbers and herbaceous borders.

ANNUALS: Children like to see the result of their work as soon as possible, therefore the annuals would seem to be the best to start with. They are mainly planted in springtime and, depending of course on the variety chosen, they will flower during the summertime. Suggest that your child plants them in small clumps of five or six plants wherever desirable over the garden rather than in rows. They will get great pleasure from seeing splashes of colour dotted all over the garden, rather than a regimented row in one place. Ask your local gardening shop for help in choosing the best varieties. You may prefer to plant from seed, alternatively if you wait until late spring, you can buy seedlings from the local nursery.

WHICH TO PLANT: Choose from any flowers in these lists to help start you off. They are generally easy to grow. The planting times depend on the variety and you will have to check this. Most flowering plants like light soil and a sunny spot. The dianthus is a lovely border plant and sweet peas are always a great favourite.

Annuals

Antirrhinum
Aster
Marigold
Cornflower
Pansy

Lobelia
Nasturtium
Petunia
Sweet pea
Sunflower

Biennials:

Pansy
Foxglove

Evening Primrose
Hollyhock

Perennials:

Michaelmas Daisy
Campanula
Delphinium
Dianthus
Helenium

Hemerocallis (yellow or pink lily)
Hosta
Iris
Red hot poker
Lupins

Bulbs and corms:

Daffodils
Snowdrops

Tulip
Crocus

DELIGHTING IN FLOWERS: One of the many attractive things about growing flowers is that your child can pick them and arrange them in vases in his or her own room or indeed take a tiny bunch of them to give as presents to relations or neighbours. They may also like to make a flower arrangement for the dining table.

ALL YEAR ROUND: You can grow flowers for different times of the year. Hyacinth bulbs give lovely blooms at Christmas time if grown indoors. Violets and primroses make good decorations for Easter tables, as do tulips, daffodils and narcissi. The snowdrop – called February fair maid by country people – is also a great favourite. It is one of the earliest flowers to appear and has a lovely scent.

OTHER IDEAS: The list of vegetables to grow with your child is endless: peas, radishes, potatoes, spinach, tomato, etc. Take it easy at first. Let younger children only grow one or two things simultaneously, so that they can digest every stage of its growth – before finally digesting it entirely. However, watching plants grow is fun – but so is watching living things develop, so now read on.

Living things

CREEPIE-CRAWLIES: If you live in a flat, or can't have a large pet for some reason, the insects and small creatures can provide a good substitute to be watched and looked after at very little cost. Like any other animal, they have to be fed, cleaned and housed, a good way to introduce children to the responsibilities involved in keeping a pet. II Children must be taught to wash their hands before and after touching their pet. There are some ideas below.

CATERPILLARS: These not only make good pets but they introduce children to the fascinating life cycle from caterpillars themselves into pupae and finally into moths. You can find caterpillars on hedges and in flower beds; look out for the tell-tale sign of nibbled leaves. Collect them carefully, using a paintbrush or an old teaspoon, and also take some of the plant on which you found them, to provide food. You might like to grow cabbages especially to see whether you will get caterpillars feeding on them (see page 280). You shouldn't have more than three or four in your caterpillar farm, and you shouldn't mix types. Keep the caterpillars in a jar with holes punched in the lid for air. Inside the jar, the plant on which they are living should touch the sides of the jar. This is because the caterpillar will use the surface of the jar to crawl up to reach the leaves. Make sure you remove any dead leaves, together with the caterpillars' waste.

The caterpillar will shed skins and make a pad of silk upon which to hang. Then they will take two or three weeks to change from a pupa into a butterfly. If they don't emerge, try spraying the pupa with a little water or breathing upon it. When the butterfly has emerged, do release it, as they are now becoming rare.

ANT FARM: Ants are some of the busiest and most interesting creatures to keep. You can collect them by picking them up on an old paintbrush; make it more attractive by dipping it in sugary water or jam, then build an ant farm in which to keep them. Make a square container out of three pieces of wood (two make the ends and the other for the base) and two sheets of clear perspex to make the sides. Make it about 30 cm (12 inches) square, using dead wood. Fill the container with fine soil, to a depth of about 15 cm (6 inches), then stand it in a bowl of water, so that the water is just below the top edge of the container. Put a couple of drops of detergent in the water and this will stop the ants climbing out over the top of their farm.

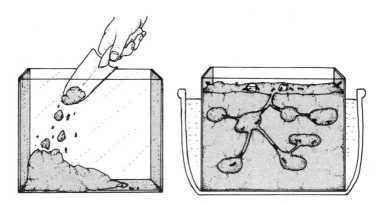

The ants should be fed on sugar cubes, dollops of jam and water. The time to give them food is whenever the last lot has disappeared. Keep the surface of the soil moist and release the ants in July or August, so that they can mate.

EARWIGS AND WOODLICE: These can usually be found, around February and March, on flowers like chrysanthemums and dahlias. Woodlice also lurk beneath the bark of dead or dying trees. They're not happy in the light, so they would have to be kept inside a cupboard most of the time, but you could start a collection inside a glass container with a lid punched with air holes and take it out of the dark occasionally. As they're scavengers, feed them on vegetables and dead flies. Earwigs and woodlice should be kept separately but you could have more than one of each per jar.

SILKWORMS: These have been reared by the Chinese for over 500 years. They will live happily on lettuce, but in order to produce real silk, they need to be fed on mulberry leaves. Silkworms have to be bought from pet shops, and should be kept in the same way as caterpillars; the silk production leads into the same pupa and moth cycle as their common garden cousins.

WORMS: You will find worms on the surface of the soil after it has rained. Alternatively, fishing shops sell solutions designed to attract worms to the surface. Keep worms in a muslin-covered glass jar (an average-sized jam jar is ideal), filled with alternating layers of soil and sand each 2.5 cm (1 inch) thick. Keep the soil damp and put a layer of dead leaves on the surface. Alternatively keep them in a discarded fish tank. Sometimes the worms will be able to be seen as they pull the leaves down from the surface along the glass sides.

WILD ANIMALS: It is important to teach children that it is cruel to trap or to keep wild animals – but it is quite alright to befriend them.

Do remind children though, that the wild animals which visit a back garden come to rely on the food which is left for them, so it is irresponsible to start feeding them, then suddenly stop.

HEDGEHOGS: If you regularly put out a dish of bread and milk, you may be able to attract a friendly hedgehog. They will usually visit in the early evening, or after rain, but they are very shy creatures and they do often carry fleas, so keep your distance. Hedgehogs are not only lovely little animals, but they are also good for the garden, killing slugs and other insects.

SQUIRRELS: These are a delight to watch from your house if you are lucky enough to have some living close by, although not all gardeners would consider this an advantage as they can be a pest. You may see them gathering nuts. You will have to tell your child to sit very still for they will flee at any sound or movement.

BIRDS: All food for birds should either be hung up on a wall, or placed on a bird table, to discourage cats. Half a coconut will attract tits during the winter, as will a string of peanuts hung from an overhanging eave (see page 127). You could also fill a yogurt pot with kitchen scraps (see page 126). Never leave them salted nuts or desiccated coconut, but do put out, especially in winter when the ponds and puddles have frozen, a dish of water.

MUSEUMS AND SOCIETIES: At the back of this book, on page 362, are some addresses to help you follow up your interest in natural history. Many others can be found at your local library or museum.

READ ALL ABOUT IT!: Children who have found pleasure and interest in keeping a little friend may well enjoy reading about them as well. The school and local library will have books on the study of insects and stories about how they develop.

7. Cooking

Useful things to have

Ingredients (see individual recipes)
Overall or pinafore
Damp cloth/kitchen paper (to wipe up spillages)

General hints

Increasing the repertoire: In part one there are recipes for simple things to cook. Now it's time to be more adventurous. Children love cooking but sometimes the more complicated dishes are beyond them. Try to find dishes that only involve one saucepan or cooking pot. If you are having a dinner party try to get the child involved in at least one dish.

Cooking as an adventure: There are endless ways to involve children in real cooking; party food, food for special occasions and special dishes are a few of the ways described, but do remember, everything they do will be really fascinating for them, even if it's just helping to cook the potatoes. Show them as many of the basic cookery skills as you can and liven it up with foods from other countries. It will not only help them with an understanding of cookery, but also with an appreciation of food, so that when they are asked to a friend's home to eat, they will be prepared to try new foods and not just stick to the familiar ones.

Preparation hints: The 'Surprise Mousse', on page 294, you will find very easy to make and your child will be delighted to help you. No cooking is involved in this but it helps your child learn about preparation techniques. Use scales and measuring spoons to get the correct amounts from the recipes even though you probably do not always bother with these yourself and do be prepared for a little mess. Also take into account that you will need to allow more time on the preparations. Children will have little experience at this age of the quite complicated co-ordination that takes place when cooking. A tablespoon full of flour takes the work of half a second for us to put into a bowl, whereas the manoeuvring of this for a child will take quite a bit longer.

Types of recipes: The following recipes are a guide to the types of food that children in this age group should be able to cook. Of course if they are at the younger end of the scale, you will have to help them more.

Good habits to get into: Once children get into the habit of starting off well and finishing off tidily, the following should become automatic.

(a) Wash hands, nails, tie back hair, wear an apron/overall.
(b) Read the recipe right through before starting.
(c) Assemble all the ingredients in advance.
(d) Collect together all the necessary utensils.
(e) Set the oven to the right temperature at the beginning.
(f) Clear up afterwards, or preferably, as you go along!

Cautionary notes on cooking: !! The following are some extra safety notes on cooking sessions with children.

Knives
1. Give children the following instructions before they use knives:

  – Always pick up a knife by the handle, never by the blade.
  – Always hold the knife blade downwards.
  – Always cut away from you, never towards yourself.
  – Use a proper cutting board or work surface.
  – Always wipe a knife from the back of the blade.

2. Always supervise your child carefully, if necessary holding your hand over his to help him. If at any time you are in doubt about your child using a knife – do it yourself and wait until he is older before letting him try it out on his own again.

3. Take great care when a child is using a sharp knife in the kitchen. Make sure that the work surface is at a comfortable height. If your work surface is too high, then make sure that your child sits at a table of the correct height.

4. If the sharp knife has a pointed end, put a cork over it. This stops any accidental movements causing the point to stick into the child.

5. Make sure sharp knives are safely put away after use.

Cookers

1. The child should wear an apron of a kind that can be removed easily should anything hot fall on to him.

2. Do make sure that if your child is putting things in or taking them out of a hot oven, he is wearing oven gloves, can reach the oven easily and has an adult standing by to help.

3. It is also advisable for the child to wear a close-fitting, long-sleeved garment, as the arms may touch the sides of the oven.

4. Always shut the oven door after use.

Hobs

1. Although you can have control over the heat on the top of the cooker, so a child may stir the ingredients in a saucepan, it is imperative that the child can see into the saucepan. Raise him on to a steady chair.

2. Turn the saucepan handles towards the back, so they cannot be knocked off in passing. Don't ever let a child be tempted to pull the saucepan towards himself in order to see what's happening.

3. Never leave the kitchen whilst gas/electric rings are on. Electric rings stay hot for a long time – don't touch them.

4. Finally – switch off all equipment after you have finished.

Recipes

A SCONE DOUGH

Equipment required: mixing bowl
225 g (8 oz) self-raising flour
pinch of salt
50 g (2 oz) margarine, cut into pieces
about 150 ml (¼ pint) milk, for mixing

This is a good introduction to pastry-making methods. The dough is needed for the pizza recipe which follows.

Sift the flour and salt into a mixing bowl. Rub in the margarine until the mixture resembles fine breadcrumbs. Then stir in the milk to make a fairly soft but not sticky dough.

PIZZA

!! **Equipment required:** frying pan, baking tray
25 g (1 oz) lard
1 large onion
1 heaped tablespoon of plain flour
1 × 400 g (14 oz) can tomatoes, liquidized
1 tablespoon of tomato purée
2-3 teaspoons mixed herbs
salt
freshly ground black pepper
pinch of granulated sugar
1 quantity Scone Dough (see above)
160 g (5 oz) Cheddar cheese, grated

!! Melt the lard in a frying pan and cook the onion slowly until soft but not coloured. Stir in the flour and when it is smooth add the tomatoes, tomato purée, mixed herbs, salt, pepper and sugar. Stirring the mixture all the time, bring it to the boil, i.e. when it is bubbling well. Leave on one side to cool.

Using the Scone Dough as shown above, roll an oblong shape approximately 23 × 30 cm (9 × 12 inches) and place on baking tray. Spread the filling over the dough to about 1 cm (½ inch) from edge, then scatter the grated cheese over the top. Cook the pizza in the centre of a hot oven (200°C, 400°F, Gas Mark 6) for approximately 25 minutes. The dough should then be well risen and the cheese browned.

SURPRISE MOUSSE

Equipment required: liquidizer or whisk
250 g (10 oz) full-fat soft cheese
1 × 295 g (10 oz) tin beef consommé
small pinch of garlic salt
small pinch of curry powder
chopped parsley, to garnish
1 lemon, to garnish
hot toast, to serve

This recipe is particularly easy and requires no cooking. It really is very good and tastes extremely expensive, though in fact it is very cheap.

The only thing that has to be done is to mix the cheese with the beef consommé as thoroughly as possible. !! Do this in a liquidizer or using a whisk. Crush the clove of garlic with the pinch of curry powder; mix both into the cheese and consommé mixture. Blend until it is very smooth and probably a bit frothy, then put the mixture into 6 individual dishes or into one large dish and put into the refrigerator until it sets. This will take about an hour or so and it sets rather like a soft jelly. Decorate it with chopped parsley and slices of lemon and serve with hot toast. This keeps quite a while and could be made the day before you need it, so, if you are giving a dinner party perhaps your child could make this as the 'starter' for you.

ALBANY SALAD

Half a lettuce, shredded very finely
3 carrots, grated
half a cucumber, chopped very, very finely
2 tomatoes, chopped very finely
2 apples, with the skin on, chopped very finely
half an onion, chopped very finely
4 or 5 walnuts, chopped
4 raw mushrooms
¼ green pepper, chopped very finely
as many pink and white marshmallows as you would like
lemon or orange juice, for sprinkling
salt
freshly ground black pepper

A lot of children always think that preparing food has to be with heat and saucepans and forget that sometimes some of the salads you can get

take more preparation than a roast dinner.

Try out this very unusual salad, that I first had in Albany, New York State, with your children.

Mix all but the marshmallows into a bowl, then cut up the marshmallows into the smallest cubes you can. This is a very messy, sticky job; more of the marshmallows will be eaten than put in. Put the remains in the salad and sprinkle lemon or orange juice over the top, together with a little salt and pepper. Mix it all in. This really is a delightful salad.

POTATO AND CHEESE PIE

Equipment required: 2½ litre (5 pint) saucepan, ovenproof casserole
1½ kg (3 lb) potatoes
salt
butter or margarine, for greasing
275 g (10 oz) cheese
freshly ground black pepper
3 tomatoes

This has a dryish texture which goes well with a moist dish such as baked beans.

‼ Pre-heat the oven to 200°C, 400°F, Gas Mark 6. Peel the potatoes and cut them into slices which are ½ cm (¼ inch) thick. Put sufficient water in a 2½ litre (5 pint) saucepan to cover the potatoes, add some salt and bring to the boil. Let the potatoes boil for approximately 6 minutes – this will part cook them, but still leave them in slices. Drain off the water. (You will need to help your child do this.)

Grease the inside of an ovenproof casserole. To do this use grease-proof paper spread with butter or margarine and wipe all over the surface of the dish.

Grate the cheese. Put a layer of potatoes on the bottom of the casserole, using half the slices. Cover this layer with grated cheese and sprinkle over with a little pepper. Add the remaining potatoes in a layer, then add the rest of the cheese and again sprinkle with pepper.

!! Slice the tomatoes as finely as possible and decorate the top of the pie with them.

Put the dish in the preheated oven for approximately 30 minutes. If you want to brown the top of the cheese pie – when the pie is cooked, take it out of the oven and place under a grill for a few minutes.

GAJAR – KA HULVA

Equipment required: large heavy saucepan
1 kg (2 lb) carrots
1.2 litres (2 pints) milk
225 g (8 oz) sugar
225 g (8 oz) butter
50 g (2 oz) sultanas
50 g (2 oz) ground mixed nuts
15 g (½ oz) turmeric
2 teaspoons rose water

This is a wonderful Indian sweet. Children not only enjoy cooking this but also love eating it. They could help you cook it the day before it is needed either for an adult dinner or for an unusual sweet at a children's party. They could do a collage with foodstuffs while they wait for the carrots (see page 204).

Scrub and grate the carrots, then put them with the milk into a thick-bottomed saucepan. **!!** Bring the mixture to the boil, that is it should be bubbling well. Turn the heat down and simmer, covered, for 2 hours. Let your child stir this whenever he or she wants (provided you are there) using a wooden spoon. Make sure the mixture doesn't stick to the pan, it needs lots of occasional stirring.

When the mixture is a thick orange pulp – and it will reduce to a third of its original size – add the sugar and butter. Turn up the heat and cook and stir for 15 minutes. Remove from the heat and add the sultanas and nuts, then mix in the turmeric. Pour the mixture into a dish and leave to cool, then sprinkle with rose water – it should set quite firmly, but is delicious when still warm and not completely set.

Serve it either warm with cream or leave until cold, then the children can, with clean hands, roll the mixture into ball shapes and serve them with plain biscuits. This is a very unusual sweet, tasting a little of marzipan. You can have fun asking people to guess the ingredients.

FRENCH ONION SOUP
(4-6 servings)

!! **Equipment needed:** large heavy saucepan

3 large onions, peeled
50 g (2 oz) butter
1 teaspoon flour
1.2 litres (2 pints) water
1 beef or chicken stock cube (the French use beef stock but I prefer chicken)
salt
freshly ground black pepper
4 slices of bread
50 g (2 oz) grated cheese (Cheddar, Mozzarella or Parmesan)

This soup is a meal in itself that your child could help you prepare for lunch or for a starter for a dinner party. It has lots of processes that are quite time consuming for you but which a child would love to do for you. Children love nothing better than grating cheese and cutting bread into small squares, so this is an ideal recipe. Do however remember that a child will take a little longer to do these things than you would yourself.

!! Chop the onions as finely as possible. Depending on the age of your child either you could do this or you could let him or her do it under supervision.

Put the butter into a heavy-bottomed saucepan over a low heat. Add the onions, carefully turning them over with a wooden spoon. Sprinkle the flour over the onions as they are cooking. Cook until they are transparent or an even golden brown colour. Be careful that they don't stick to the pan.

Add the water a little bit at a time and keep stirring. When all the water is added, crumble in the stock cube, then add salt and pepper to taste. Bring to the boil and then simmer, covered, for 20 minutes.

While the soup is simmering, either fry the slices of bread in a little oil, or toast them lightly. The French prefer to fry the bread, but when children are helping they prefer to toast it. Cut the toasted or fried bread into small squares (cut it into 'soldiers' first and then cut the 'soldiers' across the other way).

Pour the soup into 4 or 6 flameproof soup dishes (or 1 flameproof soup tureen). Add the bread and cover with the grated cheese. Pop under the grill and cook until cheese is bubbling and just turning brown.

‼ You will then have to remove the dishes from the grill yourself, as they will be hot and the soup easily spilt. Serve and eat.

ONIONS WITHOUT TEARS: One tip to prevent tears when chopping onions is to hold a slice of raw potato between your teeth. A child will love doing this more for the fun than the effect. However, I don't know why it works – but it does!

LEFTOVER SOUP

Equipment needed: heavy-bottomed saucepan
Leftover potatoes, peas, cabbage, carrots, cauliflower (all or any of these will do, but try to make sure there are some potatoes, this helps thicken the soup), total weight 225 g (8 oz)
50 g (2 oz) butter
1 teaspoon flour
450-600 ml (¾-1 pint) water
1 stock cube – chicken or beef
salt
freshly ground black pepper

Mash all the vegetables in a bowl with a fork or a potato masher.

Put the butter into a saucepan over a low heat. Add the vegetables and turn with a wooden spoon until they are well covered with butter. Sprinkle the flour over the vegetables and stir for a short time. Don't let the vegetables stick to the pan.

Add the water a little at a time until the soup looks the right consistency. How much you use depends on how many vegetables you have and how thick or thin you like your soup.

Add the stock cube and salt and pepper to taste. Stir for 2 minutes to allow the seasoning to mix in.

‼ Bring to the boil and simmer, covered, for 20 minutes. ‼ Remove from the heat and serve. For this age group it is best that you pour the soup into the bowls for your child, to prevent undue splashing with hot soup. But some 10-11 year olds are capable of doing this themselves.

As a further refinement to this recipe, you could let the soup cool down, then liquidize to remove the lumps, reheat then serve.

Party food

MINIMIZE THE LEFTOVERS: There is often a lot of food left over at the end of a party. Children are usually far too excited on these occasions to want to eat too much, so make as many varied tastes as possible but not too much of any one thing. I prefer not to let children have or make too many sweet things, to safeguard their teeth and their health. However, most children's parties don't start with sweet things, they start with sandwiches, so they can fill up on those first before having a few sweets. Let your child help you with these, by buttering the bread and mixing the fillings.

ADVENTUROUS FILLINGS: As your children get older they might like to help you make some more exciting sandwiches than the usual cheese or sliced meat fillings.

1) Banana and Cucumber – either slice or mash the banana and put on the bread. Dice up the cucumber into very small pieces and lay on top of banana. Cover with second slice of bread.

2) Sardines – mash a tin of sardines into a bowl, add a few drops of vinegar or lemon juice and some salt and pepper.

3) Bacon and banana – grill the bacon until crisp. Leave it to cool. Cut or tear into small pieces, then add to the mashed banana in a bowl and spread on sandwich.

4) Apple and pork – if you have some pork left over from a joint, grate it up finely and add diced apple.

5) Egg and salad cream – mash hard-boiled eggs with a little salad cream and salt and pepper.

6) Cottage cheese and shrimps – this need not be quite as expensive as it sounds, since if you get your child to cut the shrimps or prawns into small pieces, they will spread quite a long way when mixed with the cottage cheese.

7) Scrambled egg and tomato sandwiches. Make scrambled egg your own way – leave to cool, then add salt and pepper. Spread the bread with the scrambled egg mixture and top with slices of tomato.

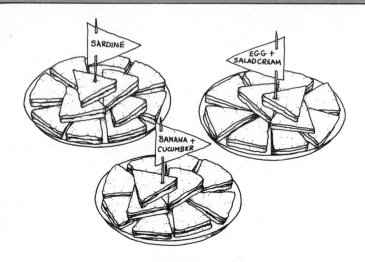

DISPLAYING THE SANDWICHES: Cut the sandwiches into triangles and arrange on plates keeping all the same fillings together. Then cut out some triangles of writing paper. Get your child to write the type of filling on this, stick one end of a cocktail stick through the paper (like a sail) and the other into the sandwich.

OTHER PARTY FOODS: Things on cocktail sticks are fun. They are normally time-consuming to prepare but this is made easier with a willing helpmate. Try small, whole sausages on sticks or cubes of cheese and pineapple.

SIMPLE FRUIT SALAD

Segments of orange and tangerine
Slices of peeled or unpeeled apple (depending on your taste)
Grapes, pips removed
Slices of banana
Add slices of any other fruit that may be in season such as plums, peaches, apricots.

Prepare enough fruit to fill your serving dish. Sprinkle a little sugar over the top of the fruit and also some lemon juice. Store in a cool place until ready to eat. The sugar causes the fruit to give up its juices, so no extra fluid is needed. Serve with cream or evaporated milk or custard or just on its own. If your child is helping you to make a fruit salad for one of your own dinner parties, then you could add diced cucumber, sultanas and nuts to give extra taste.

TRIFLE

12 sponge fingers
1 small can fruit salad, or small quantity fresh fruit salad
½ × 135 g (4¾ oz) packet strawberry jelly
300 ml (½ pint) made-up thick custard or blancmange (see below)
150 ml (¼ pint) double or whipping cream

To decorate:
nuts (almonds, walnuts or hazelnuts)
glacé cherries, halved

Trifle is always a party favourite and involves various different processes, such as jelly making, custard making and whipping cream. Children will enjoy doing all of these provided you supervise.

Line the bottom of a 1.2 litre (2 pint) serving dish with the sponge fingers. Pour on the fruit salad, just enough to cover the sponge fingers.

‼ Make up the half packet of strawberry jelly according to the packet instructions in a separate bowl. When cool but not set, pour the jelly over the sponge fingers and fruit salad.

Leave to set. You could do this part the day before the party and leave to set overnight.

Make 300 ml (½ pint) custard or blancmange (see below). Allow to cool, then pour over the set jelly. Leave the custard to set. Whip up the cream until thick and spread this over the top of the custard. Decorate with nuts and/or cherries.

You will find that children enjoy making as much of this as you will allow them.

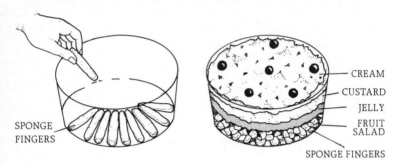

SPONGE FINGERS

CREAM
CUSTARD
JELLY
FRUIT SALAD

SPONGE FINGERS

Custard for Trifle

The easiest way to make a custard is from the instructions on the back of a custard powder recipe. If you are making one for a trifle add a little more custard powder or a little less milk then the recipe states, to ensure that it will be a thick custard that will set. You could make a sweet sauce instead which is, in fact, a recipe for making blancmange (see below).

BLANCMANGE

Equipment needed: milk saucepan
25 g (1 oz) cornflour
600 ml (1 pint) milk
40 g (1½ oz) caster sugar
1 teaspoon vanilla essence
15 g (½ oz) butter
a few drops of yellow food colouring or 1 egg yolk (optional)

Mix the cornflour in a bowl with a little of the cold milk.

Warm the rest of the milk in a saucepan, then remove from the heat and add the cornflour paste.

!! Bring to the boil and simmer for 3 minutes. The mixture will then thicken up considerably. You can test if it has reached the right consistency by dropping a small blob of the mixture on to a cold saucer. It should form a skin straightaway. Remove from the heat and add the rest of the ingredients, stirring for about 1 minute. The yellow food colouring or the egg yolk will make it the colour of custard. Pour into a bowl, or put on top of a fruit salad or trifle. Leave to set.

If you want to make a blancmange, use the above recipe but don't add the colouring or egg yolk. If you want to put the blancmange into a mould that can be turned out to sit wobbling on the party table, the above recipe is for a 600 ml (1 pint) mould. But rinse the mould with cold water before you pour the blancmange mixture into it – this helps it come free from the sides, when it is set and ready to be turned out.

DIFFERENT FLAVOURINGS FOR BLANCMANGE: Make the blancmange according to the above recipe but omit the vanilla essence and the yellow food colouring or egg yolk.

Lemon Blancmange – add 1 teaspoon finely grated lemon rind and a few drops of yellow food colouring to the milk when it is warming.

Orange Blancmange – add 1 level teaspoon finely grated orange peel and a few drops of orange food colouring to the milk when warming.

Coffee Blancmange – add 2-3 level teaspoons of coffee powder to the milk when it is warming.

Chocolate Blancmange – add 2-3 level teaspoons of cocoa or chocolate powder to the milk when it is warming. If the chocolate powder is of the sweetened variety only use 15 g (½ oz) caster sugar in the main recipe.

Strawberry or raspberry blancmange – add fruit essences and red food colouring to taste and colour.

FRUIT FOOLS

Equipment needed: large heavy saucepan
450 g (1 lb) fruit (apples, gooseberries, raspberries, etc.)
150 ml (¼ pint) double or whipping cream, stiffly whipped
100 g (4 oz) sugar
a little water

‼ These are very good for children's parties and can easily be made by children under supervision.

Wash the fruit. Cut any large fruit and remove the skin from hard-skinned fruit. Place the fruit in a heavy-bottomed pan with the sugar and a little water. Cook over a gentle heat until soft and tender. Rub through a sieve to remove any skin or pips or liquidize then sieve, then leave until cold. Fold in the cream until well mixed and a good, even colour. Serve in individual dishes.

Cakes

LITTLE OR LARGE: The following recipes are all variations on a basic theme, designed for children to help you make. The basic recipe is also that of a Victoria Sponge Sandwich, but cooked in smaller portions. To make a sponge sandwich, use the recipe but put the whole mixture into 2 greased and floured 18 cm (7 inch) sponge tins. Cook as for the Fairy cakes, then turn out on to a wire rack to cool and fill (as for an ordinary sandwich) with butter cream and/or fresh cream and jam.

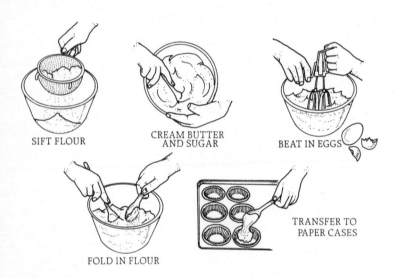

SIFT FLOUR

CREAM BUTTER AND SUGAR

BEAT IN EGGS

FOLD IN FLOUR

TRANSFER TO PAPER CASES

FAIRY CAKES

100 g (4 oz) self-raising flour
100 g (4 oz) butter, softened
100 g (4 oz) caster sugar
2 eggs

Sift the flour into a bowl.

Cream the butter and sugar together using a wooden spoon in another bowl, until very pale in colour and light and fluffy.

Beat the eggs into the butter and sugar one at a time.

Add the sifted flour, a little at a time, folding it in very gently to avoid flour spraying everywhere.

Transfer equal amounts (about 1 dessertspoonful) into 18 paper cases and stand in ungreased bun tins. Bake in the centre of a preheated oven: 190°C, 375°F or Gas Mark 5 for 20-25 minutes. They will then be well risen and a light golden brown.

!! Transfer to a wire rack to cool.

CHOCOLATE CHIP CAKES

Follow the recipe for the Fairy cakes but add 50 g (2 oz) plain chocolate chips after adding the flour.

CURRANT OR SULTANA FAIRY CAKES

Follow the recipe for the fairy cakes but add 50 g (2 oz) currants or sultanas.

BUTTERFLY CAKES

Make up the Fairy cakes. When cool, cut a slice off the top of each cake. Cut these slices in half for wings. Put a spoonful of Butter cream frosting (see below) or a large blob of strawberry jam on the bottom part of the cake, then stick the 'wings' into this at an angle. Dust the 'butterfly cakes' with sifted icing sugar.

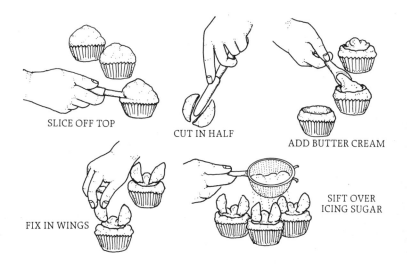

SLICE OFF TOP

CUT IN HALF

ADD BUTTER CREAM

FIX IN WINGS

SIFT OVER
ICING SUGAR

BUTTER CREAM FROSTING

100 g (4 oz) butter
225 g (8 oz) sifted icing sugar
2 tablespoons cold milk
food colouring (optional)

Beat the butter with a fork until soft. Add the sugar and milk. Continue beating until light and frothy. Add the food colouring drop by drop until you have the required colour.

Some food for special occasions

PANCAKES

Equipment needed: frying pan
1 egg, size 2, separated
salt
100 g (4 oz) plain flour
300 ml (½ pint) milk
25 g (1 oz) margarine or butter

Shrove Tuesday was the last time that eggs, flour and dairy produce could be used before the fasting days of Lent, so people made pancakes to help use up any of these things that were left in the house. You will need to supervise the frying of the pancakes.

Beat the egg yolk, together with a pinch of salt.

Sift the flour into a bowl and add the milk, beating until it is the consistency of thick cream. Beat in the egg yolk mixture.

Beat the egg white until stiff, then fold into the batter. !! Heat a little butter in a frying pan, just enough to grease the surface. Pour in enough batter to cover the base of the frying pan thinly. Cook over a fairly high heat for about 1 to 2 minutes.

Turn the pancake over using a spatula and cook the other side for about 1 minute. The pancakes should be a light golden brown colour. Your child could have a go at tossing the pancakes, but it is risky.

Turn out on to greaseproof paper. Cover with another piece of greaseproof paper and make more pancakes until the batter is used up.

To serve, sprinkle each pancake with sugar and lemon juice, then roll up. This is the traditional filling, there are many others. You could use jam, fruit, cheese, nuts, chocolate spread or maple syrup.

ST VALENTINE'S DAY HEARTS OF CREAM

Equipment needed: heart-shaped metal or pottery moulds with drainage holes, lined with muslin. (If you don't have any proper moulds, clean yogurt cartons with holes punched in the bottom can be used instead.)
225 g (8 oz) unsalted cream cheese or cottage cheese
300 ml (½ pint) double cream
4 teaspoons caster sugar
2 egg whites
few drops of red food colouring (optional)
strawberries (frozen or picked from a jar of whole strawberry jam)

Press the cheese through a sieve, into a bowl. Mix in the double cream and sugar.

Beat the egg whites until stiff, then fold into the cheese mixture. Add a few drops of colouring if wished. Spoon the cheese mixture into lined moulds.

Place the moulds on a wide plate in the refrigerator overnight to drain and chill. Next day, carefully turn out the moulds and decorate with strawberries. Serve with single cream.

EASTER EGGS

The best thing to do with your child at Easter is to get him to hard boil an egg with some food colouring added to the water to make the shells an interesting colour.

8. Books, Listening And Writing

General hints

For useful things to have, see the following pages

Take a tip from the past: Years ago children were brought up on the myths and legends of our culture. These were stories that had been handed down from one generation to another and were spread by word of mouth. There is a lifetime's worth of reading in these stories alone. So carry on the tradition.

Reading at home: It's important for children to see their parents reading and children's books should be out on the coffee table beside your own – although children should also have a special place to keep their own books as treasured possessions. Try not to give children books which are tatty or torn, as this will encourage careless treatment.

Book cassettes: If your child still hasn't quite mastered the art of reading at this age, why not get some of the excellent storytelling cassettes that are in the shops? Quite often they have picture books to look at while the cassette is playing and they can help and encourage children to read the story for themselves once they have heard the cassette. These cassettes are also very useful when taking a child on a long car or train journey. Some children, as well as adults, feel a bit sick when reading in a car, so having a story told to them from a cassette will overcome this problem. It also keeps them very quiet when stuck in those interminable traffic jams!

The world of science fiction: The modern equivalent of myths and legends is the science fiction story. Again there are characters of good and evil and, though the fight for supremacy is sometimes more dwelt on, the apparent violence does not have a harmful effect, as it is always accepted as fantasy. Fantasy games have been developed using SF stories too.

Fantasy games: If you are interested in finding out more about these and all other types of fantasy games contact the Games Workshop (see page 360 for their address). There is also a magazine called the 'White Dwarf' which tells of clubs all over the British Isles.

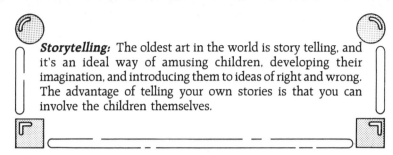

Storytelling: The oldest art in the world is story telling, and it's an ideal way of amusing children, developing their imagination, and introducing them to ideas of right and wrong. The advantage of telling your own stories is that you can involve the children themselves.

Telling stories

STARTING OFF: Start the story by sitting close to the children in a comfortable spot and make sure there are no distractions around. This close contact and peace and quiet is all part of building a world where the imagination can run wild.

MAKE IT A SERIAL: If you turn your story into a serial of several episodes, you have an instant means of quietening down some other lively play session. Stories should last for between five and ten minutes, and you should always stop at the most exciting moment so that they're eager to hear you begin again next time.

INVOLVING THE LISTENERS: Encourage the children to ask questions about the story, and ask them what they think will happen next and why. Use the names of their friends, and mimic people and voices that they know. You'll find out a lot about your child too. If at some point he/she says, 'I think we ought to kill that character off – he's awful', you could point out that lots of other things not quite so bad could happen, or perhaps you could try to find something good in the character.

COMMUNITY LINKS: One of the best things about storytelling is that the older people in the community and your children's grand-parents can be involved. Often true stories from their childhood will fascinate young listeners. If you have a tape recorder or cassette player perhaps the children could record the stories, to replay to their class at school. Many school teachers are trying to involve children more in community relations. Perhaps you could suggest this at a parents' meeting at school. It will fill many an empty hour during the holidays or weekends once the contacts are made.

Reading

READING BOOKS: Library and Book Associations will happily supply lists of recommended books for children of all ages according to their reading ability. Other addresses of some of the places to write to are given on pages 359 and 360.

JOIN A BOOK CLUB: There are a number of book clubs which encourage children to read, write and involve themselves with books. Some are national organizations, while others are run by individual publishers. They all run newsletters, competitions, games, exhibitions and other activities based on children's books. Ask at the school or local library for details.

Libraries

ABSORBING INFORMATION: Show children how to get information out of books. If a child asks a question, instead of simply answering yourself, suggest that you see together what a book has to say. Teach them how to answer their own questions by using reference books and show them the difference between dictionaries, encyclopaedias and so on.

JOINING THE LIBRARY: Membership of public libraries is free for both children and their parents. Go along with your children on their first visit, and fill in their membership form; then a librarian will usually be free to explain to the child where the different kinds of books are.

USING THE LIBRARY: Go round with the children and try to help them in their choice, making sure that the books they select aren't too difficult (although a couple to stretch the imagination can be quite educational for the child). Make sure that children understand that the books will have to go back, cannot be kept for good, and that they must be looked after especially carefully.

FINDING A LIBRARY: If you're not sure where your nearest children's library is, contact the Library Association, see page 360 for the address.

MORE THAN A COLLECTION OF BOOKS: During the summer holidays, most libraries organize children's activities. These include slide and cartoon film shows; book displays and exhibitions; games and competitions; and local history projects. Your own library will be able to supply the details.

Writing

BECOMING A WRITER: Encourage children to write their own stories by cutting out pictures from magazines, then asking them to write about what is happening in the picture. Alternatively, get them to continue a story that they know well, e.g. what do they think happened to the Seven Dwarfs after Snow White went away with the Prince?

FACT-FINDING MISSIONS: If your children are more interested in fact than fiction, set them a project on a particular subject by writing and sticking pictures into an exercise book. Give them books and magazines to help, and show them how to find out more from reference books. Typical subjects might be: our pets; water; a visit to the park; trees; the four seasons.

KEEPING A DIARY: Diaries are great fun. Children are perhaps familiar with your appointments diary but introduce them to the more personal sort, where you write down not just what you did, but why you did it and how you felt about it. Use a large diary or an exercise book, so that they have lots of space in which to write, and if they are stuck for things to write about, talk over the day's events with them, and point out things which they might want to remember from the things they have done.

A CONTINUING TRADITION: If you ever kept a diary when you were young, show it to your child. As you know, they love to hear about all the things that happened to you and you could point out that they can do the same when they have children.

SOCIAL HISTORY: Suggest to children that they put in the diary how much things cost when talking about buying things. I recently had enormous fun with my children when I found an old shopping list with the prices written by the side. It lead to at least an hour's worth of reminiscing which, to my total surprise, then found its way into an essay that my younger son was writing for his homework.

KEEPING SECRETS: Don't forget the fun that can be had by using codes in the diary. With all the best will in the world, it is very hard for anyone to resist peeping into someone else's diary when it has been left lying around. So to stop prying eyes knowing their deep thoughts, show your children how to use some codes.

Very secret sentences: Reverse the alphabet. This means that they have to make a chart, like this:

Z Y X W V U T S R Q P O N M L K J I H G F E D C B A
A B C D E F G H I J K L M N O P Q R S T U V W X Y Z

So that, 'Bought Mum her birthday present – perfume' would read

YLFTSG NFN SVI YRIGSWZB KIVHVMG – KVIUFNV

and would mean very little to anybody else.

NON-LETTER CODES: Asterisks and special marks can be used too to conceal people's names. I remember writing about a boy that I thought was super. Whenever I even caught a glimpse of him I would write 'saw * in the library today'. The unfortunate thing is that now I can no longer remember his real name – he will forever be asterisk to me.

FAMOUS LAST WORD: Many famous people keep diaries – you do not know if your children will be famous one day!

Wordgames

I-SPY: A good way of amusing children and developing their under-standing of language at the same time is through wordgames. One of the simplest is I-Spy – make allowances, but gently correct any mistakes about the letters with which words begin.

THE NEVER ENDING SENTENCE: Try playing the Never Ending Sentence, in which three children provide successive words for a possible sentence but each one tries not to be the one to give the word which will end the sentence. The first one who cannot think of a word to continue the sentence begins a new one and the child before loses a point, because he has completed the sentence. For example (the children are numbered 1, 2 and 3):

1   2   3   1   2   3   1   2   3   1
The cat sat on the mat and looked at the

2   3   1   2   3   1 2   3
fire which crackled and glowed in the fireplace

1   2   3   1   2   3   1   2
by the tall grandfather clock which was just

3   1   2   3   1   2
striking four o' clock, the time when, etc

ENDING A LIMERICK: A fun game, which incidentally increases children's understanding of the sounds and rhythms of speech, is to teach them about limericks. Once they understand that the first, second and last lines rhyme with each other and so do the fourth and fifth, they will have great fun, adding their own final line. Here are some suggestions:

There was an old man from Rangoon
Who went to live on the moon
It's a nice place to stay
And just takes a day

(Suggested answer could be – On the back of a hot air balloon.)

When watching a programme on Telly
And eating a plateful of jelly
Lord John missed his mouth
The jelly fell south

(Suggested answer could be – And went straight down inside his left welly.)

HANGMAN: Older children can play Hangman. Think up a word, then put down dashes to represent each letter on a piece of paper. Your child has to guess what the word is. To do this he suggests what letters might be in the word. For each letter he gets wrong, a detail is added to a drawing of a hanged man. If the drawing is finished before he's guessed the word, then he loses the game.

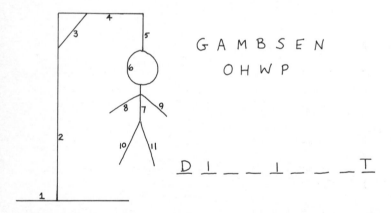

SILLY WILLY: This is a game which adults and children can play together easily or children can play on their own. Surprisingly enough it is often the adults who can't play the game. The idea is that you say two things that Silly Willy likes and then two things that he doesn't like, but the other person doesn't know exactly what it is that Silly Willy does or doesn't like. For example, if Silly Willy likes the colour yellow, you could say Silly Willy likes butter and dandelions but not cabbages and post boxes. If he likes words with double letters in them, you could say Silly Willy likes boots and balloons but not shoes and bats. If the other person doesn't guess straightaway, you have to go on giving clues.

Here's an example:

Silly Willy likes raspberries and tomatoes but not apples and oranges
Silly Willy likes London buses and post boxes but not country buses
and cabbages
Silly Willy likes American Indians and poppies but not cowboys and
lilies
Silly Willy likes blood and tomato sauce but not gravy and sausage

(Answer – have you worked it out? – Yes, it's red.)

ASSOCIATION GAME: You clap three times and say a word. The
next person claps three times and has to say a word that the first word
reminds him or her of. For instance: (X = clap)

X X X – Uncle
X X X – Aunt
X X X – Dolly (Auntie Dolly – if you have one)
X X X – Toy
X X X – Game
X X X – Chess

You can also play this game by making the rules slightly different. Each
new word having to start with the following letter in the alphabet.

X X X – Apple
X X X – Banana
X X X – Cricket
X X X – Dog
X X X – Elephant
X X X – Farthing

This version could be made slightly harder by restricting the words to a
particular theme, such as school subjects:

X X X – Arithmetic
X X X – Biology
X X X – Chemistry
X X X – Divinity
X X X – Exercise

It's surprising how the enforced rhythm makes these games much more
difficult than they at first appear.

ADD A LETTER: This is an infuriating word game that will help with spelling and vocabulary. The first player writes down a letter. The second has to write a word with two letters that starts with the letter chosen. The third has to give a three letter word and so on. So if the first player started with A the list could go like this:

A
AN
ANT
ABLE
ATTIC
AUGUST
AUNTIES
ANTIQUES
ARTICHOKE
AUSTRALIAN

You could use a dictionary with this game to start with – but it is cheating a little – see if you can manage without.

ANAGRAMS: Mix up the letters of a word, then see if your child can unravel them and vice versa. You could start with three-letter words and gradually increase the number. Give a clue to the word's identity or keep to a particular theme, e.g. fruit:

MULP = PLUM
GERANO = ORANGE
LEPAP = APPLE
EMNLO = LEMON
TPOAIRC = APRICOT

HOW MANY WORDS?: This game has to be played within a given time limit, say one minute. You ask the children to write down as many words as they can think of beginning with a particular letter, or which have a certain vowel in them, or a mixture of letters like th, ch, ph, oo, ll, ee. The winner has the largest number of (correctly spelt) words.

GENTLY DOES IT: All the word games suggested here are an excellent way for a sick or convalescent child to pass away the time, for they only take mental not physical energy. They are also useful quiet games to play after tea at a children's party.

IT STARTS AT THE END: This is a very simple word game that helps a child with spelling. The idea is that someone says a word and the next person has to say another word that starts with the last letter in the previous word. For example:

PANS
STATION
NOSE
EGG
GREEK
KNOW
WINDOW
WALL
LORRY
YES
SOLD

When the child becomes proficient at this game, try to do it to the clapping word game rhythm (see page 317). It isn't easy. Also make a rule that no word can be repeated within the game.

9. Entertaining Ideas For Particular Occasions

Useful things to have

(see also individual games)

Empty plastic bottles
Pebbles
Empty washing-up bottles
Ping-pong balls
Large bucket or bowl
Balloons

Blindfold
Empty picture frame
Feathers
Pack of cards
Calculator

General hints

The newness of it: As a useful way into the whole business of computers, calculators and electronic displays, make a list of all the things you have in your home which come in this group and discuss with your child how relatively recently each one has become a part of everyday life. There are digital displays on watches, clocks, radios and even thermometers, there are calculators, cassettes and an ever-growing trend towards micro-computers.

Making use of it: Not everyone has access to all the modern gadgetry, but most people have a television or at least have seen one. Don't just sit glued to it – try to make use of it. There are endless quiz programmes and game programmes on both the radio and the television. Why not make up some that you could play at home, based on the ideas given in the shows that you have seen and heard?

Party play ideas

SILLY SQUIRT: This is a game to be played by all ages, and can last as long as the concentration lasts. It's a game which obviously has to be played outdoors; in the garden or in a playground or even on a patio. Place six pebbles in the bottom of six empty plastic orange squash (or similar) bottles to stabilize them. Remove the caps from the bottles. Place ping-pong balls on the open top of the bottles. Fill six washing-up

liquid bottles with water from a large bucket. These act as water pistols. Stand at a suitable distance away from the plastic bottles and try to shoot the ping-pong balls off the top of the bottles by squirting them with water. In this game, the idea is to see how many ping-pong balls you can get off the top of the bottles while somebody is counting. In fact, all the other players could stand by and count one-two-three-four-five-six out loud.

WATER BOMBS: This is definitely an outdoor game, preferably when the weather is very warm, as the participants will get quite wet. **!!** It should be played in a park or fairly large garden or indeed by a paddling pool or at the seaside. This is the kind of game which is a great success at the seaside but should it be played in the garden, it would be a good idea to wear old clothes.

Fill a balloon half full of water and blow up the remainder with air, then tie off.

Measure out a certain distance, say 100 metres. The idea of the game is to hold the water-filled balloon between the knees and walk along from the starting post to the finish as quickly as possible trying not to break the balloon, which is easier said than done.

TREASURE HUNT: This is a game that I found kept my children amused for hours and hours on end. It is especially useful when there are visiting friends or relations. The adults have to make a list of things for the children to obtain and obviously it depends on where you live as to what will be available. The following is a list of suggestions, which should help you on your way:

Leaf	One penny piece
Twig	Piece of string
Bus ticket	Sweet paper wrapper
Button	Feather
Blade of grass	Piece of wool
Blue, pink, yellow flower	Stone or pebble

The game can be played inside as well as outside, but always include one difficult thing, for instance an envelope addressed to somebody else or an old stamp, a piece of paper signed by a policeman or by the lady next door (!! providing she isn't the visitor and you can trust your child outside the house on his or her own). The winner is the one who is the first to get all the objects or has the most of them after a certain period of time. At the end of each game there is to be a small prize – an individual carton of fruit juice or a packet of crisps or an apple or 5 pence – whatever the parents wish to give.

TRY SOMETHING NEW AS WELL: Children are by now used to, and indeed love, the traditional games but they also will enjoy any new game. Traditional games for the 7-11 year old age group include, Hunt the Thimble, Musical Chairs, Postman's Knock. Below are a few you might not know.

NEPTUNE'S CAVE: This is played by children but made up and organized by parents. It is a fairly messy game and therefore is best played in the kitchen.

While the children sit in the lounge playing with one parent, another can prepare Neptune's cave in the kitchen. The children must not see what is going on. Fill a bucket or bowl with all the bits of party food leftovers, with orange juice, tea bags, bits of sandwiches, trifle: in fact as much of a mess as possible. Then drop some 10p and 20p pieces into this bucket. Fill a second bucket with water and drop money in this too. One of the adults then sits on a chair with a rug draped over his or her shoulders and a broom held in the hand. The bucket or bowl with the food leftovers is placed on the table in front of him or her.

Another adult now goes into the room where the children are playing carrying the bucket of clear water, shows it to the children and describes it like this: 'I've just been down to the bottom of the sea and found all this money in Neptune's cave. Would anyone else like to come to Neptune's cave with me and see if they can find some money?' Hopefully they all want to play. They are taken one by one into the kitchen, but first of all they must be blindfolded. One of the parents pretends that the child is being touched with seaweed by wafting a damp teatowel over face, arms and legs. Then the child is invited to feel Neptune's spiky hair (the top of a broom). Now he must feel Neptune's rough skin (a rug). He's then asked to listen to Neptune speak (someone blows into a glass of water through a straw). And now he is told that there are jelly fish, sponges and other deep sea creatures trying to stop him getting Neptune's treasure. Does he still want to try? If he does, he has to plunge his hand into Neptune's treasure chest to try to find a coin. As you've guessed, the party food bucket is the one the child plunges his hands in. Lots of oohs and aaghs and the child can keep the coin he finds – only one coin!

When the first child has had his/her turn, he stays in the room to help by being seaweed and Neptune's voice.

YOU'VE BEEN FRAMED: This is another good but fairly quiet game to play once the children have used up a lot of energy. All the children except one sit on the floor. The remaining child stands or sits in front of them holding an empty picture frame in front of his or her face and he or she then strikes a pose and tries to stay like that without moving. All the rest of the children take it in turns to say different things to make the child move or laugh. For instance 'Look there's a mouse behind you' or they could try to tell a joke. The child who has stayed still long enough wins a prize. An adult has to keep a check on the times.

FEATHER FLIGHT: If you have some small light feathers (e.g. from old pillows or duvets) you can make use of them with this game. Give each player a feather and see how long they can keep the feather in the air by just blowing, huffing and puffing. Whenever a feather goes out of control the player has to sit down leaving the others to play. The child keeping his or her feather in the air the longest is the winner and may receive a prize if you wish it.

BALLOON GOAL: You'll need a balloon for this and some chairs. Divide the children into two teams. Have two rows of chairs facing each other but about 2 metres (5 feet) apart. Sit the teams on the chairs. The children may not lift their bottoms off the chairs. Toss a coin to see which side starts with the balloon. They have to knock or pat the balloon with their hands or heads from one side to the other. A goal is scored when the balloon either touches the floor or cannot be returned to the other team.

PAIRS: This is a card game for which you'll need two packs of cards. It can be played with two to six children. More than this is difficult to arrange. Turn all the cards face downwards on the floor. They shouldn't touch each other, but they do not have to be in straight rows. Each player takes it in turn to turn up two cards. They can be from anywhere in the display. The idea is to find two cards with the same value. If the cards do not make a pair they are both turned face downwards again in the same place. It becomes a game of memory to see if the children can remember where they last saw a card. If a player does find a matching pair he removes it from the floor and keeps it by him. At the end of the game the number of pairs each player has is counted and the one with the most is the winner.

Games

THREE LITTLE WORDS: There is a programme called 'Three Little Words' which should be great fun to play at home. Explain the rules, start the children off and then leave them to it. It is a game in which you have three chances to try to convey one word by using another to describe it. For example if the word is

MAN
you could say
BOY

then let the child guess. If the answer is wrong, you have two more chances. You may choose ADULT as the second word; if they still don't give a correct answer, you could say DADDY. Then let the child choose the word and give you three guesses at it. To make sure that the game is played properly, you should both write down the original words chosen, so that you keep a check on them. This game not only stretches the imagination but the vocabulary as well.

If you have more than one child, or your child has a friend visiting, this could be a game in which there is a chairman. Write out several cards with one word on each of them. Shuffle them face downwards and divide them between the two players at the start, so that everything is fair, then let them play the game. Award a small prize to the winner. If there are even more children, you could play it as a knockout competition and award the overall winner a prize. Here are some more words and their 'three little words' to start you on your way.

HOME	BUILDING – HOUSE – YOURS
TEAPOT	CONTAINER – TEA – POURS
PENCIL	WRITING – PEN – WOODEN

If they get close to the word but have put it in the plural when it should be in the singular or vice versa you may say as one of your words SINGULAR or PLURAL. You may also use the words SHORTER or LONGER if they have the root word correctly but the tense wrong. For example, if the main word is PAINT but they say PAINTING, you may say SHORTER and then they should say PAINT. Remember only one word may be used at a time.

UNIVERSITY CHALLENGE OR MASTERMIND: These are general knowledge and specialized knowledge games. There are many general knowledge quiz books on the market that you could buy to help play these sorts of games. But why not go through your children's school books or books you know they are reading, or even use television programmes that you know they watch and ask them questions from any of these. You may find that your child wants to set you some questions, too. You'll be surprised how much they know when asked this way – and possibly how much they know that you don't! You could either compile general knowledge quizzes covering a whole range of subjects or concentrate on a narrower area, such as a pop quiz or a sports quiz or a news quiz.

CHARADES: This is a game played on TV but has also been a popular parlour game for many years. You choose the title of a book, play, song or musical and mime the words in it, so that the other players can guess which it is. There are set mimes and rules here. Firstly, hold up the number of fingers to tell how many words there are in the title. Then, to let people know if it's a book, you close the palms of your hands in the praying position and then open them out as if they were a book opening;
for a song title you open your mouth as if singing and spread your arms widely;

for a television show you draw a square in the air;
for a play you mime curtains opening;
for a film you mime looking through a camera and turning a handle.

Next there are a few conventions about miming the words. The word THE is signalled by making a T shape by putting one first finger across the top of the other.

A small word is signalled by the first finger and thumb of one hand opening and closing.

If a word has one or more syllables you may break the word down and mime each syllable. To do this you show the number of syllables in the word by putting that number of fingers on the upper part of the opposite arm.

A proper name is shown by patting your head.

Here are some fairly easy titles for you to start with.

Star Wars (film)
Three Blind Mice (song)
Butterfly Ball (book and film)
The Lion, the Witch and the Wardrobe (book)
The Railway Children (film and book)
Jack and the Beanstalk (book)

Your child should choose something that most children will be familiar with. At least half the children should know the title once the game has ended for it to be a fair game. There are lots more rules to this game that you can either invent yourselves or get passed on to you from other people who have played the game. It's a good game to play at parties.

I KNOW WHAT YOU LIKE: This can be played by quite a few players. The idea is to find out how much you know about each other. The questions are about one member of the family or a friend and they have to be answered by the others and then justified by the person concerned. See who knows you best. Your husband, your child or your mother – or perhaps your best friend. And also see how well you know your child. First, write out a series of questions. Here are a few examples:

1) What does this person like best?

– going to the theatre/watching television/reading

2) What does this person like to eat most?

– cheese/fish and chips/sweets

3) What is this person's favourite type of television programme?

– sport/daily serial/pop programmes

4) What is this person's favourite colour?

– red/blue/green

Always give only three possible answers, for this makes scoring easier. You will need a chairman to choose the questions. Each member playing should write his or her answers down, as well as the person who the questions are about. It is really a fun game. You'll be surprised how observant some of your family are – and how unobservant others are.

Videos

FOR THE SECOND TIME OF ASKING: Video a quiz programme and you can play it again so that children can have another go at answering the questions. They have the advantage of memory the second time around but this is something that children love to do as well as being a fun way of increasing general knowledge.

REPEAT PERFORMANCE: Video a classic play and see the number of times your children will go back over and over again to watch it. It is an entirely painless way of becoming familiar with the style and subject matter of such well-known literature.

COMPUTERS: Most primary schools now have computer study pro-grammes but you can all have entertainment from one if you are able to have one in your own home. Read up on the subject first – there are many excellent books. Several of these are written for children and will give them a good start on the necessary jargon. Of course children will want to play only the games at first, but it really doesn't take too long for them to want to do other things with the computer as well. Composers of games and puzzles are often teenagers or younger. Your child could help you with household accounts, for instance.

TV GAMES: Most TV games have a switch for playing the games at different skill levels, so that they do have scope for increasing children's eye and hand co-ordination. They are a useful rainy day standby but can become addictive and are not particularly worthwhile.

Calculators

CALCULATED SHOPPING: A calculator can be a useful aid when you go shopping with your children. Get them to add up the price of everything as it goes in your basket. This means you have a running total of the cost of the shop and can always check your calculations with that of the check-out till as an extra insurance.

CALCULATOR TALK: Here are some games children can play with a calculator. The idea is to enter figures into the print out, which when turned upside down show as a word instead of figures.

Tell your child that the calculator wants to talk to them and that the code numbers to use for it to speak to them are 0.7734. Get them to punch those numbers. Turn the calculator upside down and it spells out

HELLO

Then say that if the child punches another set of numbers it will print out the calculator's name.
Choose from any of these numbers:

7718 = BILL   7719 = GILL   808 = BOB

Ask the child to ask the calculator what his job is and then punch out:

5508.918

and it will read out (upside down)

BIG BOSS

then get the child to ask it who it works for and punch out:

710.77345

which says he works for:

SHELL OIL

Ask the child to ask it how big the Shell Oil building is and punch

4614

and it will say

HIGH

You can make up masses of answers and questions like this. The basic thing to remember is that whatever you punch in you will have to punch in reverse order to get the answer you need.

Make up the words from these letters.

H = 4	O = 0
E = 3	B = 8
L = 7	G = 9 or 6
I = 1	S = 5

You will also find that you have to punch a decimal point after an 0 if the word ends in O. Or a decimal point to get the gap between two words in order to make the gap.

SUMMING IT UP: You may also find that you can make up small sums to get the written answers. For instance: If Jill took 7000 small steps – punch in 7000 – and Jack took 714 large steps – punch in + then 714. Where were they going? Punch the = sign, turn the calculator upside down – the answer is Hill.

THE AGE GAME: By using a calculator your child can play a trick on his friends by guessing their ages. To add to the general air of mystery, the child gives the friends the calculator and they do all the operations themselves.

What to do
1. Tell the friend to hide the screen from view and then press in his age.
2. Tell him to multiply his age by 2.
3. Then add 1.
4. Multiply the total by 5.
5. Add 5.
6. Multiply the total by 10.
7. Subtract 100.
8. Ask your friend to tell you the answer.
9. To find out the friend's age, you ignore the last two digits. The number you are left with will be your friend's age.

When your child is doing this game, please make sure that anyone concerned really **wants** to tell his or her age. Aunt Jemima could be very upset if her real age was shouted out to everyone.

THE SAME NUMBER TRICK: You can do a similar trick to the above one but this time you will be finding out what random number your friend has keyed in is.

1. Get a friend to enter any number up to seven digits on the calculator. They should also write down this number somewhere hidden, in case they forget it.
2. Multiply by 3.
3. Add 2.
4. Multiply again by 3.
5. Add the number which is 2 greater than the first number.
6. Ask for the answer.
7. Leave out the last number he says and repeat the number to him. It will be the one he first put in.

For example:

Entered number –

$$
\begin{array}{r}
1873659 \\
3 \ \times \\
\hline
5620977 \\
2 \ + \\
\hline
5620979 \\
3 \ \times \\
\hline
16862937 \\
1873661 \ + \\
\hline
18736598 \\
\end{array}
$$

Knock off the last number and you have your friend's first number: 1873659. It works with smaller beginning numbers as well.

10. Visits

General hints

Working it out beforehand: A lot of the traditional sights and visits for children, whether entertaining or educational, can be made a lot more fun and a lot more worthwhile if they're approached in the right way. The ideas in this chapter are for family outings, although within the visits, say to museums, there is scope for children to explore their own ideas.

Outdoor activities: When the weather is fine, there are many ways to entertain your children. Outdoor games and visits are just two of the ways. And they are fun, hopefully. Try to remember what it was like when you were the same age as your children and look at everything you do as if it were new to you. You'll be surprised how much you missed first time round. This will also prevent you from 'mother henning' the children, and you might allow them more freedom to wander around looking at things their own way.

Freedom to wander: !! Suggest meeting points where children should collect every five or ten minutes. You'll be surprised how often a child stays really quite close to you when freedom is offered – deny freedom and they'll run away. So let go of the reins a bit when you can. Let children find out things for themselves and listen to the pride in their voices when they tell you what *they* themselves have done or found out. Of course don't let this go to extremes – just keep looking after them when they play outside or go on a visit – but let go some of those apron strings. Also do impress on children where the 'lost children section' is, should the worst happen. Make sure they know their own first name and surname and their address. If you are on holiday give them a piece of paper with the address of the place you are staying – don't trust this one to memory – and finally always tell the children how nice policemen and policewomen are, even if your opinion differs; without them there would be many a sad lost child.

Museums

A LITTLE GOES A LONG WAY: Children learn a lot more from seeing and touching objects than from studying them in books. But don't simply go to a museum and try to see as much as possible. Decide in advance to visit only particular areas of the museum and look at those really closely, rather than glancing around the whole building.

KEEPING A RECORD: A lot of museums have an educational department, which can recommend particular tours of the exhibits and can often provide you with educational aids. Make sure the children have paper, pen and a clipboard of some kind, so that they can make notes and draw the exhibits. When you leave, buy them postcards or posters of their favourite exhibits, and encourage them to follow up their interests.

A MUSEUM QUIZ: A good way of stimulating children's interest is to set them a quiz. Think of ten simple questions connected with the department you've decided to look around and offer a small prize for the right answers. As well as encouraging children to take a real interest in the exhibits, it trains them in discovering information for themselves.

SPECIAL EVENTS: It is worth keeping a check on museums during the summer holidays, as many have special children's exhibits and events, and most museums are open on Sundays and Bank Holidays too. Local museums are listed in your telephone directory.

A TOURIST AT HOME: Unfortunately quite a lot of the major museums are to be found in London, but there are also similar specialist museums dotted about the country. One important thing to remember is that most towns or cities have a tourist bureau. This is not just for people from overseas. Try being a tourist in your own town and you will be surprised what interesting things there are on your own doorstep.

CAPITAL MUSEUMS: However, as most people try to visit the capital city, here is a list of some London Museums.

British Museum, Great Russell Street, London, WC1. 01-636-1555. Vast range of world antiquities; children particularly like the Egyptian mummies. There is also a new Roman Britain gallery with a trail of questions for children to follow.

Bethnal Green Museum of Childhood, Cambridge Heath Road, E2. 01-980-2415. Toys, dolls, puppets, etc., from bygone times.

Museum of Mankind, 6, Burlington Gardens, W1. 01-437-2224. Ethnography museum showing how different cultures live and lived.

Imperial War Museum, Lambeth Road, SE1. 01-735-8922. Exhibits mainly from the two World Wars.

London Transport Museum, 39, Wellington Street, WC2. 01-379-6344. An extremely lively, noisy museum of working transport exhibits.

Natural History Museum, Cromwell Road, SW7. 01-589-6323. Their pre-historic exhibits are particularly popular with children. They also have a human biology exhibition with audio-visual effects, slide shows and games.

Science Museum, Exhibition Road, SW7. 01-589-3456. Has an entire floor devoted to children's exhibits, with lots of buttons to press and things to do. There is also a life-size tableau of the Apollo moon landing.

R.A.F. Museum, Hendon, NW9. 01-205-2266. A collection of historical and modern aeroplanes.

Museum of London, London Wall, EC2. 01-600-3699. The history of the capital, with many special shows and talks. Exhibits include the Lord Mayor's Coach, a recreation of the Great Fire and reconstructed Victorian shops.

National Maritime Museum, Romney Road, SE10. 01-858-4422. Naval exhibits, together with the 0° longitude line, so you can stand with one foot in each half of the world.

Victoria & Albert Museum, Cromwell Road, SW7. 01-589-6371. Exhibits of weapons, jewels and the history of dress all appeal to children.

The Horniman Museum, Forest Hill, London, SE23. 01-699-2339. This has a demonstration room and craft room. It has a wonderful collection of musical instruments, Egyptian artifacts and tropical fish.

Pollocks Toy Museum, London. 01-636-3452.

Greenwich Planetarium, Greenwich Park, London, SE10.

Commonwealth Institute: This is a great place to visit if you are taking your child on a special outing to London for the day (see page 368 for the address). They have special children's exhibits with lots of colour slides to see, things from commonwealth countries to look at and in some cases to touch as well, and numerous exhibits that can be activated at the press of a button.

FARM VISITS: Even if you live in a city, it's possible to get your children back to nature for a day. There are now lots of small farms which have been set up in towns to teach children about farm animals and agriculture. Contact the National Federation of City Farms, see page 362 for their address.

NATURE TRAILS: In the countryside surrounding cities, there are a number of organized nature trails, designed to teach children about the natural world around them. For more details, see page 362.

ZOOS: Children always like visiting zoos, but it's important to combine some education with their pleasure. The Young Zoologists' Club builds upon their interest in animals and teaches them more about

the world's creatures, while also involving them more closely with the animals in the zoo itself. Details from London Zoo, Regents Park, London, NW1 – where, incidentally, the children's section contains animals that children can touch and stroke.

PARKS: You can find facilities like boating ponds, small zoos, Bank Holiday fairs, ducks, paddling pools, sailing and rowing all in your local park. During the summer there are often special entertainments like Punch and Judy shows and children's plays. In London there is a G.L.C. Parks Information Service on 01-633-1707.

WILDLIFE PARKS: Many people nowadays seem to prefer to take a whole day out visiting a wildlife park to see animals in a natural surrounding rather than in a zoo. Do remember, however, to observe the rules of the park. If it says 'Please close all windows' – it really does mean just that, so never get out of a car and wander free. The animals are just as described – wild. And although they sometimes look very cuddly on the TV screen, I certainly wouldn't advise you to try it! There are some addresses of popular wildlife parks on pages 363 to 364.

LONDON: Even resident parents are bewildered by the wealth of children's activities in London, so don't feel bashful about seeking advice on a visit to the capital. There's a Children's Information service available on 01-246-8007, which details some of the most appealing current children's events. The Capital Children's Line, on 01-222-8070, is another source of advice about London events for children.

AIRPORTS: Major airports nearly always have an observation terrace or spectators' gallery, where children can watch aeroplanes landing and taking off. 'Phone your airport before setting off though, as bad weather conditions can sometimes close the terraces.

RIVER TRIPS: Wherever there is a river, there is usually a boat or barge that provides pleasure trips. In London, there are boats on the Thames from Kew, Greenwich and Westminster Pier, running approximately every half hour.

TRIPS FOR CHILDREN: Junior Jaunts is for children in and around London. It arranges, during school holiday periods, a programme of outings, pottery lessons, ice-skating and so on, which is continually being varied (for example pantomimes at Christmas, outdoor events in summer). Details on page 368.

Traditional customs

A TRADITIONAL FLING: Foreigners traditionally think of the British, and particularly the English, as being a rather serious, stiff-upper-lipped lot, although you have only to see the New Year Celebrations in London's Trafalgar Square or attend a wild Hogmanay Party in Scotland to realise that the po-faced image is way off the mark. We can let our hair down with the best of them. But, of course, it's not just at New Year that we have traditional celebrations; there are a host of unusual and interesting customs and celebrations taking place all over the British Isles throughout the year. Many of them are well worth a visit, either as a way of filling in a day of your holiday schedule or as a special family trip out. They are ideal subjects for children to photograph or draw and the family could produce a fascinating scrap-book combining photographs, postcards, drawings and written descriptions of calendar customs throughout the year, which could include everything from the universally celebrated Christmas, right down to small local events.

MAKING THE TRIP WORTHWHILE: This chapter contains details of the more spectacular events (one from each main area of the country) but it represents only a few of the hundreds of traditional customs and festivals to be seen throughout the year. Some are large-scale affairs, attended by thousands of people, others are very personal to perhaps one village or family and are noticed by just a handful of passers by. But large or small all our customs are important and give us an insight into our history, our beliefs and our traditional character. Some of the events are related to moveable feasts and so you should check with the local vicar, police or tourist information office before setting off on a long car journey, just to confirm dates and times.

WHO IS THE BURRY MAN?: Well, if you do not know, stick with me! First have a look at the map of the British Isles on page 337 to find out where everything is going on. It might be a good idea to pin or stick a map to your child's bedroom wall and put in coloured drawing pins to show the places that you have visited. Now read on . . .

HAXEY HOOD GAMES: (Haxey, Humberside) Twelfth Day – January 6th. Following a sing song in the two village pubs and a speech by the 'Fool' outside the church, the 'Lord' and his thirteen attendants or 'Boggans' lead the crowds up to a field on the outskirts of the village. Here a muddy free-for-all ensues for possession of one of the thirteen 'Hoods'. The 'Hoods' are canvas rolls about 18 inches long and 3 or 4 inches in diameter. The last 'Hood' to be thrown to the crowd is covered in leather and the various groups try to get it back to their own particular pub. A muddy event, but exciting to watch. Brave visitors can get into the 'sway' (scrum) if they wish.

CHINESE NEW YEAR CELEBRATIONS: (Gerrard Street, London) Sunday late January or early February. Spectacular street entertainment by Soho's Chinese community. The main event is the Dragon Dance performed by a local martial arts school, in which a dozen or so dancers get under the long snake-like body, with its huge Chinese dragon head, and dance through the crowds.

PANCAKE RACE: (Olney – Buckinghamshire) Shrove Tuesday. One of the most famous of the many pancake races held all over the country is said to have been held in Olney since 1445, when a local woman, on hearing the church bells calling everyone to the Shrove Tide service, ran to church still clutching the frying pan in which she'd been cooking a pancake. The modern race is over a 415 yard long course to the church door. Only women can participate and they have to toss a pancake three times in their frying pans during the course of the race. The winner gets a kiss from the church bell-ringer and a prayer book from the vicar. Pancake races are also held at Bodiam in Sussex and North Somercotes in Lincolnshire.

SHROVETIDE FOOTBALL: (Sedgefield, County Durham; Alnwick, Northumberland; Ashbourne, Derbyshire; Atherstone, Warwickshire) Shrove Tuesday. At one time Shrove Tuesday football matches were held in dozens of towns and villages all over the British Isles. A primitive cross between football and rugby, with any number of players, often played with goals three miles apart, these massive heaving matches were frequently barred due to the danger to life and limb. They did, however, survive in the above towns and if you do not mind risking *your* life and limbs, you can join in, or perhaps more sensibly, just take some photos.

MARBLES CHAMPIONSHIP: (Tinsley Green, Crawley – Sussex) Good Friday. The annual Marbles Championship has been battled out in the six foot diameter 'ring' at Tinsley Green since 1932 by teams with such colourful names as The Tinsley Green Tigers; The Black Dog Boozers and the Copthorne Sharpshooters. The aim of the game is for each competitor of a team of six to try to knock out of the ring as many of the 49 marbles (set up at the beginning of the game) as possible with his glass Folly, which he grasps between forefinger and thumb and shoots without moving his whole hand. The local explanation for the Sussex interest in marbles is that it all began in the 1600's, when two Sussex rivals fought a marbles battle for the hand of a beautiful village girl. But some people think this is a load of marbles!

PACE EGG PLAY: (Performances at Midgley, Hebden Bridge, Mytholmroyd, Luddenden and Todmorden – Yorkshire) Good Friday. This is an Easter version of the mid-winter Mumming Play, with its action of single-combat and death, followed by the resurrection of the hero by a comic doctor (see page 221). Some people see this variously as symbolizing the struggle between good and evil, summer and winter, etc., but whatever its origin, it is now just a piece of amusing and colourful street theatre.

BOTTLE KICKING AND HARE PIE SCRAMBLE: (Hallaton – Leicestershire) Easter Monday. A large hare pie is cut up and half of it is distributed calmly to the crowds by the Rector, the rest of the pie is scrambled for by everybody on the Hare Pie Bank. Then follows the 'bottle-kicking', a sort of Rugby match between the villages of Hallaton and Medbourne, who try to carry the 'bottles' (small beribboned beer casks) over their respective goal lines. The winners climb to the top of the old butter cross to drink to their success.

WELL DRESSING: (Derbyshire – Well dressings can be seen in a number of Derbyshire villages and towns during the summer. For specific dates contact: The Peak Park Planning Board, Aldern House, Bakewell, Derbyshire.) May – September. All over the Peak District during the summer months, dedicated local people create the most beautiful floral pictures to decorate the local wells. Legend has it that the practice dates back to the plague times, when people decorated the wells to thank God for the pure well waters that helped to keep some free from disease. However, people have been decorating and worshipping wells and springs since pre-Christian times and the origins of the custom are probably to be found in these Pagan rites. Whatever its origins it's a delightful and colourful custom.

A set of colour photographs of all the wells for one year makes a beautiful collection and can give you a really good excuse for exploring the Peak District over several weekends during the summer. There are plenty of small hotels, bed and breakfast places and camping sites and lots to see quite apart from the Well Dressings.

PADSTOW 'OBBY 'OSS: (Padstow – Cornwall) May Day. This must be the most stirring custom we have in the British Isles. Dozens of drummers and accordionists in the two Hobby Horse teams set up an hypnotic primitive rhythm to accompany the wild, black, leaping and swinging Padstow hobby horses as they prance through the small fishing town, scattering all before them as they bring in the Summer and good luck and fertility to the attendant crowds.

The Hobby Horses are large, circular black canvas or P.V.C. covered frames, which rest horizontally on a fisherman's shoulders. Long swaying skirts reach to the ground and a grotesque mask is perched on top. This must be the nearest thing we have to an African Tribal ritual. A visit to Padstow on May Day also offers an opportunity to try some of the really huge Cornish pasties that are a speciality of the local bakers.

CHEESE ROLLING: (Cooper's Hill, between Cheltenham and Gloucester) Spring Bank Holiday Monday. A spectacular 'sport' in which local young men and girls and lunatic visitors race down a steep grass slope (gradient 1 in 3) trying to catch speeding Double Gloucester Cheeses.

The participants are Gloucestershire's answer to the Japanese Kamikaze pilots – Kamicheezes!!

THE BURRY MAN: (South Queensferry – Lothian) Second Friday in August. On the second Friday in August, a strange figure who looks as if he's stepped straight out of a sci-fi movie perambulates the town boundaries of South Queensferry near Edinburgh. He is covered from head to toe in a tight-fitting garment covered with thistle and teazle burrs – hence the 'Burry Man', and also wears a head-dress containing seventy roses. From ten in the morning he walks around the town visiting every pub and collecting money from anyone he meets in exchange for good luck. There's a local tale to explain the origins of the custom. It says that the 'Burry Man' commemorates the escape of King Malcolm III of Scotland from the English by covering himself with burrs and flowers. He must have been in a right prickle!

OULD LAMMAS FAIR: (Ballycastle – Co. Antrim) August – last Monday & Tuesday. The 'Ould Lammas Fair in Ballycastle – o' is Northern Ireland's most famous traditional fair and well worth a visit. (Combine it with a tour of other Ulster 'musts' such as the Giant's Causeway.) The fair is a thriving livestock and amusement fair as well as having over 200 stalls selling everything from patent medicines to antiques. The most famous items on sale are 'yellowman' (a local type of toffee) and 'dulse' (edible seaweed).

FURTHER VISITS: Further information on traditions and customs can be obtained from national organizations, such as the English Folk Dance and Song Society, and the appropriate regional tourist authority, see page 368.

FURTHER READING: If you would just like to be an armchair traveller to these wonderful events, find out more from the books in your local library about traditional British Customs.

11. Hobbies

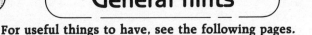

General hints

For useful things to have, see the following pages.

Collecting: This is one of the most useful hobbies, for it may turn out to be a very lucrative one in times to come. The item collected doesn't have to be an expensive one – just something that interests your child. The main problem about a collection is storage space. Unless you live in a rambling mansion try to avoid letting your child collect things like billiard tables!

Reading: Background reading on hobbies is a good idea. This will also often help solve the question about what to give a child as a birthday or Christmas present.

When does the interest start?: The ideas in this chapter are, as with the whole of this second part, designed for seven to eleven year olds, but the physical and mental development of children in this age group is so individual that it is impossible to generalize about what should be done at what age. Just try out some ideas and see and if they don't interest your child at one stage, they may well do so at another. Remember that at this age, children's enthusiasms are quickly roused, but may as quickly fade.

Hobbies and clubs: Many of the ideas in this chapter are backed up by national clubs. The addresses for these are given in the next chapter, starting on page 359. That chapter will also provide further ideas to supplement this one.

Collections

STARTING OFF: Hobbies are a very personal thing and never more so than in the desire to collect one thing rather than another. However, whatever your child has decided upon, try to get him to keep a catalogue from the very beginning of the collection. List where and when each item was bought or acquired, how much it cost (if anything) and where it came from.

IN MINT CONDITION: The main thing to remember about helping your child to collect anything is that the condition of the object should be as pristine as possible. It is worth keeping the original packaging, such as the box, in which it comes, if you are buying it new.

KEY RINGS: A popular item for collecting is the key ring. As there is hardly a place that does not produce a souvenir key ring, they can be a continuing reminder of holidays or visits. The collection could be organized into those from towns in England, those from Wales, Scotland, Ireland and so on. Other key rings come from organizations or clubs, so you could have collections from zoos, art galleries or museums.

COMICS: These can be made into an intriguing collection, and will extend the usefulness of such things, especially if the comic has quite a small circulation. Try to keep them in chronological order and try not to miss an issue.

MODEL CHILD: Models of all kinds are instantly collectable, whether they are toy soldiers, model aeroplanes, boats, ships or cars.

PENKNIVES: !! Young boys often have an overwhelming desire for these but do be careful. Make absolutely sure that you give them all the necessary warnings about how to handle them.

DOG COLLARS: This may sound strange but only recently some 17th century dog collars fetched as much as £600 each at auction. You never know – what Fido has round his neck today may be worth a fortune later.

TEDDY BEARS: These have an appeal to many adults, as well as children and are lovely things to collect, especially if there are some old ones tucked away in a family attic to help start you off.

DOLLS: Dolls, especially those in typical costumes of the times in which they were made, can be fascinating to collect. So even if your child has only very modern dolls don't think that they are worthless. Help your child make mini replicas of currently fashionable clothes with which to dress it. Remember how quaint and lovely the Victorian dolls seem to us now: it is quite likely your children's doll will appear to be just as intriguing to their great grandchildren. Dolls in national costume come in all shapes and sizes, from the intriguing Russian wooden dolls to the more elaborate flamenco dancers in Spain. Many different sorts are available here but, if bought abroad, they can, like the key rings, be a fascinating reminder of holidays.

THIMBLES: Some of these are very cheap and have the advantage of being small, so they can be displayed on tiny shelves in your child's room adding a personal touch of decor. Also raiding grannie's sewing box (with her approval, of course) may turn up some really pretty old ones. They used to be made of ivory. Nowadays thimbles are sometimes made purely for decorative rather than practical use and pottery and glass ones make very special presents for the collector.

COMMEMORATIVE WARE: Mugs, plates, salt cellars or tins are produced to mark a special event, whether it is connected with the Royal Family or just with a particular firm's anniversary or even to celebrate Christmas every year. The pieces produced for the engagement and wedding of the Princess and Prince of Wales, for example, must have started many collections. Perhaps, as with thimbles, you could make a shelf for your child in his or her room to display the commemorative ware should they wish to collect them. Children may also like to write about what they were doing on the day commemorated or if it wasn't in their lifetime, to find out what the official events were on the day celebrated.

BOTTLES AND JAR TOPS: Collecting these is very much a modern cult though conversely, it could perhaps even start a child off on an interest in archaeology. !! You'll be surprised what a bit of judicious digging in your garden, or the perusal of the back of dark cupboards in a grannie's house will uncover. Cleaned and polished old coloured bottles decorated with some of the bread flowers (as described on page 241) can make very attractive presents or even good things to sell to raise money at school fêtes.

LETTERS AND POEMS AND DIARIES: Try to encourage your child to write letters or poems. If possible get him or her to have a pen pal. The information written about themselves often makes interesting reading later on, so making a copy of the letters and storing them with the reply received is not only fascinating for the child to read later on – but a wonderful insight into their lives for their grandchildren. The same can be said for encouraging diary writing (even if it is sporadic) and the writing of poetry.

MORE THINGS TO COLLECT: The list of things to collect could be enormous if it were to cover each individual's special interests. However, here are some of the more popular ideas to help your child start off:

horseshoes; pennants; beer mats; theatre programmes; sports programmes; autographs; matchboxes; teaspoons; handkerchiefs; feathers; paperweights; photographs; records and cassettes; books on specialized subjects; artificial flowers; badges; shells; carvings; fossils; postcards; stamps.

Sports and pastimes as hobbies

SPECTATOR SPORTS: You or your child do not need necessarily to be able to perform a sport to be interested in it. There are millions of football, cricket and rugby fanatics who have rarely participated in the sport but have a walking encyclopaedic knowledge of it. The craze of media coverage on darts and snooker over the recent years has increased this type of sports following enormously.

SUPPORTERS' CLUBS: If your child is enthusiastic about one particular sport, there are many supporters' clubs he or she can join and endless scarves, badges, key rings, programmes and tickets for them to collect. Alongside sport supporters' clubs there are many other clubs and societies for your child to join. Ask at your local library – they have all the addresses you will need.

SPORTS AND LEISURE CENTRES: Most central areas nowadays have wonderful sports and leisure centres organized by the local councils and the class entrance fees are usually quite nominal, also the kit needed for whatever the interest is can be hired out. This is a distinct advantage as it is better not to buy anything until you really know that any hobby that your child has is a lasting thing. It may all be a 'five minute wonder'! However, a developed hobby may turn into a career; as ice skater John Curry proves.

NATIONWIDE GROUPS: One of the best ways of helping your child join a club, in my opinion, is to introduce him or her into the cubs, brownies, scouts or guides. These groups in themselves provide opportunities for initiation into a wealth of other activities, to which you yourself may not be able to expose your child (see chapter 12 for the addresses).

BIRDWATCHING: This is a great hobby for children in this age group. They can start by watching the birds in their own garden and you can help with the identification by looking them up in books on British birds. Dropped feathers can also be identified and collected. Once a child has shown some interest in birds you can buy some binoculars and take them out to the surrounding countryside to see more birds. Get them to list the number of different species seen and also to write down where they were seen and at what time of year. There are a number of clubs, gardens and hides to visit should your child wish to take this hobby further (see page 363).

FISHING: This is a quiet and peaceful sport that attracts girls as well as boys these days. The main thing is to make sure that they are wearing warm clothing and take some flasks of warm drinks. Sitting still for hours waiting for a fish to bite is very cold work. But serious angling can be an expensive pastime with rods costing from £30 upwards. Try to borrow equipment to start with until your child shows sustained interest. You will find the address of your local club in the public library (see also page 360). There are, however, all sorts of permits and licences needed for fishing. You will have to contact the appropriate water authority for a rod licence.

DANCING: All forms of dancing have always been popular with children of both sexes and all ages. If you child hasn't settled on one particular type turn to page 365 for information about the different types of dancing available. These different organizations will also have details about your nearest clubs.

HORSE RIDING: A child can begin having lessons at five years of age. Riding schools have to be licensed by law, so check that they are. This again can be a very expensive hobby especially if the child wants his or her own horse. But to start with many schools will loan equipment. For advice, write to the British Equestrian Centre (see page 367) and ask for information on established riding schools.

SWIMMING: Anyone can learn to swim from a very early age. If, by the time your child is in the 7-11 age range, he still cannot swim, it is a good idea to encourage him to learn. Most schools do have swimming lessons in their curriculum, but if not why don't you take your child to the local swimming baths and teach him to swim yourself? Alternatively, suggest he joins a local swimming club, where he can get expert

tuition. Addresses in your area can be found either at the local library or from the local leisure centre.

PHOTOGRAPHY: Your child could join a local photographic club – address from local library. There is no need to have a very expensive camera: some of the best photographs taken are from old box brownie cameras. However, it is worth bearing in mind the cost of developing the pictures. The important thing is to learn how to take a shot. So often the photographer only looks at the person or object being photographed and forgets the background. The club will help the young photographer with this kind of observation. If your child wishes to take the interest further, he might like to join The Royal Photographic Society, see page 361 for the address.

TRAINSPOTTING: Many children love to spend hours on stations collecting the engine number of every train that passes through. They then compare these numbers with their friends, trying to see who can collect the most train numbers. If your child is interested in this, it is worth bearing in mind when visiting other parts of the country. Set some time aside for him to go to the station to spot some different trains from usual. You could also take the children to one of the railway museums (see page 369), so that they can get the numbers of some of the famous old engines.

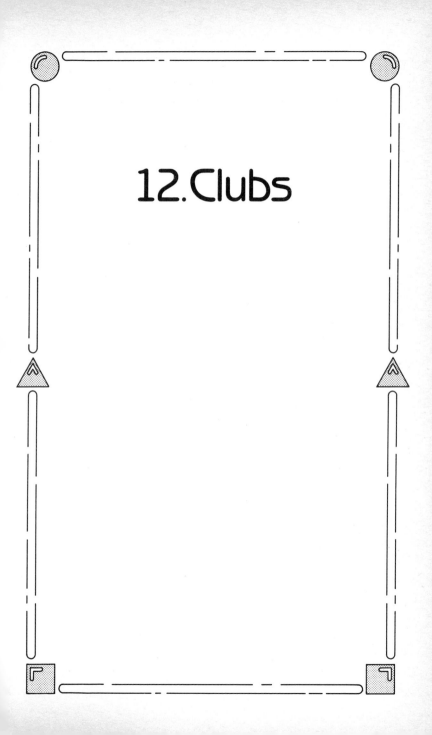

12. Clubs

General hints

Organized clubs: Children adore clubs, for a number of reasons. They need never be bored if they've got a club to go to, a club magazine to read, and a host of club activities organized for them. They learn and enjoy all sorts of activities that they might otherwise never have known about. They make a lot of new friends and they feel that their badges and membership cards make both themselves and their hobby something really special. There are dozens of clubs and societies open to children. Many are nationwide and have local branches; others are run by post, and mail out newsletters with information, quizzes, competitions and so on. Some are based around specialized activities, such as stamp-collecting, bird-watching or a love of animals. Others try to include as many different activities as possible, such as the Scouts or Guides. This chapter lists many different clubs grouped under various themes.

Local clubs: To find whether there is an organized club in your area which caters for the activity you and your child are interested in, check first of all with the local library, which will have details of all the groups and societies in your area, then contact the national headquarters. If you still can't find a local club, then why not start one of your own?

Starting your own club: If you are particularly enthusiastic and want to start a club for a particular activity, begin with a poster in the local library, a card or two in local newsagents' windows, and a small advertisement in the 'Announcements' column of your local newspaper. You'll know from the response whether there's enough interest to support the club you have in mind. At a local level, a club will probably need only one or two adults to supervise activities.

Where to meet: You'll need a place to meet regularly, which, depending on the kind of club, might be as large as the village hall (for big group activities and games) or simply somebody's front room (for a stamp club meeting, say). If you need to hire a room or hall, then you'll probably have to charge a membership fee to cover the costs, but a lot of smaller clubs based around an indoor activity can usually be run for next to nothing. And

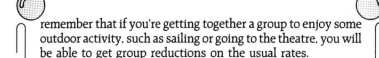

remember that if you're getting together a group to enjoy some outdoor activity, such as sailing or going to the theatre, you will be able to get group reductions on the usual rates.

How organized is it?: Decide for yourselves how formal you want the club to be. Will you need membership cards? An elected committee? Badges? Or would you like to keep it all on a friendly, informal basis? These are things for the members themselves to decide.

Involving children: Encourage the children to run as many of the club activities themselves as they can. Obviously adults will have to take care of all the financial arrangements, but give the children as much responsibility as possible. If you're interested in the club's activity yourself, so much the better, but if not, then perhaps the children's parents can supervise activities on a rota basis.

National help: The national headquarters for a particular activity can usually give advice and often provide leaflets to help you start your club.

Local activities: To find out what's on and where at any time, but especially during school holidays, the first place to try is your local library. It is also worth checking in the local press for special children's events.

Books, etc

Organizations giving details of good books to read or games to play.

Bible Reading Fellowship, 2 Elizabeth Street, London SW1W 9RQ
Supplies children with illustrated passages from the Bible to read each day, together with games, quizzes and puzzles.

Children's Book Centre, 229 Kensington Church Street, London W8
Supplies reading lists for 8-11 year olds (and 11-14 year olds) free of charge.

Games Workshop, Head Office, 27-29 Sunbeam Road, London NW10
Provides details of fantasy games.

Library Association, Ridgemount Street, London WC1E 7AE
Supplies details of nearest children's library.

National Book League, Book House, 45 East Hill, London SW18 2QZ
Has lists of recommended books for children.

Children's holidays

Older children can have lots of fun on holidays organized for un-
accompanied children, where the activities are specifically developed
for them. Children gain a sense of independence and the holiday makes
a useful break for both them and their parents.

Children's Country Holidays Fund, 1 York Street, Baker Street,
London W1H 1PZ.

Cyclists' Touring Club, 69 Meadrow, Godalming, Surrey GU7 3HS.

National Association of Youth Clubs, Keswick House, 30 Peacock
Lane, Leicester LE1 5NY.

Youth Hostels Association, 14 Southampton Street, London WC2.

General interests and pastimes

Archaeological Society, Council for British Archaeology,
112 Kensington Road, London SE11 6RE
Local digs for historical and prehistoric remains.

British Chess Federation, 9a Grand Parade, St. Leonards-on-Sea, East
Sussex TN38 0DD
Will advise on the location of your nearest club; since some of the
world's top players are children, the clubs are open to players of all ages
and abilities.

British Waterways Fisheries Officer, Willow Grange, Church Road,
Watford, Hertfordshire WE1 3QA
Information on fishing in specific canals.

Red Cross Youth, The British Red Cross Society, 9 Grosvenor Crescent, London, SW1X 7EJ.
Membership of Red Cross Youth is open to boys and girls from 5 to 10/11 as Junior Members, while those aged 10/11 up to 18 may become Youth Members. Training is offered in First Aid, Nursing, Child Care, Rescue, Communication, Survival, Camping, etc. Members help at holidays with handicapped young people and undertake a variety of service activities within their community. They are encouraged to make contact with Youth Members abroad.

The Royal Photographic Society, The Octagon, Milsom Street, Bath BA1 1DN.
Arranges field trips and exhibitions. Has reduced rates for young people.

St John's Ambulance Brigade, 1 Grosvenor Crescent, London SW1X 7EF
Cadets between 8 and 11 years old are known as St John Juniors, and enjoy the activities and help in the medical aid offered by St Johns.

Stamp Bug Club, FREEPOST, PO Box 109, Baker Street, High Wycombe, Buckinghamshire HP11 2TD
Members of this stamp collecting club receive a glossy newspaper six times a year and a special Stamp Bug album each year for special issues.

Growing things

For those children who show special interest in gardening or natural history, here are some special organizations with details on the area they cover. They're in alphabetical order.

The Countryside Commission, John Dover House, Crescent Place, Cheltenham, Gloucestershire GL50 3RA
Has details of organized nature trails in the countryside near cities to help teach children about the natural world around them. (Send S.A.E.)

Crusade Against all Cruelty to Animals, Humane Education Centre, Avenue Lodge, Bounds Green Road, London N22 4EU
Young Crusaders get a badge and magazine which teaches children how to care for stray, abandoned or injured animals.

Museums to help follow up an interest in natural history

British Museum (Natural History) Department of Entomology, Cromwell Road, London SW1.

City Museum and Art Gallery, Queen's Road, Bristol BS8 1RL.

National Museum of Wales, Cathays Park, Cardiff CF1 3NP.

Merseyside Country Museum, Education Department, William Brown Street, Liverpool L3 8EN.

Royal Scottish Museum, Department of Education and Public Relations, Chambers Street, Edinburgh EH1 1JF.

National Federation of City Farms, The Old Vicarage, 66 Fraser Street, Windmill Hill, Bristol BS3 4LY
Lists (send S.A.E.) of small farms set up in towns to teach children about farm animals and agriculture.

Watch, 22 The Green, Nettleham, Lincoln LN2 2NR
An ecological organization that gets children to monitor a particular aspect of their local environment.

Young Ornithologists' Club, RSPB, The Lodge, Sandy, Bedfordshire SG19 2DL
Bird-watching trips supervised by adults, newsletters, and education about birds. Details on how to start your own bird-watching group. Leaflets on how to make bird feeders and bird tables. Badges and a list of local leaders, local hides and local visits.

Young Zoologists' Club, London Zoo, Regents Park, London NW1 4RY
Magazines, meetings, films, lectures, and special reduced rates for admission to zoos.

Wildlife Parks

The Bird of Prey Centre, North Lodge, Chilham Castle, Kent
Golden eagles, hawks, owls, falcons. You can also watch them being exercised.

Bridgemere Wildlife Park, Bridgemere, near Nantwich, Cheshire
British animals, water fowl, birds of prey as well as 90 different types of animals and birds from Europe. Also pumas, tigers and wild cats. Large picnic area.

Buxton Country Park, Pools Cavern, Green Lane, Buxton, Derbyshire
100 acres of woodlands. Good nature trails and exhibitions. Picnic sites.
Natural limestone cave.

The Cotswold Wildlife Park, Burford, Oxfordshire
Animals from all over the world, including rhino, camel and zebra.
Adventure playground, plus an animal brass rubbing centre.

Cricket St. Thomas Wildlife Park, Cricket St Thomas, near Chard,
Somerset
Exotic birds; wapiti; leopards; jaguars; lynx. Heavy horse centre.
Agricultural countryside museum. Venture playground. Woodland
walks and nature trails.

Dartmoor Wildlife Park, Sparkwell, near Plymouth, Devon
British and European mammals and birds – some in enclosures.

The Falconry Centre, Newent, Gloucestershire
Golden eagles, hawks, owls, falcons. You can also watch them being
exercised.

Lions of Longleat, Longleat House, Warminster, Wiltshire BA1Z 7NN
Lions, tigers, pumas, Ankole cattle, chimps, birds. Other attractions
include boat trips, Longleat House and a pets corner.

Mole Hall Wildlife Park, Widdington, Saffron Walden, Essex
Many birds; chimps; capuchins; lemurs; Canadian otters; Arctic foxes;
water fowl and dwarf Zebu cattle

Windsor Safari Park, Winkfield Road, Windsor, Berkshire
Mixture of animals, also children's farmyard, nature walk and marine
mammal complex with a killer whale and dolphins.

Woburn Wild Animal Kingdom, Woburn Park, Woburn, Bedfordshire
Mainly African animals, including wildebeest, eland and ostrich.
Skytrip ride, boat rides and dolphinarium are added attractions.

Sounds, Music and Drama

The following are societies or centres which deal with singing, dancing and stage work. For details of local ballet or dance classes, try your local library.

Cardiff Community Dance Project, 56 Ruby Street, Adamsdown, Cardiff, CF2 1LN.
Creative movement workshop classes, pre-school sessions, multi-media week for children every summer.

English Folk-Dance & Song Society, 2 Regent's Park Road, London NW1 7AY
The headquarters often hold Saturday afternoon children's dances for 7-13 year olds, and can supply details of local song and dance clubs, Morris dancing, clog dancing, maypole dancing.

Incorporated Society of Musicians, 10 Stratford Place, London W1N 9AE
For qualified music teachers in your area.

National Association of Youth Orchestras, Ainslie House, 11 St. Colme Street, Edinburgh EH3 6AG
For information on nearest orchestra or combination – over 7 and under 14 only.

National Children's Orchestra, Fitznells, Chessington Road, Ewell, Epsom, Surrey, KT17 1TF
For really talented players.

National Operatic and Dramatic Association, 1 Crestfield Street, London WC1H 8AU
Children who enjoy singing and acting are often in demand for stage productions, such as pantomimes or 'Oliver'. There are also junior societies which put on all-children productions.

Oval House, 54 Kennington Oval, London SE11
Dance technique for 5-10 year olds.

Pineapple Dance Centre, 7 Langley Street, London WC2
All types of dancing including belly dancing. Special holiday courses.

Sports clubs

There are clubs scattered around the country which cater for every conceivable sport. If you don't find the particular one you want here, write for details, specifying the sports in which you're interested, to the **Sports Council**, 16 Upper Woburn Place, London WC1H 0QP.

Amateur Boxing – Amateur Boxing Association, Francis House, Francis Street, London SW1P 1DE

Archery – The Grand National Archery Society, 7th Street, National Agricultural Centre, Stoneleigh, Kenilworth, Warwickshire CV8 2LG

Athletics – Amateur Athletic Association, Francis House, Francis Street, London SW1P 1DL

Badminton – The Badminton Association of England, National Badminton Centre, Bradwell Road, Milton Keynes, Buckinghamshire MK8 9LA

Baseball – British Amateur Baseball and Softball Federation, 197 Newbridge Road, Hull, North Humberside HU9 2LR

Basketball – English Basketball Association, Calomax House, Lupton Avenue, Leeds L89 7DD

Canoeing – The British Canoe Union, Flexel House, 45-47 High Street, Addlestone, Weybridge, Surrey KT15 1JV

Cricket	– National Cricket Association, Lord's Cricket Ground, London NW8 8QN
Croquet	– The Croquet Association, The Hurlingham Club, Ranelagh Gardens, London SW6 3PR
Cycling	– The British Cycling Federation, 16 Upper Woburn Place, London WC1H 0QE
Football	– Football Association, 16 Lancaster Gate, London W2 3LW
Fencing	– The de Beaumont Centre, 83 Perham Road, London W14 9SP
Golf	– English Golf Union, 12a Denmark Street, Wokingham, Berkshire RG11 2BE
Gymnastics	– British Amateur Gymnastics Association, 95 High Street, Slough, Berkshire SL1 1DH
Horse and Pony Riding	– British Equestrian Centre, Stoneleigh, Kenilworth, Warwickshire CV8 2LR
Judo	– British Judo Association, 16 Upper Woburn Place, London WC1H 0QH
Netball	– All England Netball Association, Francis House, Francis Street, London SW1P 1DE
Sailing	– Royal Yachting Association, Victoria Way, Woking, Surrey GU21 1EQ

Skating (Ice or Roller)	– National Skating Association of Great Britain, 15-27 Gee Street, London EC1V 2RU
Swimming	– Amateur Swimming Association, Harold Fern House, Derby Square, Loughborough, Leicestershire, LE11 0AL
Table Tennis	– English Table Tennis Association, 21 Claremont, Hastings, East Sussex TN34 1HA
Tennis	– Lawn Tennis Foundation, The Queen's Club, Palliser Road, West Kensington, London W14 9EQ
Trampolining	– British Trampoline Federation Ltd, 152a College Road, Harrow, Middlesex

Visits

Here are some organizations which either arrange outings or can give details of events nationwide.

English Tourist Board, 4 Grosvenor Gardens, London SW1.

Wales Tourist Board, Brunel House, 2 Fitzalan Road, Cardiff CF2 1VY.

Scottish Tourist Board, 23 Ravelstone Terrace, Edinburgh EH4 3EV.

Northern Ireland Tourist Board, River House, 48 High Street, Belfast BT1 2DS.

Commonwealth Institute, 230 Kensington High Street, London W8
Write to or phone the press office for details of special exhibitions. Opening hours: 10 am-5.30 pm Mondays to Saturdays and 2-5 pm on Sundays.

English Folk Dance and Song Society, 2 Regents Park Road, London NW1 7AY
Produce a directory of folk information and also run a Children's Section of the Society called The Hobby Horse Club, which organizes folk camps.

Junior Jaunts, 4a William Street, London SW1
Arranges events and provides details on activities in and around London.

FOR TRAINSPOTTERS AND ENTHUSIASTS:

Bowes Railway, Springwell, Gateshead, Tyne and Wear.

Bulmer Railway Centre, Whitecross Road, Hereford, Herefordshire
(Open most weekends and Bank Holidays.)

The Great Western Railway Museum, 34 Faringdon Road, Swindon,
Wiltshire.

The National Railway Museum, Leeman Road, York, Yorkshire.

Youth organizations

Nationwide organizations geared towards children. They cover a wide
range of all-year-round activities and usually hold regular meetings.

Boys' Brigade, Brigade House, Parsons Green, London SW6 4TH
A uniformed Christian club which organizes a huge variety of indoor
and outdoor activities.

CHURCH-BASED CLUBS:

There are a number of clubs for children which are run from local church
premises to promote Christian thought. They include:

Campaigners, Campaigner House, St. Mark's Close, Colney Heath,
St. Albans, Herts AL4 0NQ
Proficiency badges, games, local campaigns and projects.

Covenanters, 104 Bloom Street, Manchester M1 6HU
In addition to the main group meetings, children join in a range of
activities, national contests, camping holidays and competitions.

Pathfinders, Falcon Court, 32 Fleet Street, London EC4Y 1DB
Lively Sunday meetings, games, outings, festivals and sports. Also
training for confirmation.

All these headquarters can supply details of local groups, or you can
inquire from your own vicar. If your religion is not C of E, your own
church may have similar youth groups.

Girls' Brigade, (address as for Boys' Brigade)
A similar uniformed Christian club, including community work, nursing and home care among its games and sporting activities.

Girl Guides Association, 17-19 Buckingham Palace Road, London SW1W 0PT
There are now 7½ million Guides around the world, wearing the familiar uniforms of the Brownies and Guides. They describe their activities themselves as: you'll get to know people, enjoy the outdoors, give service, explore the arts, keep fit, become a homemaker, learn to keep the Guide laws and – above all – think for yourself.

Scout Association, Baden-Powell House, Queen's Gate, London SW7 5JS
The Scouts and their younger Cubs are immensely popular, with over 16 million members around the world. Most troops hold weekly indoor meetings with games and competitions, regularly go on camps and enjoy open-air activities.

Association for Jewish Youth, 50 Lindley Street, London E1
Provides local social events and service to the community.

Jewish Lads' and Girls' Brigade, 3 Beechcroft Road, South Woodford,
London E18
Uniformed club enjoying sports, camps, activities and community
service.

Woodcraft Folk, 13 Ritherdon Road, London SW17
An active, mainly outdoor group, based on a spirit of fellowship; like a
socialist Scouts.

Index

(Figures (**1**) and (**2**) refer to activities more appropriate to the younger and older child respectively)